THE ALEXANDER

General Editor
R.B. Kennedy

Edited by Collin Symes

TWELFTH NIGHT

William Shakespeare

COLLINS
CLASSICS

Harper Press
An imprint of HarperCollins*Publishers*
77–85 Fulham Palace Road
Hammersmith
London W6 8JB

This Harper Press paperback edition published 2011

A catalogue record for this book is available from the British Library

ISBN-13: 978-0-00-790238-5

Printed and bound in Great Britain by Clays Ltd, St Ives plc

MIX
Paper from
responsible sources
FSC™ C007454

FSC
www.fsc.org

Life & Times section © Gerard Cheshire
Shakespeare: Words and Phrases adapted from
Collins English Dictionary
Typesetting in Kalix by Palimpsest Book Production Limited,
Falkirk, Stirlingshire

10 9 8 7 6 5 4 3 2 1

Prefatory Note

This Shakespeare play uses the full Alexander text. By keeping in mind the fact that the language has changed considerably in four hundred years, as have customs, jokes, and stage conventions, the editors have aimed at helping the modern reader – whether English is their mother tongue or not – to grasp the full significance of the play. The Notes, intended primarily for examination candidates, are presented in a simple, direct style. The needs of those unfamiliar with British culture have been specially considered.

Since quiet study of the printed word is unlikely to bring fully to life plays that were written directly for the public theatre, attention has been drawn to dramatic effects which are important in performance. The editors see Shakespeare's plays as living works of art which can be enjoyed today on stage, film and television in many parts of the world.

CONTENTS

An Elizabethan playhouse. Note the apron stage protruding into the auditorium, the space below it, the inner room at the rear of the stage, the gallery above the inner stage, the canopy over the main stage, and the absence of a roof over the audience.

The Theatre in Shakespeare's Day

On the face of it, the conditions in the Elizabethan theatre were not such as to encourage great writers. The public playhouse itself was not very different from an ordinary inn-yard; it was open to the weather; among the spectators were often louts, pickpockets and prostitutes; some of the actors played up to the rowdy elements in the audience by inserting their own jokes into the authors' lines, while others spoke their words loudly but unfeelingly; the presentation was often rough and noisy, with fireworks to represent storms and battles, and a table and a few chairs to represent a tavern; there were no actresses, so boys took the parts of women, even such subtle and mature ones as Cleopatra and Lady Macbeth; there was rarely any scenery at all in the modern sense. In fact, a quick inspection of the English theatre in the reign of Elizabeth I by a time-traveller from the twentieth century might well produce only one positive reaction: the costumes were often elaborate and beautiful.

Shakespeare himself makes frequent comments in his plays about the limitations of the playhouse and the actors of his time, often apologizing for them. At the beginning of *Henry V* the Prologue refers to the stage as 'this unworthy scaffold' and to the theatre building (the Globe, probably) as 'this wooden O', and emphasizes the urgent need for imagination in making up for all the deficiencies of presentation. In introducing Act IV the Chorus goes so far as to say:

> . . . we shall much disgrace
> With four or five most vile and ragged foils,
> Right ill-dispos'd in brawl ridiculous,
> The name of Agincourt, (lines 49–52)

In *A Midsummer Night's Dream* (Act V, Scene i) he seems to dismiss actors with the words:

The best in this kind are but shadows.

Yet Elizabeth's theatre, with all its faults, stimulated dramatists to a variety of achievement that has never been equalled and, in Shakespeare, produced one of the greatest writers in history. In spite of all his grumbles he seems to have been fascinated by the challenge that it presented him with. It is necessary to re-examine his theatre carefully in order to understand how he was able to achieve so much with the materials he chose to use. What sort of place was the Elizabethan playhouse in reality? What sort of people were these criticized actors? And what sort of audiences gave them their living?

The Development of the Theatre up to Shakespeare's Time

For centuries in England noblemen had employed groups of skilled people to entertain them when required. Under Tudor rule, as England became more secure and united, actors such as these were given more freedom, and they often performed in public, while still acknowledging their 'overlords' (in the 1570s, for example, when Shakespeare was still a schoolboy at Stratford, one famous company was called 'Lord Leicester's Men'). London was rapidly becoming larger and more important in the second half of the sixteenth century, and many of the companies of actors took the opportunities offered to establish themselves at inns on the main roads leading to the City (for example, the Boar's Head in Whitechapel and the Tabard in South-wark) or in the City itself. These groups of actors would come to an agreement with the inn-keeper which would give them the use of the yard for their performances after people had eaten and drunk well in the middle of the day. Before long, some inns were taken over completely by companies of players and thus became the first public theatres. In 1574 the officials of the City of London issued an order which shows clearly that these theatres were both popular and also offensive to some respectable people, because the order complains about 'the inordinate haunting of great multitudes of people, specially youth, to plays interludes and shows; namely occasion of frays and quarrels, evil practices of incontinency in great inns . . .' There is evidence that, on public holidays, the theatres on the banks of the Thames were crowded with noisy apprentices and tradesmen, but it would be wrong to think that audiences were always undiscriminating and loudmouthed. In spite of the disapproval of Puritans and the more staid members of society, by the 1590s, when Shakespeare's plays were beginning to be performed, audiences consisted of a good cross-section of English society, nobility as well as workers, intellectuals as well as simple people out for a laugh; also (and in this respect English theatres were unique in Europe), it was quite normal for respectable women to attend plays. So Shakespeare had to write plays which would appeal to people of widely different kinds. He had to provide 'something for everyone' but at the same time to take care to unify the material so that it would not seem to fall into separate pieces as they watched it. A speech like that of the drunken porter in *Macbeth* could provide the 'groundlings' with a belly-laugh, but also held a deeper significance for those who could appreciate it. The audience he wrote for was one of a number of apparent drawbacks which Shakespeare was able to turn to his and our advantage.

Shakespeare's Actors

Nor were all the actors of the time mere 'rogues, vagabonds and sturdy beggars' as some were described in a Statute of 1572. It is true that many of them had a hard life and earned very little money, but leading actors could become partners in the ownership of the theatres in which they acted: Shakespeare was a shareholder in the Globe and the Blackfriars theatres when he was an actor as well as a playwright. In any case, the attacks made on Elizabethan actors were usually directed at their morals and not at their acting ability; it is clear that many of them must have been good at their trade if they were able to interpret complex works like the great tragedies in such a way as to attract enthusiastic audiences. Undoubtedly some of the boys took the women's parts with skill and confidence, since a man called Coryate, visiting Venice in 1611, expressed surprise that women could act as well as they: 'I saw women act, a thing that I never saw before . . . and they performed it with as good a grace, action, gesture . . . as ever I saw any masculine actor.' The quality of most of the actors who first presented Shakespeare's plays is probably accurately summed up by Fynes Moryson, who wrote, '. . . as there be, in my opinion, more plays in London than in all the parts of the world I have seen, so do these players or comedians excel all other in the world.'

The Structure of the Public Theatre

Although the 'purpose-built' theatres were based on the inn-yards which had been used for play-acting, most of them were circular. The walls contained galleries on three storeys from which the wealthier patrons watched, they must have been something like the 'boxes' in a modern theatre, except that they held much larger numbers – as many as 1500. The 'groundlings' stood on the floor of the building, facing a raised stage which projected from the 'stage-wall', the main features of which were:

1 a small room opening on to the back of the main stage and on the same level as it (rear stage),
2 a gallery above this inner stage (upper stage),
3 canopy projecting from above the gallery over the main stage, to protect the actors from the weather (the 700 or 800 members of the audience who occupied the yard, or 'pit' as we call it today, had the sky above them).

In addition to these features there were dressing-rooms behind the stage and a space underneath it from which entrances could be made through trap-doors. All the acting areas – main stage, rear stage, upper stage and under stage – could be entered by actors directly from their dressing rooms, and all of them were used in productions of Shakespeare's plays. For example, the inner stage, an almost cavelike structure, would have been where Ferdinand and Miranda are 'discovered' playing chess in the last act of *The Tempest*, while the upper stage was certainly the balcony from which Romeo climbs down in Act III of *Romeo and Juliet*.

It can be seen that such a building, simple but adaptable, was not really unsuited to the presentation of plays like Shakespeare's. On the contrary, its simplicity guaranteed the minimum of distraction, while its shape and construction must have produced a sense of involvement on the part of the audience that modern producers would envy.

Other Resources of the Elizabethan Theatre

Although there were few attempts at scenery in the public theatre (painted backcloths were occasionally used in court performances), Shakespeare and his fellow playwrights were able to make use of a fair variety of 'properties', lists of such articles have survived: they include beds, tables, thrones, and also trees, walls, a gallows, a Trojan horse and a 'Mouth of Hell'; in a list of properties belonging to the manager, Philip Henslowe, the curious item 'two mossy banks' appears. Possibly one of them was used for the

> bank whereon the wild thyme blows,
> Where oxlips and the nodding violet grows

in *A Midsummer Night's Dream* (Act II, Scene i). Once again, imagination must have been required of the audience.

Costumes were the one aspect of stage production in which

trouble and expense were hardly ever spared to obtain a magnificent effect. Only occasionally did they attempt any historical accuracy (almost all Elizabethan productions were what we should call 'modern-dress' ones), but they were appropriate to the characters who wore them: kings were seen to be kings and beggars were similarly unmistakable. It is an odd fact that there was usually no attempt at illusion in the costuming: if a costume looked fine and rich it probably was. Indeed, some of the costumes were almost unbelievably expensive. Henslowe lent his company £19 to buy a cloak, and the Alleyn brothers, well-known actors, gave £20 for a 'black velvet cloak, with sleeves embroidered all with silver and gold, lined with black satin striped with gold'.

With the one exception of the costumes, the 'machinery' of the playhouse was economical and uncomplicated rather than crude and rough, as we can see from this second and more leisurely look at it. This meant that playwrights were stimulated to produce the imaginative effects that they wanted from the language that they used. In the case of a really great writer like Shakespeare, when he had learned his trade in the theatre as an actor, it seems that he received quite enough assistance of a mechanical and structural kind without having irksome restrictions and conventions imposed on him; it is interesting to try to guess what he would have done with the highly complex apparatus of a modern television studio. We can see when we look back to his time that he used his instrument, the Elizabethan theatre, to the full, but placed his ultimate reliance on the communication between his imagination and that of his audience through the medium of words. It is, above all, his rich and wonderful use of language that must have made play-going at that time a memorable experience for people of widely different kinds. Fortunately, the deep satisfaction of appreciating and enjoying Shakespeare's work can be ours also, if we are willing to overcome the language difficulty produced by the passing of time.

Shakespeare: A Timeline

Very little indeed is known about Shakespeare's private life; the facts included here are almost the only indisputable ones. The dates of Shakespeare's plays are those on which they were first produced.

1558	Queen Elizabeth crowned.	
1561	Francis Bacon born.	
1564	Christopher Marlowe born.	William Shakespeare born, April 23rd, baptized April 26th.
1566		Shakespeare's brother, Gilbert, born.
1567	Mary, Queen of Scots, deposed. James VI (later James I of England) crowned King of Scotland.	
1572	Ben Jonson born. Lord Leicester's Company (of players) licensed; later called Lord Strange's, then the Lord Chamberlain's and finally (under James) the King's Men.	
1573	John Donne born.	
1574	The Common Council of London directs that all plays and playhouses in London must be licensed.	
1576	James Burbage builds the first public playhouse, The Theatre, at Shoreditch, outside the walls of the City.	
1577	Francis Drake begins his voyage round the world (completed 1580). *Holinshed's Chronicles of England, Scotland and Ireland* published (which	

Shakespeare later used
extensively).

1582		Shakespeare married to Anne Hathaway.
1583	The Queen's Company founded by royal warrant.	Shakespeare's daughter, Susanna, born.
1585		Shakespeare's twins, Hamnet and Judith, born.
1586	Sir Philip Sidney, the Elizabethan ideal 'Christian knight', poet, patron, soldier, killed at Zutphen in the Low Countries.	
1587	Mary, Queen of Scots, beheaded. Marlowe's *Tamburlaine (Part I)* first staged.	
1588	Defeat of the Spanish Armada. Marlowe's *Tamburlaine (Part II)* first staged.	
1589	Marlowe's *Jew of Malta* and Kyd's *Spanish Tragedy* (a 'revenge tragedy' and one of the most popular plays of Elizabethan times).	
1590	Spenser's *Faerie Queene* (Books I–III) published.	
1592	Marlowe's *Doctor Faustus* and *Edward II* first staged. Witchcraft trials in Scotland. Robert Greene, a rival playwright, refers to Shakespeare as 'an upstart crow' and 'the only Shake-scene in a country'.	*Titus Andronicus* *Henry VI, Parts I, II and III* *Richard III*
1593	London theatres closed by the plague. Christopher Marlowe killed in a Deptford tavern.	*Two Gentlemen of Verona* *Comedy of Errors* *The Taming of the Shrew* *Love's Labour's Lost*
1594	Shakespeare's company becomes The Lord Chamberlain's Men.	*Romeo and Juliet*

1595	Raleigh's first expedition to Guiana. Last expedition of Drake and Hawkins (both died).	*Richard II* *A Midsummer Night's Dream*
1596	Spenser's *Faerie Queene* (Books IV–VI) published. James Burbage buys rooms at Blackfriars and begins to convert them into a theatre.	*King John* *The Merchant of Venice* Shakespeare's son Hamnet dies. Shakespeare's father is granted a coat of arms.
1597	James Burbage dies, his son Richard, a famous actor, turns the Blackfriars Theatre into a private playhouse.	*Henry IV (Part I)* Shakespeare buys and redecorates New Place at Stratford.
1598	Death of Philip II of Spain	*Henry IV (Part II)* *Much Ado About Nothing*
1599	Death of Edmund Spenser. The Globe Theatre completed at Bankside by Richard and Cuthbert Burbage.	*Henry V* *Julius Caesar* *As You Like It*
1600	Fortune Theatre built at Cripplegate. East India Company founded for the extension of English trade and influence in the East. The Children of the Chapel begin to use the hall at Blackfriars.	*Merry Wives of Windsor* *Troilus and Cressida*
1601		*Hamlet*
1602	Sir Thomas Bodley's library opened at Oxford.	*Twelfth Night*
1603	Death of Queen Elizabeth. James I comes to the throne. Shakespeare's company becomes The King's Men. Raleigh tried, condemned and sent to the Tower	
1604	Treaty of peace with Spain	*Measure for Measure* *Othello* *All's Well that Ends Well*
1605	The Gunpowder Plot: an attempt by a group of Catholics to blow up the Houses of Parliament.	

1606	Guy Fawkes and other plotters executed.	*Macbeth* *King Lear*
1607	Virginia, in America, colonized. A great frost in England.	*Antony and Cleopatra* *Timon of Athens* *Coriolanus* Shakespeare's daughter, Susanna, married to Dr. John Hall.
1608	The company of the Children of the Chapel Royal (who had performed at Blackfriars for ten years) is disbanded. John Milton born. Notorious pirates executed in London.	Richard Burbage leases the Blackfriars Theatre to six of his fellow actors, including Shakespeare. *Pericles, Prince of Tyre*
1609		Shakespeare's Sonnets published.
1610	A great drought in England	*Cymbeline*
1611	Chapman completes his great translation of the *Iliad*, the story of Troy. Authorized Version of the Bible published.	*A Winter's Tale* *The Tempest*
1612	Webster's *The White Devil* first staged.	Shakespeare's brother, Gilbert, dies.
1613	Globe theatre burnt down during a performance of *Henry VIII* (the firing of small cannon set fire to the thatched roof). Webster's *Duchess of Malfi* first staged.	*Henry VIII* *Two Noble Kinsmen* Shakespeare buys a house at Blackfriars.
1614	Globe Theatre rebuilt in 'far finer manner than before'.	
1616	Ben Jonson publishes his plays in one volume. Raleigh released from the Tower in order to prepare an expedition to the gold mines of Guiana.	Shakespeare's daughter, Judith, marries Thomas Quiney. Death of Shakespeare on his birthday, April 23rd.
1618	Raleigh returns to England and is executed on the charge for which he was imprisoned in 1603.	
1623	Publication of the Folio edition of Shakespeare's plays	Death of Anne Shakespeare (née Hathaway).

Life & Times

William Shakespeare the Playwright

There exists a curious paradox when it comes to the life of William Shakespeare. He easily has more words written about him than any other famous English writer, yet we know the least about him. This inevitably means that most of what is written about him is either fabrication or speculation. The reason why so little is known about Shakespeare is that he wasn't a novelist or a historian or a man of letters. He was a playwright, and playwrights were considered fairly low on the social pecking order in Elizabethan society. Writing plays was about providing entertainment for the masses – the great unwashed. It was the equivalent to being a journalist for a tabloid newspaper.

In fact, we only know of Shakespeare's work because two of his friends had the foresight to collect his plays together following his death and have them printed. The only reason they did so was apparently because they rated his talent and thought it would be a shame if his words were lost.

Consequently his body of work has ever since been assessed and reassessed as the greatest contribution to English literature. That is despite the fact that we know that different printers took it upon themselves to heavily edit the material they worked from. We also know that Elizabethan plays were worked and reworked frequently, so that they evolved over time until they were honed to perfection, which means that many different hands played their part in the active writing process. It would therefore be fair to say that any play attributed to Shakespeare is unlikely to contain a great deal of original input. Even the plots were based on well known historical events, so it would be hard to know what fragments of any Shakespeare play came from that single mind.

One might draw a comparison with the Christian Bible, which remains such a compelling read because it came from the collaboration of many contributors and translators over centuries, who each adjusted the stories until they could no longer be improved. As virtually nothing is known of Shakespeare's life and even less about his method of working, we shall never know the truth about his plays. They certainly contain some very elegant phrasing, clever plot devices and plenty of words never before seen in print, but as to whether Shakespeare invented them from a unique imagination or whether he simply took them from others around him is anyone's guess.

The best bet seems to be that Shakespeare probably took the lead role in devising the original drafts of the plays, but was open to collaboration from any source when it came to developing them into workable scripts for effective performances. He would have had to work closely with his fellow actors in rehearsals, thereby finding out where to edit, abridge, alter, reword and so on.

In turn, similar adjustments would have occurred in his absence, so that definitive versions of his plays never really existed. In effect Shakespeare was only responsible for providing the framework of plays, upon which others took liberties over time. This wasn't helped by the fact that the English language itself was not definitive at that time either. The consequence was that people took it upon themselves to spell words however they pleased or to completely change words and phrasing to suit their own preferences.

It is easy to see then, that Shakespeare's plays were always going to have lives of their own, mutating and distorting in detail like Chinese whispers. The culture of creative preservation was simply not established in Elizabethan England. Creative ownership of Shakespeare's plays was lost to him as soon as he released them into the consciousness of others. They saw nothing wrong with taking his ideas and running with them, because no one had ever suggested that one shouldn't, and Shakespeare probably regarded his work in the same way. His plays weren't sacrosanct works of art, they were templates for theatre folk to make their livings from, so they had every right to mould them into productions that drew in the crowds as effectively as possible. Shakespeare was like the helmsman of a sailing ship, steering the vessel but wholly reliant on the team work of his crew to arrive at the desired destination.

It seems that Shakespeare certainly had a natural gift, but the genius of his plays may be attributable to the collective efforts of Shakespeare and others. It is a rather satisfying notion to think that *his* plays might actually be the creative outpourings of the Elizabethan milieu in which Shakespeare immersed himself. That makes them important social documents as well as seminal works of the English language.

Money in Shakespeare's Day

It is extremely difficult, if not impossible, to relate the value of money in our time to its value in another age and to compare prices of commodities today and in the past. Many items *are* simply not comparable on grounds of quality or serviceability.

There was a bewildering variety of coins in use in Elizabethan England. As nearly all English and European coins were gold or silver, they had intrinsic value apart from their official value. This meant that foreign coins circulated freely in England and were officially recognized, for example the French crown (écu) worth about 30p (72 cents), and the Spanish ducat worth about 33p (79 cents). The following table shows some of the coins mentioned by Shakespeare and their relation to one another.

GOLD	British	American	SILVER	British	American
sovereign (heavy type)	£1.50	$3.60	shilling	10p	24c
sovereign (light type)	66p–£1	$1.58–$2.40	groat	1.5p	4c
angel royal	33p–50p	79c–$1.20			
noble	50p	$1.20			
crown	25p	60c			

A comparison of the following prices in Shakespeare's time with the prices of the same items today will give some idea of the change in the value of money.

ITEM	PRICE British	American	ITEM	PRICE British	American
beef, per lb.	0.5p	1c	cherries (lb.)	1p	2c
mutton, leg	7.5p	18c	7 oranges	1p	2c
rabbit	3.5p	9c	1 lemon	1p	2c
chicken	3p	8c	cream (quart)	2.5p	6c
potatoes (lb)	10p	24c	sugar (lb.)	£1	$2.40
carrots (bunch)	1p	2c	sack (wine) (gallon)	14p	34c
8 artichokes	4p	9c	tobacco (oz.)	25p	60c
1 cucumber	1p	2c	biscuits (lb.)	12.5p	30c

INTRODUCTION

Shakespeare wrote *Twelfth Night* around 1600, about half way through his career as a playwright. It is the last, and perhaps most successful of the Comedies. The cycle of the English History Plays was virtually complete; the great Tragedies and the so-called 'Dark Comedies' were still to come. The first recorded production was given in the Hall of the Inner Temple, London, in 1602, although it is possible the play was actually written to be performed on January 6th the previous year – hence the title (January 6th is the twelfth day after Christmas, and marks the end of the seasonal festivities).

The Language of the Play
A living language is constantly changing. In particular, spoken English changes very rapidly: certain words or expressions become popular, get over-used, and then are replaced by others. New words are invented, or old words acquire new meanings. In a play like *Twelfth Night*, written nearly four hundred years ago, there are bound to be difficulties of understanding for modern audiences. Sir Toby Belch and Feste, for example, use colloquial expressions or catch-phrases of their own time that now seem unintelligible at first sight. Notes are provided in this edition to explain these and other problems of the meanings of words or groups of words. The notes will also explain another staple ingredient of comedy of all ages: topical allusions. All audiences enjoy references to contemporary events and, in the case of *Twelfth Night*, we have to have a little background information if we want to appreciate the jokes and allusions. This verbal humour is obviously a marked feature of *Twelfth Night* but it is not the most important aspect of Shakespeare's use of language. On a much deeper level, he uses both prose and poetry to express subtle moods, to emphasize

differing emotions, and to contrast one character with another. The mood of Orsino at the beginning of the play is that of a man enjoying the role of the romantic, disappointed lover:

> If music be the food of love, play on,
> Give me excess of it, that, surfeiting,
> The appetite may sicken and so die.
> That strain again! It had a dying fall;
> O, it came o'er my ear like the sweet sound
> That breathes upon a bank of violets,
> Stealing and giving odour!
>
> (Act I, Scene i, lines 1–7).

This speech has a languid movement and a careful rhythmic pattern attuned to the music that accompanies it. However, towards the close of the play, Orsino has another speech that is altogether more determined in tone:

> But hear me this:
> Since you to non-regardance cast my faith,
> And that I partly know the instrument
> That screws me from my true place in your favour,
> Live you the marble-breasted tyrant still;
> But this your minion, whom I know you love,
> And whom, by heaven I swear, I tender dearly,
> Him will I tear out of that cruel eye
> Where he sits crowned in his master's spite.
>
> (Act V, Scene i, lines 116–23)

Orsino has moved from an unreal world created in his own imagination

> So full of shapes is fancy
> That it alone is high fantastical
>
> (Act I, Scene i, lines 14–15)

to a different world where he is genuinely angered. Shakespeare creates the new mood in the verse by running one sentence across eight line-divisions; thus the anger that is in the words is supported by the surge of the poetry. Equally powerfully, Malvolio is set apart from all other characters in the play by his contemptuous dismissal of Feste:

> I marvel your ladyship takes delight in such a barren rascal; I saw him put down the other day with an ordinary fool that has no more brain than a stone. Look you now, he's out of his guard already; unless you laugh and minister occasion to him, he is gagg'd. I protest I take these wise men that crow so at these set kind of fools no better than the fools' zanies.
>
> (Act I, Scene v, lines 77–83)

Here Shakespeare includes a number of key words for the actor to emphasize to give just the right edge to his voice and so convey a mood of sardonic disdain.

What is remarkable about the language of *Twelfth Night* is its range and adaptability. The play is full of passages of lyrical beauty, like Viola's intense assurance to Olivia:

> Make me a willow cabin at your gate,
> And call upon my soul within the house;
> Write loyal cantons of contemned love
> And sing them loud even in the dead of night;
> Halloo your name to the reverberate hills,
> And make the babbling gossip of the air
> Cry out 'Olivia!'
>
> (Act I, Scene v, lines 257–63)

There is an immediate contrast between speeches such as this and all those sections of the play that are written in prose. Apart from Viola's exchanges with Olivia, all the scenes in Olivia's house are prose scenes. This creates a clear distinction between a world of romantic love and a more down-to-earth world occupied by Sir Toby, Fabian, and Maria. Nothing could be further removed from the delicacy of Viola's speech just quoted than Malvolio's confrontation with Sir Toby in the early hours of the morning:

Malvolio: My masters, are you mad? Or what are you?
            Have you no wit, manners, nor honesty, but
            to gabble like tinkers at this time of night?
            Do ye make an ale-house of my lady's house,
            that ye squeak out your coziers' catches
            without any mitigation or remorse of voice?
            Is there no respect of place, persons, nor
            time, in you?
Sir Toby: We did keep time, sir, in our catches. Sneck up!
                            (Act II, Scene iii, lines 81–8)

Yet to underline, as it were, this variety of tone in the
play's dialogue, Shakespeare introduces into the same
scene one of his most poignantly beautiful songs for Feste
to sing:

> What is love? 'Tis not hereafter;
> Present mirth hath present laughter;
> What's to come is still unsure.
> In delay there lies no plenty,
> Then come and kiss me, sweet and twenty;
> Youth's a stuff will not endure.
>   (Act II, Scene iii, lines 44–9)

Not only does this song contrast with the scene in a
general way; in particular, the words themselves throw
light on a different kind of experience. They glance
obliquely at another world, in which Olivia has rejected
life to go into mourning for her brother, and hint at the
way in which romantic love will alter her feelings. Even
Sir Andrew's and Sir Toby's comments on the song are
grotesque parodies of the romantic judgements of the
power of music that come from Orsino:

Sir Andrew: Very sweet and contagious, i' faith.
Sir Toby: To hear by the nose, it is dulcet in contagion.
                            (Act II, Scene iii, lines 52–3)

Such allusions highlight the marked contrast between
different types of language in *Twelfth Night*. Similarly,

images and vivid turns of phrase have a cumulative effect as the play proceeds. Throughout all the poetry and much of the prose, Shakespeare causes his characters to think in comparisons: that is, their speech is constantly moving from one picture in words to the next, and all these pictures or images compare one thing with another, or create relationships between things that the reader or listener may not have noticed had any similarity. In some cases this imagery may just verbally 'set the scene', but there are also recurrent ideas expressed in a variety of ways scattered through the play; references to the sea, or dreams, for example. A whole theme of the work may be developed entirely in terms of a chain of such images. Our enjoyment of the play depends on an appreciation of the poetic language – its beauty in isolation, and the pattern of cross-references, recurrent ideas, and imaginative worlds evoked.

Characterization

Shakespeare created his characters to be interpreted by actors, and the considerable variation in such interpretations throughout the history of *Twelfth Night* has sometimes been used as evidence of the flexibility of Shakespeare's writing. To some extent this is true: actors and directors who examine the text carefully are constantly discovering new subtleties and find the parts particularly rewarding ones to play. Feste is a notable example of a character open to interpretation: somewhat neglected in the eighteenth and nineteenth centuries, in the twentieth (especially in more recent productions), the Fool has become a key figure. Actors and theatre critics alike expect him to be old rather than young, thoughtful and a shade melancholy, detached and self-contained, rather than enjoying the company of any of the other characters. Malvolio, also, has been subject to extremes of interpretation.

In a theatrical production, the actors and actresses, or

more frequently nowadays the director, will decide what approach they are to take towards the play as a whole and the way in which the respective parts must be played. When you read the play, you too should decide these matters for yourself by examining the characters carefully and trying to determine their nature from the evidence of the text. The material supplied in the 'Summing Up' (page 229) provides some useful guidelines as well. Some broad conclusions are inescapable: that Viola is enterprising, quick-witted, and lively; that Malvolio is self-important and inflexible, for instance. But beyond these surface judgements lies the interest of interpreting the characters in a more profound way. Just as one forms opinions about people in real life, the more you know, the more reliable your view will be. If you have the opportunity to see the play, you will be able to measure your estimation of the characters against the representations of them in that particular production.

Plot

Act I   Duke Orsino, governor of Illyria, is love-sick for the Lady Olivia; his suit to her is rejected since she vows to mourn the recent death of her brother for seven years. By chance, Viola is shipwrecked on the coast and her twin brother, Sebastian, is thought to have been drowned in the disaster. Viola decides to seek service with Orsino, since the only other noble household close at hand is that of Olivia and she is shut up in mourning. Olivia's uncle, Sir Toby Belch, abuses his privileged position in her house by indulging in hard drinking and riotous behaviour, despite warnings by Maria, Olivia's attendant gentlewoman, that he will have to mend his ways. Sir Toby has brought Sir Andrew Aguecheek, a rich and foolish knight, into Olivia's house and persuaded him that he must woo and marry

Olivia. Within three days, Viola, now disguised as a male courtier (to escape attention for the time being) and having assumed the name of Cesario, has won the trust and admiration of Orsino. He entrusts to her the courtship of Olivia on his behalf. Viola accepts this duty but has already fallen in love with Orsino. Olivia, whiling away the time with her professional clown, Feste, mildly rebukes her steward, Malvolio, for his critical attitude towards jesters. She is interrupted by the arrival of Cesario, whose persistence is rewarded with a private conference to express Orsino's love. Olivia is so impressed that she falls in love with 'Cesario' and invites 'him' to visit her again on Orsino's behalf. To ensure his return she sends Malvolio after him with a ring.

Act II   Sebastian, twin brother to Viola (to whom he bears a marked resemblance), has been rescued from death in the shipwreck by Antonio, a sea-captain. Assuming in his turn that his sister must have perished in the storm, Sebastian determines to visit Orsino. Despite having been a notable enemy of the Duke in a previous sea battle, Antonio resolves to follow Sebastian. Malvolio catches up with Viola/Cesario and throws down the ring when she refuses to accept it. Viola, already in love with Orsino, now concludes that Olivia has fallen in love with her in her guise as Cesario. The same night, Sir Toby, Sir Andrew, and Feste stay up drinking and singing after midnight. Maria comes to warn them that Malvolio has been ordered by Olivia to turn them out of the house. Malvolio comes to tell Sir Toby that his mistress requires him to reform or leave but Sir Toby continues to sing and abuse the steward until he goes away in disgust. Maria proposes a plan to deceive Malvolio into thinking

Olivia is in love with him. At Orsino's court, Viola/Cesario listens to the Duke's views of love and expresses her love for him in a concealed way. She is then sent upon a further visit to present the Duke's love to Olivia. Fabian, Sir Toby, and Sir Andrew conceal themselves to watch Malvolio find a letter, forged by Maria in Olivia's handwriting, apparently expressing Olivia's love for Malvolio. The letter instructs him to wear yellow cross-gartering, to smile, and to behave in a haughty manner towards everyone but Olivia. Malvolio is convinced and Sir Toby and Maria are delighted with the success of their ruse.

Act III When Viola/Cesario again pleads the Duke's love, Olivia declares her love for Cesario. Obviously, Cesario must reject her but is urged to come once more on the Duke's behalf. Sir Andrew now despairs of winning Olivia because she seems to give more attention to Cesario. He decides to go home but Fabian and Sir Toby persuade him that Olivia's favours to Cesario are merely provocation; he must show his courage and challenge Cesario to a duel. Maria arrives to urge them all to come and witness Malvolio dressed absurdly and behaving as he was instructed to by the letter. Antonio, the sea-captain, has accompanied Sebastian to the city, given him his own purse, and arranged to meet him at their lodgings at the Elephant, since he fears detection if he walks the streets openly. Olivia, anxiously awaiting the return of Cesario, desires the serious company of her steward but he presents himself dressed in yellow cross-gartering, smiling, and quoting the letter he has found. Olivia, thinking him mad, asks for him to be attended to by Sir Toby and hastens to meet the newly-arrived Cesario. Sir Toby, Fabian and Maria treat Malvolio as a madman until he leaves angrily. Sir Andrew brings his challenge of a duel to Cesario/Viola, written out in ridiculous terms. He then goes to lie in wait in the orchard, though Sir Toby intends to challenge Cesario face to face to make sure the duel takes place. Meanwhile, as a token of love, Olivia gives Cesario her jewelled picture and urges him to return on the morrow. Left alone, Viola/Cesario is surprised to find herself challenged by Sir Toby on Aguecheek's behalf; Fabian tells Cesario that Sir Andrew is a skilled and violent swordsman while Sir Toby tells Aguecheek that Cesario is equally expert and eager for the duel. The two, mutually terrified, draw their swords but are interrupted by the arrival of Antonio who, taking Cesario for Sebastian, offers to defend him. Sir Toby intervenes until officers of the Duke interrupt the brawl and, recognizing Antonio as an enemy of Orsino, arrest him. Antonio, still assuming that Cesario is Sebastian, appeals to him for the purse he gave him but, naturally, Viola finds this unintelligible: appalled by this betrayal, as he sees it, Antonio is carried off to prison. As Antonio addressed her as Sebastian, Viola begins to have some hope her brother may be alive. She leaves hurriedly, thus convincing Sir Toby and Sir Andrew of her cowardice and leading them to pursue her.

Act IV Feste, coming across Sebastian, mistakes him for Cesario and tells him to visit Olivia. Sebastian is mystified and tries to get rid of the attentions of Feste when Sir Toby, Fabian and Sir Andrew arrive. The latter strikes Sebastian, assuming him to be the cowardly Cesario, but Sebastian instantly draws his sword and responds to Sir Toby. Olivia then enters and orders Sir Toby and his companions to leave. She in her turn takes Sebastian for

Cesario and urges him to accompany her to her house. Sebastian, thinking this to be some wonderful dream, readily agrees. Meanwhile Feste, disguised as a priest, makes fun of Malvolio who is shut in a dark room. Sir Toby and Maria, after enjoying this, leave Feste to assume his own identity and promise Malvolio the means to secure his release. Sebastian, still amazed at his good fortune, finds Olivia in love with him and they go to be married in secret immediately.

Act V   The Duke and Viola/Cesario come to visit Olivia to woo her once more. Antonio is brought in and while Viola commends him as her rescuer from the duel he denounces her apparent ingratitude in refusing to give him his purse. Olivia enters and rebukes Cesario for breaking his trust with her. The Duke urges his love for Olivia but is rejected: angrily, he says he will take Cesario away with him for ever. Viola is all too ready to go, but Olivia produces the priest who asserts that Olivia and Cesario are married. The Duke is furious at this treachery and, acknowledging that Cesario has deceptively won Olivia, he commands that Viola/Cesario must never meet him again. This is interrupted by Sir Andrew calling for a surgeon since Sir Toby and himself have been wounded by Sebastian, whom they think is Cesario. Sir Andrew rebukes Cesario who denies any responsibility. While Sir Toby and Sir Andrew are taken away to have their wounds attended to, Sebastian comes to apologize to Olivia for injuring her kinsman. Antonio and Sebastian recognize each other and are reconciled. Finally, Viola and Sebastian joyfully acknowledge that they are brother and sister. Olivia having married Sebastian, the Duke is delighted to take Viola as his wife. Feste comes with a letter from Malvolio complaining of his ill-treatment. He is released and comes to hear that the letter was forged by Maria as a plot devised by all those who disliked Malvolio and sought revenge. Malvolio leaves swearing to get revenge himself and, with the wedding between the Duke and Viola in prospect, the play ends with a song from Feste.

An outline such as this gives the bare bones of the plot and nothing more. It is useful, especially in a comedy involving disguise and mistaken identities, to be sure of what happens and to understand all the events. We can be fairly certain, however, that Shakespeare was interested in stories as a means to an end rather than as stories, pure and simple. One indication of this is the fact that in all the plays he wrote he only invented one plot for himself: all the others, including *Twelfth Night*, are adaptations of existing stories. As in other plays, there are a few inconsistencies in the adaptation of the material of *Twelfth Night*. Viola, in Act I, Scene ii, intends to present herself as a eunuch at Orsino's court, but there are no further references to this, for obvious reasons! The sea-captain, also in this scene, seems to promise to play a prominent part but, except for a mysterious reference to him in Act V, Scene i, he disappears. Sir Toby and Sir Andrew are wounded by Sebastian in an unspecified brawl of which we have no direct knowledge. Events occupying about three days seem at another moment to have been occurring over a period of three months. Feste was to have been present at the gulling of Malvolio but his place is taken by Fabian without explanation. None of these minor details, however, is noticeable in the rapid movement of the play on stage. They may be taken as further indications that it was the broad sweep of a story that interested Shakespeare, and the opportunity such a story afforded him for presenting a varied and entertaining selection of characters and situations.

Dramatic Structure and the Thematic Pattern

There are three stories in *Twelfth Night*: the main plot concerns Orsino and his attempts to woo Olivia by employing Viola/Cesario, with the resultant complications when Olivia falls in love with Viola, and Viola falls in love with Orsino. Running parallel to this is another plot concerning Sir Toby Belch, Sir Andrew Aguecheek, Maria, Fabian, and Feste, their activities culminating most notably in the 'gulling' of Malvolio. Thirdly, there is Sebastian, supported by Antonio, and the things that happen when he intervenes, as it were, in the other two plots and is mistaken for Cesario. The structure of the play is formed by the interweaving of these stories and the balancing of contrasting elements. Reference has already been made to one clear contrast: all the scenes with Sir Toby in Olivia's house are in prose, while scenes concerned with romantic love are in verse. Two distinctly different atmospheres are thereby created.

Another important factor is the order of scenes, which ensures a flow of action that has the maximum contrast and variety while advancing the plots simultaneously. By examining, for example, the first nine scenes of the play (Act I, Scene i to Act II, Scene iv inclusive), it is easy to see how all the stories are set in movement and how carefully they are dovetailed together. Thereafter the various traps are sprung over the succeeding eight scenes (Act II, Scene v to Act IV, Scene iii inclusive), leaving one long scene (Act V, Scene i) to resolve all the confusions. The balance of the sections, sometimes called Exposition, Development, and Resolution, gives to *Twelfth Night* a masterly symmetry. The characters, notably Viola and Feste, move from one plot to another, and form one of the ways in which the stories are blended together.

In a more subtle way, the play is united by two themes. The first is that of love; the second, the importance of a true, realistic view of the world as opposed to a dream, or even madness. The first theme is established by showing all the principal characters experiencing various manifestations of love: Orsino is affected and excessively romantic, enjoying the idea of a grand passion; Olivia, initially, is determined to mourn her brother in an equally deluded excess of sisterly affection. Both change their allegiances with surprising facility. Viola falls in love with Orsino and, in her role as Cesario, is loved by Olivia. Sir Toby is, in his own boisterous way, in love with Maria who loves him in return. He is so delighted with Maria's ingenuity in tricking Malvolio that he exclaims: 'I could marry this wench for this device!' Sir Andrew is persuaded that he must hope to marry Olivia and pathetically claims that he 'was ador'd once too'. Malvolio, also, provides a further variation by being 'sick of self-love'. Related to all this is the second theme. On numerous occasions, characters comment upon the unreality of their experience. The same words recur: sometimes love is seen as a kind of madness, 'a most extracting frenzy' as Olivia calls it; alternatively, in the confusion of events, it is a dream. Sebastian sees it as such when he is taken for Cesario by Olivia:

> What relish is in this? How runs the stream?
> Or I am mad, or else this is a dream.
> Let fancy still my sense in Lethe steep;
> If it be thus to dream, still let me sleep!
>
> (Act IV, Scene i, lines 58–61)

The 'gulling' of Malvolio and his appearance before Olivia, causes her to exclaim: 'Why this is very midsummer madness', and indeed, he is eventually locked away in a dark room as a lunatic. Yet Olivia also recognizes in her love for Cesario that she is on a par with Malvolio's distracted state:

> I am as mad as he
> If sad and merry madness equal be.
>
> (Act III, Scene iv, lines 14–15)

Shakespeare develops the part of Feste, referred to throughout the play as 'the Fool', to give him a special role within this theme of madness. Feste wryly comments upon the foolish behaviour of others, which he implies is universal:

> Foolery, sir, does walk about the orb like the sun –
> it shines everywhere.

> (Act III, Scene i, lines 38–9)

Viola is quick to recognize that Feste is 'wise enough to play the fool':

> For folly that he wisely shows is fit.
> But wise men, folly-fall'n, quite taint their wit.

> (Act III, Scene i, lines 66–7)

She points out a certain detached insight he provides into the events of the play: a role which is examined in more detail in the 'Summing Up' on p. 239.

This 'Summing Up' section may help you in forming an overall view of *Twelfth Night*. Although a thorough knowledge of its component elements is important, a sense of the play as a whole is vital.

LIST OF CHARACTERS

Orsino	Duke of Illyria
Sebastian	brother of Viola
Antonio	a sea captain, friend of Sebastian
A Sea Captain	friend of Viola
Valentine *Curio* }	gentlemen attending on the Duke
Sir Toby Belch	uncle of Olivia
Sir Andrew Aguecheek	
Malvolio	steward to Olivia
Fabian *Feste* a clown }	servants to Olivia
Olivia	a rich countess
Viola	sister of Sebastian
Maria	Olivia's waiting woman

Lords, Priest, Sailors, Officers, Musicians, and Attendants

The Scene: A city in Illyria; and the sea-coast near it.

ACT ONE SCENE I

Notice how quickly and effectively Shakespeare introduces two of his main characters, the Duke in person, and Olivia by report. It is never his practice to leave us guessing just for the fun of it. The delicate, almost sugary atmosphere of the scene, with the richly clad nobles elegantly relaxed around the Duke, the music, and the lyrical declarations of love-sickness, all tell us a great deal – perhaps all there is to know – about Orsino. There is a touch of unreality about his distress, as if he is unconsciously enjoying the situation, and being the Duke, with no shortage of courtiers to echo his mood, he can indulge his emotions in comfort. The cause of his desperation, Olivia's coolness, and her reasons for it, are made plain. And so, furnished with this essential piece of the main plot, and with a fairly strong impression of Orsino already forming in our minds, we can move on to learn the other piece of the pattern, in the next scene.

1–3. What Orsino is saying here is that he wants the musicians, with their evocative music, to help him to 'use up', as it were, all the love-sick thoughts that are torturing him, and so be rid of them. (But does he really want this? Is he not unconsciously enjoying every minute of it? Look at lines 41–2.)

2. *surfeiting:* having more than it can contain.

4. *fall:* cadence or concluding phrase (a musical term).

5–7. A subtle comparison between sound and scent which is spoiled if we try to render it in prose.

9. *spirit*. This is pronounced as one syllable, 'sprite', or more probably 'spreet'. 'Sprite' and 'spirit' were virtually the same word. ***quick:*** lively.

10. We should probably insert the words 'the fact that' after ***notwithstanding***.

12. *validity:* value. ***pitch:*** height (probably a hawking term).

13. *abatement and low price*. These two are synonymous here, meaning 'worthless condition'. Orsino's description of the working of love is somewhat involved. He seems to be saying that it matters not who they are who fall in love, or how passionately, the effect on them is the same. They are alike reduced to the same condition of helplessness.

14–15. Again, the meaning is obscure. Orsino seems to be saying that a love-sick person's thoughts (***fancy***) are so occupied imagining fond things (***shapes***), that they end up in an utterly unreal world (***high fantastical***).

16. *go hunt:* go hunting.

19–23. Orsino describes his love-at-first-sight. He is referring to an ancient Greek myth in which Actaeon, when out hunting, came upon the goddess Diana while she was bathing, which so displeased her that she turned him into a stag, to be savaged by his own hounds. Orsino is saying that, as soon as he saw Olivia, his passion, like Actaeon's hounds, began to torture him, and has gone on doing so ever since.

ACT ONE
SCENE I

The Duke's palace

[Enter ORSINO, *Duke of Illyria,* CURIO, *and other*
LORDS; MUSICIANS *attending]*

Duke
  If music be the food of love, play on,
  Give me excess of it, that, surfeiting,
  The appetite may sicken and so die.
  That strain again! It had a dying fall;
  O, it came o'er my ear like the sweet sound   5
  That breathes upon a bank of violets,
  Stealing and giving odour! Enough, no more;
  'Tis not so sweet now as it was before.
  O spirit of love, how quick and fresh art thou!
  That, notwithstanding thy capacity   10
  Receiveth as the sea, nought enters there,
  Of what validity and pitch soe'er,
  But falls into abatement and low price
  Even in a minute. So full of shapes is fancy,
  That it alone is high fantastical.   15

Curio
  Will you go hunt, my lord?

Duke
                  What, Curio?

Curio
  The hart.

Duke
  Why, so I do, the noblest that I have.
  O, when mine eyes did see Olivia first,

20. *purg'd the air of pestilence!* Elizabethans were still preoccupied with the physical manifestations of evil. Darkness, fog and bad weather generally were to them more than just unpleasant natural conditions. They saw them almost as the outward signs of the evil forces surrounding mankind. So when Orsino describes the effect of Olivia's beauty, it is not surprising that he will think first of this aspect of her beneficent influence.

22. *fell:* fierce.

25–33. Valentine has been sent to woo the Countess Olivia (or at least take the first steps) on behalf of Orsino, who apparently feels that, as Duke, he can hardly go in person at this stage. (The kind of courtship practised by Orsino follows the medieval style, with its long and not dishonourable history, and we should not think of the Duke as behaving in an unconventional way in all this.)

25. *might not be admitted:* was not allowed in.

27. *element:* sky; ***seven years' heat:*** seven summers (and so, seven years).

28. *at ample view:* in public.

29. *cloistress:* nun (who keeps to the cloisters, which are part of a monastery or nunnery, and is thus withdrawn from the outside world).

30–1. *water . . . brine:* a poetic way of saying that she will weep every day. 'Brine' is salt-water, and tears are thought to be salt; ***'eye-offending'***, because weeping makes our eyes sore.

31. *season.* We season food with salt, to bring out the full flavour and to keep it fresh. Olivia is trying to keep alive the memory of her dead brother by weeping over him. The use of this elaborate imagery perhaps leaves us today with a feeling of artificiality. Is Olivia really as heart-broken as she believes she is? Is she possibly getting a kind of satisfaction out of the strict conditions of mourning she has set herself, in just the way that Orsino appears to enjoy his love-sickness?

34–40. Ever hopeful, Orsino reasons that if Olivia can have had such affection for a brother, she will be even more whole-hearted when she falls in love – with himself, as he hopes!

36–8. *How will she love . . . live in her:* Once she has fallen in love, affection for everyone and everything else will cease.

36. *rich golden shaft.* Cupid, the love-god, shot golden-tipped arrows at people to make them fall in love.

38–9. *liver, brain, and heart. These sovereign thrones.* The physical organs were still generally held to be the seat of emotion and thought. They are spoken of here as 'sovereign (all-powerful) thrones' because it was believed that whatever occupied them would then be in effective control of the whole person, like a king on his throne, ruling his subjects.

40. *one self king!* one and the same king. The 'sole ruler' Orsino hopes for in Olivia's case is 'love', and he is duly dazzled as he conjures up the prospect.

41–2. On which optimistic note, Orsino can now turn and enjoy his romantic mood again, this time in the garden!

Methought she purg'd the air of pestilence! 20
That instant was I turn'd into a hart,
And my desires, like fell and cruel hounds,
E'er since pursue me.

[Enter VALENTINE]

How now! what news from her?
Valentine
So please my lord, I might not be admitted, 25
But from her handmaid do return this answer
The element itself, till seven years' heat,
Shall not behold her face at ample view;
But like a cloistress she will veiled walk,
And water once a day her chamber round 30
With eye-offending brine; all this to season
A brother's dead love, which she would keep fresh
And lasting in her sad remembrance.
Duke
O, she that hath a heart of that fine frame
To pay this debt of love but to a brother, 35
How will she love when the rich golden shaft
Hath kill'd the flock of all affections else
That live in her; when liver, brain, and heart,
These sovereign thrones, are all supplied and fill'd,
Her sweet perfections, with one self king! 40
Away before me to sweet beds of flow'rs:
Love-thoughts lie rich when canopied with bow'rs.

[Exeunt]

SCENE II

This is an abrupt change from the security and leisureliness of Orsino's palace. Here we see bedraggled survivors from the sea, under much greater actual stress than Orsino and Olivia, for all their protestations of emotion. We get our first glimpse of Viola, an integrated, resourceful creature who impresses us at once with her 'no-nonsense' genuineness. Her arrival in Illyria spells the end of what promised to be a quite predictable pattern of courtly wooing. The whole of the main plot will turn upon the interaction of these three with their utterly distinct personalities. As well endowed with feelings as any, Viola is as yet in no position to show them. All she has time for is simply to ensure her survival.

Again, much sheer information is packed into this scene; and Viola's reason for taking this most crucial step – joining Orsino's service – is explained and justified quite acceptably.

2. *Illyria:* probably the Adriatic coast; though we might feel that any country with a coast-line would do as well. The actual locality has little significance in this play.

4. *Elysium:* the equivalent of Heaven in the religion of the Ancient Greeks.

5. A very natural touch: Viola suddenly clutches at a hope, and at once turns to the sailors for their support.

6. *perchance:* only by chance.

7–8. The Captain comforts her by describing her brother's brave efforts to save himself from the wreck, which, as far as he can see, may well have been successful.

11. *driving:* being driven by the wind.

12. *provident:* taking appropriate action.

14. *liv'd:* managed to keep afloat.

15. *Arion:* a semi-mythical poet of the ancient Greeks, who managed to foil a murderous attempt to drown him, by charming a dolphin with one of his songs, to carry him to safety on its back.

16. *hold acquaintance with:* keep on struggling against.

18–20. Viola rewards him for this cheering news, and reasons with herself that, as she herself has escaped, so there is every cause to hope that her brother, too, is safe – especially now that the Captain's story points the same way (*serves for authority*).

21. Only now does Viola turn to her own needs – her first thoughts have all been for her brother.

SCENE II

The sea-coast

[Enter VIOLA, *a* CAPTAIN, *and* SAILORS]

Viola
What country, friends, is this?

Captain
This is Illyria, lady.

Viola
And what should I do in Illyria?
My brother he is in Elysium.
Perchance he is not drown'd – what think you,
    sailors?   5

Captain
It is perchance that you yourself were saved.

Viola
O my poor brother! and so perchance may he be.

Captain
True, madam, and, to comfort you with chance,
Assure yourself, after our ship did split,
When you, and those poor number saved with you,   10
Hung on our driving boat, I saw your brother,
Most provident in peril, bind himself—
Courage and hope both teaching him the practice—
To a strong mast that liv'd upon the sea;
Where, like Arion on the dolphin's back,   15
I saw him hold acquaintance with the waves
So long as I could see.

Viola
For saying so, there's gold.
Mine own escape unfoldeth to my hope,
Whereto thy speech serves for authority,   20
The like of him. Know'st thou this country?

Captain
Ay, madam, well; for I was bred and born
Not three hours' travel from this very place.

21

30–41. A few more useful bits of background information.

32. *fresh in murmur:* the latest piece of gossip.

35. *What's she?* 'Who's she?' (A frequent Shakespearian usage.)

40. *abjur'd:* sworn to do without.
41–4. Viola sees a chance here for herself to find some sort of safe if temporary concealment. The construction is a little involved, but the meaning is plain – she wants to serve Orsino so that for the time being she can remain in obscurity (*not be delivered to the world*) till she has found a suitable opportunity (*made mine own occasion mellow*) to assume her proper rank and position.

44. *compass:* achieve, bring about.

47–51. Viola is so well impressed by the Captain's manner that she confidently believes that he is good at heart; though she realises that an attractive exterior (*beauteous wall*) often only disguises a rotten character (*Doth oft close in pollution*).

Viola
  Who governs here?
Captain
  A noble duke, in nature as in name.   25
Viola
  What is his name?
Captain
  Orsino.
Viola
  Orsino! I have heard my father name him.
  He was a bachelor then.
Captain
  And so is now, or was so very late;   30
  For but a month ago I went from hence,
  And then 'twas fresh in murmur – as, you know,
  What great ones do the less will prattle of—
  That he did seek the love of fair Olivia.
Viola
  What's she?   35
Captain
  A virtuous maid, the daughter of a count
  That died some twelvemonth since, then leaving her
  In the protection of his son, her brother,
  Who shortly also died; for whose dear love,
  They say, she hath abjur'd the company   40
  And sight of men.
Viola
              O that I serv'd that lady,
  And might not be delivered to the world,
  Till I had made mine own occasion mellow,
  What my estate is!
Captain
              That were hard to compass,
  Because she will admit no kind of suit—   45
  No, not the Duke's.
Viola
  There is a fair behaviour in thee, Captain;
  And though that nature with a beauteous wall
  Doth oft close in pollution, yet of thee

53. *Conceal me what I am* Modern English would either say 'conceal me' or 'conceal what I am'. (Compare St Mark's Gospel, Chapter I, Verse 24 (A.V.), 'I know thee who thou art'), So 'keep my identity secret'.

54. *become:* suit.

55. *The form of my intent:* 'whatever role I decide to adopt'.

56. *eunuch.* Eunuchs (castrated males) were, for obvious reasons, frequently found as intimate servants in wealthy households particularly in the Middle East. It would clearly seem a good idea for Viola to assume this rôle; it would tend to stop people asking too many questions about her un-masculine voice and appearance. It is odd, perhaps, that this is never referred to again. But it is not allowed to become what would only be a further complication in Viola's ensuing involvement with Orsino and Olivia.

59. 'That will guarantee that I can give worthwhile service' – a suitable qualification for the job, as we would say today. Viola's musical talent will be a good recommendation in her hoped-for employment with Orsino.

60. 'The future must be left to take care of itself.'

61. 'Treat my scheme with due secrecy.' (Literally, 'make your silence appropriate to my scheme'.); *wit* has many meanings. Here, it signifies the finished product of her wit or intelligence.

62. *Be you . . . I'll be:* 'All right, you be his eunuch and I'll be your mute.' *mute:* a dumb servant. (Like a eunuch, but for different reasons, a mute would have his uses in a household – secrets would always be safe with him!)

63. 'May I be struck blind if I betray your secret.' *blabs:* betrays confidence.

SCENE III

It is now time for some light relief; the action up to now has been at a high pitch. The blank verse and stately language, therefore, give place to informal, conversational prose. (This is a fairly regular practice of Shakespeare at this stage in his career, though his later plays make increasing use of prose for serious dialogue and soliloquy.)

But the break is only in mood. The very first line takes up the thread again – Olivia's excessive mourning is in question once more, this time to be condemned by the down-to-earth common-sense of her uncle, Sir Toby Belch.

Sir Toby's position in her household is worth noting. Things were still at the stage where a person of rank and possession would be only too pleased to provide permanent hospitality to dependants, who might not be relatives. These, if able-bodied men, would provide some kind of security for the Lord and Lady of the house, who, alone, would be hard put to it to defend a large residence. So we must not think of Sir Toby as just a parasite in his niece's house. Even he could be a quite comforting person to have about the place if danger threatened.

I will believe thou hast a mind that suits   50
With this thy fair and outward character.
I prithee, and I'll pay thee bounteously,
Conceal me what I am, and be my aid
For such disguise as haply shall become
The form of my intent. I'll serve this duke: 55
Thou shalt present me as an eunuch to him;
It may be worth thy pains, for I can sing
And speak to him in many sorts of music,
That will allow me very worth his service.
What else may hap to time I will commit;   60
Only shape thou thy silence to my wit.

Captain
Be you his eunuch and your mute I'll be;
When my tongue blabs, then let mine eyes not see.

Viola
I thank thee. Lead me on.

[Exeunt]

SCENE III

_____

Olivia's house

[Enter SIR TOBY BELCH and MARIA]

Sir Toby
What a plague means my niece to take the death of
her brother thus? I am sure care's an enemy to life.

Maria
By my troth, Sir Toby, you must come in earlier o'

4. *cousin.* In Shakespeare, this could denote any close relationship, not necessarily of blood.

5. *ill hours:* bad hours (and so 'late hours').

6. *except before excepted:* word-play on a Latin legal phrase 'exceptis excipiendis'. Sir Toby is suggesting that Olivia has already taken quite enough exception to his behaviour.

7. *confine:* restrain.

9. *confine . . . finer.* Another pun, playing on the two meanings of 'fine'.

11. *an:* if (a fairly regular Shakespearian usage).

11–12. *hang themselves in their own straps.* A more vivid way of saying 'Let them be hanged'. (Modern English still has the quite common phrase, 'I'll be hanged if . . .'.) There was an Elizabethan saying, 'To be hanged in one's own garter', which may have been in Sir Toby's mind.

16. The very idea of sponsoring Sir Andrew Aguecheek as a serious suitor for the Countess was almost ludicrous, as we may well agree when he makes his appearance. There was certainly a financial interest in it for Sir Toby, even if only indirectly, to the tune of 3000 ducats a year – a sizeable fortune by any reckoning (see Note, line 20). But Sir Toby is likely motivated as much by his irrepressible sense of fun, in much the way that he joins in Maria's later device to push Malvolio into the same impossible position with his niece. We are hugely indebted to Maria and Sir Toby for their ingenuity and the sheer outrageousness of their schemes. In modern idiom, they 'think big' and it pays off.

18. *tall:* brave, or simply 'good' as in our modern phrase 'a good fellow'.

19. Somewhat cynically 'What's that got to do with it?'

20. *ducat.* There were ducats in more than one European currency. The value in England in Shakespeare's day was equivalent to something like 33p.

21. *he'll have but a year in all these ducats:* 'his whole fortune is likely to last him only a year.'

22. *prodigal:* one who spends and gives away his wealth with no thought for the future.

23. *Fie:* an expression of disapproval or disgust. Sir Toby pretends to be disgusted with Maria for saying such a thing

23–4. *viol-de-gamboys:* (for 'viola-da-gamba') bass viol, a stringed instrument like a 'cello, held between the legs

27. *natural.* Maria is here using 'natural' to mean 'half-witted', which it often meant at this period.

nights; your cousin, my lady, takes great exceptions to
your ill hours.   5

Sir Toby

Why, let her except before excepted.

Maria

Ay, but you must confine yourself within the modest
limits of order.

Sir Toby

Confine! I'll confine myself no finer than I am. These
clothes are good enough to drink in, and so be these 10
boots too; an they be not, let them hang themselves
in their own straps.

Maria

That quaffing and drinking will undo you; I heard my
lady talk of it yesterday, and of a foolish knight that
you brought in one night here to be her wooer.   15

Sir Toby

Who? Sir Andrew Aguecheek?

Maria

Ay, he.

Sir Toby

He's as tall a man as any's in Illyria.

Maria

What's that to th' purpose?

Sir Toby

Why, he has three thousand ducats a year.   20

Maria

Ay, but he'll have but a year in all these ducats; he's
a very fool and a prodigal.

Sir Toby

Fie that you'll say so! He plays o' th' viol-de-gamboys, and speaks three or four languages word for
word without book, and hath all the good gifts of 25
nature.

Maria

He hath indeed, almost natural; for, besides that he's
a fool, he's a great quarreller; and but that he

27

29. gust . . . quarrelling: taste for quarrelling.

31. have the gift of a grave: 'meet his death'. (The idea of 'gifts' of nature is thus carried further.)

32. substractors: detractors (those who take away his good name). Sir Toby's indignant outburst is not seriously meant to take anyone in. He knows as well as Maria that Sir Andrew is a figure of fun.
36. Like Falstaff, Sir Toby is adept at turning an argument against his critics. He can always talk himself out of an unfavourable situation, yet without really trying to dodge the blame he knows he deserves. His excuse in this instance – drinking his niece's health – is one he doesn't expect Maria to take seriously. It would spoil his joke if she did.

38. coystrill: worthless fellow.
40. parish-top: a large spinning-top kept in a parish to provide the parishioners with wholesome exercise when bad weather prevented them from working on the land.
40. What . . . ! simply an exclamation. **Castiliano vulgo!** This mysterious phrase suggests that Sir Toby is urging Maria to behave more seriously now that Sir Andrew is approaching, but no one knows the exact meaning.
41. Agueface. To get someone's name wrong on purpose, in this way, is a familiar trick of the comedian.

46. Accost. The confusion initiated by the introduction of this word has the desired effect of putting Sir Andrew off-balance from the start. (He is not over-endowed with poise, in any case.) Having thus drained him of self-confidence, Sir Toby now intentionally over-supplies him, with the result that he has Sir Andrew dancing to his tune, and literally so at the end of the scene. This is a delightful episode. Or is it a bit cruel, like a cat playing with a mouse? The word 'accost' is used quite properly ('Approach and start conversing'). But its abruptness here has Sir Andrew clearly bewildered.
47. What's that? This can equally mean 'Who's that?' in Shakespearian English (see Act I, Scene ii, line 35). This latter meaning is the one Sir Toby chooses to take, and answers accordingly. But Sir Andrew's reaction shows that it was the word, not the person, he wanted explained. Sir Toby may well have been wilfully misunderstanding him – he certainly does nothing to clear up the confusion, not, that is, till he has had his fun out of it.

hath the gift of a coward to allay the gust he hath in
quarrelling, 'tis thought among the prudent he would 30
quickly have the gift of a grave.

Sir Toby

By this hand, they are scoundrels and substractors that
say so of him. Who are they?

Maria

They that add, moreover, he's drunk nightly in your
company. 35

Sir Toby

With drinking healths to my niece; I'll drink to her as
long as there is a passage in my throat and drink in
Illyria. He's a coward and a coystrill that will not drink
to my niece till his brains turn o' th' toe like a parish-
top. What, wench! Castiliano vulgo! for here comes 40
Sir Andrew Agueface.

[Enter SIR ANDREW AGUECHEEK]

Sir Andrew

Sir Toby Belch! How now, Sir Toby Belch!

Sir Toby

Sweet Sir Andrew!

Sir Andrew

Bless you, fair shrew.

Maria

And you too, sir. 45

Sir Toby

Accost, Sir Andrew, accost.

Sir Andrew

What's that?

Sir Toby

My niece's chambermaid.

Sir Andrew

Good Mistress Accost, I desire better acquaintance.

Maria

My name is Mary, sir. 50

52–3. *front her, board her, woo her, assail her.* This sudden string of indelicate synonyms has Sir Andrew believing that nothing less than instant love-making is now expected of him.

56. *Fare you well, gentlemen.* Why does Maria suggest leaving just now? Is she embarrassed by all this, or simply pretending to be, to keep up the joke?
57. *An:* if. The meaning of Sir Toby's observation here is almost – 'You're not the man I took you for, if you let her go just like that'.

59. Notice how meekly Sir Andrew echoes him, almost word for word. This emphasizes neatly his pathetic dependence upon Sir Toby's judgment and experience. He is almost mesmerized by it.
60. *do you think you have fools in hand?* 'do you think you are having to deal with fools?'
62. *I have not you by th' hand.* Maria has taken 'in hand' literally – intentionally, of course.

63. *Marry:* by (the Virgin) Mary (a mild oath); ***here's my hand.*** This, for Sir Andrew, is real progress in amorousness.
64. *thought is free:* (proverbially) 'one may think what one likes.'
65. *butt'ry-bar:* rather like our modern serving-hatch, where refreshment of both kinds was dispensed (the word originally meant a place where bottles were stored, from the French word *Bouteille*, bottle).
66. *What's your metaphor?* 'What double meaning are you now implying? (Or, more simply, 'What are you hinting at now?') Sir Andrew tries hopefully to keep abreast of all this 'double-talk', but he never quite catches up. The ensuing dialogue is typical Elizabethan wordplay, if a little one-sided. By nimbly substituting now one meaning, now another, for her words, Maria has Sir Andrew helplessly trailing behind her.
68–9. *I can keep my hand dry:* Sir Andrew's meaning here is probably quite literal – he is protesting that he won't spill his liquor. But Maria has in mind a popular belief that a 'dry hand' indicated an un-amorous disposition. But the word 'dry' in *A dry jest* has yet another meaning – stupid – and this is how Sir Andrew seems to take it.
72. When Maria says she has the 'dry jests' *at her fingers' ends*, she is referring to Sir Andrew's hand which she is holding, and which amuses her because it *is* dry; and so, when she lets it go, her cause for amusement goes too. Sir Toby has been enjoying all this. He and Maria share the humour, which has gone over Sir Andrew's head.

Sir Andrew

Good Mistress Mary Accost—

Sir Toby

You mistake, knight. 'Accost' is front her, board her, woo her, assail her.

Sir Andrew

By my troth, I would not undertake her in this company. Is that the meaning of 'accost'? 55

Maria

Fare you well, gentlemen.

Sir Toby

An thou let part so, Sir Andrew, would thou mightst never draw sword again!

Sir Andrew

An you part so, mistress, I would I might never draw sword again. Fair lady, do you think you have fools in 60 hand?

Maria

Sir, I have not you by th' hand.

Sir Andrew

Marry, but you shall have; and here's my hand.

Maria

Now, sir, thought is free. I pray you, bring your hand to th' butt'ry-bar and let it drink. 65

Sir Andrew

Wherefore, sweetheart? What's your metaphor?

Maria

It's dry, sir.

Sir Andrew

Why, I think so; I am not such an ass but I can keep my hand dry. But what's your jest?

Maria

A dry jest, sir. 70

Sir Andrew

Are you full of them?

Maria

Ay, sir, I have them at my fingers' ends; marry, now

74. *canary:* a popular wine, from the Canary Islands.

77–8. *Methinks . . . an ordinary man.* Such crestfallen frankness might have elicited some sort of pity – but not from Sir Toby!

79–80. *eater of beef . . . wit.* A popular belief, that beef had this effect when eaten to excess.

82. *forswear:* do without, give up.

85. *What is 'pourquoi' . . . ?* Sir Andrew is apologetic about the gaps in his education.

89. The conversation now switches to Sir Andrew's lank, pale yellow hair, an obvious feature to make capital out of in such a scene.

91. *thou seest it will not curl by nature.* Sir Toby is punning here on the word 'tongues'. When Sir Andrew regretted his neglect of the 'tongues' he meant 'foreign languages'. But Sir Toby takes it as 'tongs' (curling tongs) which might, of course, have done something to improve Sir Andrew's hair. (There may also be a reference to the antithesis between 'art' and 'nature'.)

93. *flax on a distaff.* Flax is a plant used in the making of linen and other materials. The distaff was the spindle on to which it was spun, normally within the home, by the *huswife* (housewife). The pale yellow colour of flax gives us our word 'flaxen'.

I let go your hand, I am barren.

[Exit MARIA]

Sir Toby
　　O knight, thou lack'st a cup of canary! When did I see
　　thee so put down?　　　　　　　　　　　　　　　75
Sir Andrew
　　Never in your life, I think; unless you see canary put
　　me down. Methinks sometimes I have no more wit
　　than a Christian or an ordinary man has; but I am a
　　great eater of beef, and I believe that does harm to my
　　wit.　　　　　　　　　　　　　　　　　　80
Sir Toby
　　No question.
Sir Andrew
　　An I thought that, I'd forswear it. I'll ride home
　　tomorrow, Sir Toby.
Sir Toby
　　Pourquoi, my dear knight?
Sir Andrew
　　What is 'pourquoi' – do or not do? I would I had　　85
　　bestowed that time in the tongues that I have in
　　fencing, dancing, and bear-baiting. O, had I but
　　followed the arts!
Sir Toby
　　Then hadst thou had an excellent head of hair.
Sir Andrew
　　Why, would that have mended my hair?　　　　90
Sir Toby
　　Past question; for thou seest it will not curl by nature.
Sir Andrew
　　But it becomes me well enough, does't not?
Sir Toby
　　Excellent; it hangs like flax on a distaff, and I hope to
　　see a huswife take thee between her legs and spin it
　　off.　　　　　　　　　　　　　　　　　95

96–9. Sir Andrew's present loss of confidence we can well understand. What does surprise us is that he ever allowed himself to be talked into this courtship.

102. *there's life in't*: 'you still have a sporting chance.'

103–5. *I am a fellow . . . sometimes altogether*. A small but telling sign here of Sir Andrew's vanity, a side of his character just as fundamental as his more obvious self-deprecation. There is one cause for both – he takes himself far too seriously – hence his blithe assumption here that other people will be as fascinated as he is by what goes on in his mind.

104. *revels*: entertainments (like the very ones put on by the Inns of Court, with *Twelfth Night* as probably one of its items).

106. *kickshawses:* trivial things that entertain or amuse. (The word seems to be a corruption of the French *quelquechose* in the sense of a trifle or small delicacy.)

107–9. How cautious can he get! He says he is as good as his equals! *Compare with an old man*. This has been variously explained, but it is difficult to supply a meaning with any certainty. It may be that Sir Andrew has the phrase 'elders and betters' in mind; he has already spoken of his 'betters'.

110. *galliard:* a quick, lively dance.

111. *cut a caper*. One of the steps in the galliard was to beat the feet together in the air. The other meaning of 'caper' – a plant of which the buds are used for making sauce – is taken by Sir Toby (line 112) for an easy pun.

113. *backtrick:* a caper backwards.

115. *Wherefore are these things hid?* Almost the master-stroke in the process of flattery so successfully brought off by Sir Toby – 'If I could dance as well as you can, I'd be doing it all the time.'

116. *curtain*. These were used to protect valuable pictures, and would be drawn aside only when the picture was to be viewed.

117. *Mistress Mall's picture*. 'Mall' is probably the same as 'Moll'. There is no clear indication whose portrait is referred to.

119. *coranto:* another lively dance, similar to the galliard.

120–1. *make water . . . sink-a-pace*. 'Sink-a-pace' is a corruption of *cinque pace*, a French dance. The picture here is crude, but it certainly drives the point home!

121–2. *Is it a world to hide virtues in?* Like Falstaff, Sir Toby now and then speaks as a true philosopher.

Sir Andrew
  Faith, I'll home to-morrow, Sir Toby. Your niece will
  not be seen, or if she be, it's four to one she'll
  none of me; the Count himself here hard by woos
  her.

Sir Toby
  She'll none o' th' Count; she'll not match above her 100
  degree, neither in estate, years, nor wit; I have heard
  her swear't, Tut, there's life in't, man.

Sir Andrew
  I'll stay a month longer. I am a fellow o' th' strangest
  mind i' th' world; I delight in masques and revels
  sometimes altogether.   105

Sir Toby
  Art thou good at these kickshawses, knight?

Sir Andrew
  As any man in Illyria, whatsoever he be, under the
  degree of my betters; and yet I will not compare with
  an old man.

Sir Toby
  What is thy excellence in a galliard, knight?   110

Sir Andrew
  Faith, I can cut a caper.

Sir Toby
  And I can cut the mutton to't.

Sir Andrew
  And I think I have the backtrick simply as strong as
  any man in Illyria.

Sir Toby
  Wherefore are these things hid? Wherefore have 115
  these gifts a curtain before 'em? Are they like to take
  dust, like Mistress Mall's picture? Why dost thou not
  go to church in a galliard and come home in a
  coranto? My very walk should be a jig; I would not
  so much as make water but in a sink-a-pace. What 120
  dost thou mean? Is it a world to hide virtues in? I
  did think, by the excellent constitution of thy

123. *form'd under the star of a galliard.* This is in astrological vein. It suits Sir Toby here to pretend that Galliard is a sign of the Zodiac, conferring dancing genius on those born under it.

124. Once more Sir Andrew's vanity is tickled into motion, though it doesn't venture beyond *indifferent well* (fairly well).

125. *stock:* stocking.

126. *What should we do else?* 'What else is there to do?'

127. *Taurus:* an authentic Zodiacal sign this time (the Bull), but it was not concerned with 'sides and heart' (each sign had a particular part or parts of the human anatomy assigned to it.)

129. *legs and thighs.* Sir Toby gleefully points out Sir Andrew's error and takes the appropriate opportunity to make him dance ridiculously

SCENE IV

A brief return to the fortunes of Viola. Her scheme has worked and she is duly installed in the Duke's service, as his latest and – as he optimistically believes – most promising go-between in his courtship of Olivia. How ill-placed his optimism is, we can judge from Viola's hint at the end.

This is an excellent example of Shakespeare's skill in linking scene with scene by a dexterous economy of word and material. There is a continuous moving forward, yet not so subtly expressed that we miss the connection, nor yet so laboured that we lose interest.

1–2. *Cesario:* the masculine name Viola has adopted.

2. *like:* likely.

5–7. 'You must have doubts about his reliability, or about the way I'm doing the job, if you are so uncertain whether he will go on being nice to me.'

5. *humour:* natural tendency; *negligence:* that is, in the carrying out of her job. It is beginning to mean a great deal to her that Orsino is being so kind, but she needs a lot of reassurance, and – typical of a young person in her first job and her first romance – has her fair share of diffidence.

9. *Count.* Orsino is from now on thus addressed.

leg, it was form'd under the star of a galliard.

Sir Andrew
Ay, 'tis strong, and it does indifferent well in a flame-colour'd stock. Shall we set about some revels?   125

Sir Toby
What shall we do else? Were we not born under Taurus?

Sir Andrew
Taurus? That's sides and heart.

Sir Toby
No, sir; it is legs and thighs. Let me see thee caper.
Ha, higher! Ha, ha, excellent!   130

[Exeunt]

SCENE IV

The Duke's palace

[Enter VALENTINE, *and* VIOLA *in man's attire]*

Valentine
If the Duke continue these favours towards you, Cesario, you are like to be much advanc'd; he hath known you but three days, and already you are no stranger.

Viola
You either fear his humour or my negligence, that you   5
call in question the continuance of his love. Is he inconstant, sir, in his favours?

Valentine
No, believe me.

[Enter DUKE, CURIO, *and* ATTENDANTS]*

Viola
I thank you. Here comes the Count.

Duke
Who saw Cesario, ho?   10

12. *Stand you awhile aloof*. Spoken to all except Viola. Orsino seems to have decided already that he can confide more in Viola than in anyone else.

13. *unclasp'd*. Valuable books would, as sometimes even now, be secured by a clasp.

15. *address thy gait:* 'make your way'.

16. *Be not denied access:* 'Don't let them refuse to let you in.'

17–18. A very effective way for her to say that she won't move until they have let her in to speak to Olivia.

20. *As it is spoke:* 'as it is reported' ('spoke' was a correct Elizabethan past participle).

21. *Be clamorous:* almost 'Make a great noise'; ***leap all civil bounds:*** 'ignore (leap over) all the normal rules of polite behaviour.'

22. 'Don't come back empty-handed.'

23. Ever practical, Viola realizes that she hasn't been told what to say if she does get invited in.

25. *dear faith:* heartfelt fidelity.

26. 'You are well suited to convey my desperate feelings of love-sickness.'

28. *nuncio:* messenger. Quite naturally, since he is not prepared to do it in person, Orsino would rather someone did it who was young enough to deliver the message with conviction.

29. Viola knows just how impossible this may be.

29–34. Emphasizing her youthful appearance, in order to convince her of her suitability, Orsino probably only embarrasses her, and makes her feel that her secret is less secure than ever.

29–31. 'Your carefree, youthful appearance (***happy years***) clearly proves wrong (***belie***) those who say you are grown up.'

32. *rubious:* ruby-coloured; ***pipe:*** windpipe. Conveniently for Viola, Orsino attributes her girlish voice to the fact that it has not yet broken.

34. *is semblative:* resembles.

35. *constellation*. Astrology teaches that a person's character is affected by the position of the stars at the time of birth. 'Constellation' here means 'character, as fixed by the stars'.

36. *attend*. Here used as an imperative. Orsino is ordering them to go with Viola.

37–8. He prefers to be alone in his present mood.

Viola

On your attendance, my lord, here.

Duke

Stand you awhile aloof. Cesario,
Thou know'st no less but all; I have unclasp'd
To thee the book even of my secret soul.
Therefore, good youth, address thy gait unto her;   15
Be not denied access, stand at her doors,
And tell them there thy fixed foot shall grow
Till thou have audience.

Viola

              Sure, my noble lord,
If she be so abandon'd to her sorrow
As it is spoke, she never will admit me.   20

Duke

Be clamorous and leap all civil bounds,
Rather than make unprofited return.

Viola

Say I do speak with her, my lord, what then?

Duke

O, then unfold the passion of my love,
Surprise her with discourse of my dear faith!   25
It shall become thee well to act my woes:
She will attend it better in thy youth
Than in a nuncio's of more grave aspect.

Viola

I think not so, my lord.

Duke

            Dear lad, believe it,
For they shall yet belie thy happy years   30
That say thou art a man: Diana's lip
Is not more smooth and rubious; thy small pipe
Is as the maiden's organ, shrill and sound,
And all is semblative a woman's part.
I know thy constellation is right apt   35
For this affair. Some four or five attend him—
All, if you will, for I myself am best
When least in company. Prosper well in this,
And thou shalt live as freely as thy lord
                        39

41. *barful:* frustrating. (To bar the way to something is to hinder or frustrate whoever is trying to get to it.)

42. Some of the most significant lines in Shakespeare are conveyed in 'asides'.

SCENE V

A busy scene, which gives us our first sight of the clown, Feste, in characteristic role; and Olivia, whose fortunes take a momentous step forward; and Malvolio, who manages, though in restrained fashion as yet, to present himself in his true colours. So, by the end of Act I, we shall have made the acquaintance of all the main characters (except Sebastian and his loyal friend Antonio) intimately enough for us to size them up; and the main plot, at least, will be sufficiently under way for us to see where it is heading.

5. *fear no colours.* The word 'colours' is used here in the military sense, meaning 'ensign' or 'standard'. The complete phrase, almost proverbial, means 'fear no foe', which in turn means 'fear no one (or nothing)'.

6. *Make that good:* 'Explain that satisfactorily.'

7. A deliberate anticlimax – Feste's meaning suddenly becomes literal: 'Not only will a hanged man have no fears, he will have nothing else either!'

8. *lenten answer:* a short answer, 'rationed', like food in Lent (a penitential season in the Christian calendar).

To call his fortunes thine.

Viola

I'll do my best   40

To woo your lady. *[Aside]* Yet, a barful strife!

Whoe'er I woo, myself would be his wife.

SCENE V

_____

Olivia's house

[Enter MARIA *and* CLOWN*]*

Maria

Nay, either tell me where thou hast been, or I will not
open my lips so wide as a bristle may enter in way of
thy excuse; my lady will hang thee for thy absence.

Clown

Let her hang me. He that is well hang'd in this world
needs to fear no colours.   5

Maria

Make that good.

Clown

He shall see none to fear.

Maria

A good lenten answer. I can tell thee where that saying
was born, of 'I fear no colours'.

Clown

Where, good Mistress Mary?   10

Maria

In the wars; and that may you be bold to say in your
foolery.

Clown

Well, God give them wisdom that have it; and those
that are fools, let them use their talents.

Maria

Yet you will be hang'd for being so long absent; or to   15
be turn'd away – is not that as good as a hanging to
you?

20. *You are resolute then?* 'You have made up your mind, then?'

21. *points*. A pun – 'points', or tagged laces, were used to keep up a man's gaskins or breeches.

24–6. *if Sir Toby . . . any in Illyria:* 'It makes about as much sense to call you the wittiest woman in Illyria, as to say that Sir Toby will give up drinking.'
26. *Eve's flesh.* Eve was the first woman to be created, in the Genesis story in the Bible; hence all women are part of her 'flesh' – descended physically from her.

29. *Wit . . . fooling!* Feste calls on 'Wit', as on a god, to give him the gift of humour.
29–30. *Those wits that think they have thee:* 'Those who are clever only in their own estimation.'
32. *Quinapalus:* an authority of dubious authenticity, dragged in for the occasion!
32–3. *'Better a witty fool than a foolish wit'.* Clearly a play on the two meanings of 'fool', which, in the first part means a 'professional clown', whereas 'foolish' later has its modern meaning. This theme is touched upon several times in *Twelfth Night*. Feste here seems particularly on the defensive, resenting the superficial assessment of his real intelligence made by those who, he feels, are his inferiors mentally.
36. *dry:* dull, stupid.

38. *Madonna:* 'my lady.'
39. Feste deliberately takes the literal meaning of 'dry'.

Clown

Many a good hanging prevents a bad marriage; and
for turning away, let summer bear it out.

Maria

You are resolute then?   20

Clown

Not so, neither; but I am resolv'd on two points.

Maria

That if one break, the other will hold; or if both break,
your gaskins fall.

Clown

Apt, in good faith, very apt! Well, go thy way; if Sir
Toby would leave drinking, thou wert as witty a piece   25
of Eve's flesh as any in Illyria.

Maria

Peace, you rogue, no more o' that. Here comes my
lady. Make your excuse wisely, you were best.

[Exit. Enter OLIVIA *and* MALVOLIO*]*

Clown

Wit, an't be thy will, put me into good fooling! Those
wits that think they have thee do very oft prove fools;   30
and I that am sure I lack thee may pass for a wise man.
For what says Quinapalus? 'Better a witty fool than a
foolish wit.' God bless thee, lady!

Olivia

Take the fool away.

Clown

Do you not hear, fellows? Take away the lady.   35

Olivia

Go to, y'are a dry fool; I'll no more of you. Besides,
you grow dishonest.

Clown

Two faults, Madonna, that drink and good counsel will
amend; for give the dry fool drink, then is the fool
not dry. Bid the dishonest man mend himself: if he   40
mend, he is no longer dishonest; if he cannot, let

42. *botcher:* one who patches things, usually unskilfully. (We use the word today figuratively – 'a botched-up job'.)

43–4. *virtue that transgresses . . . patch'd with virtue.* Nonsense – or does it come near the point of deep wisdom? The clown's role is not so different from that of the playwright, in observing and commenting on life and people, and being as often as not ignored or misunderstood. This is perhaps why Shakespeare seems to have a soft spot for his clowns, and to depict them so feelingly. Some of his shrewdest lines are entrusted to them.

45. *syllogism:* a piece of systematic reasoning. (Feste is, of course, not entirely serious when he uses the word here.)

46. *cuckold.* The cuckoo's habit of laying its egg in another bird's nest – a sort of unfaithfulness – has given us this word, which denotes the husband of an unfaithful wife. His wife and her lover, by their adultery, are said to 'make him a cuckold'. But here he seems to be using the word in an active sense, to denote the one who commits the unfaithfulness, and thus refers to calamity's way of inflicting loss and humiliation. The main thing about this speech of Feste's is that he's rattling away so as to give Olivia no chance to rebuke him.

47. *so beauty's a flower.* Again, if sense is intended, this would be a comment on the transitoriness of beauty, which withers as a flower.

50–1. *Misprision:* misunderstanding; ***'Cucullus non facit monachum':*** 'The hood (part of a monk's normal dress) does not make the monk.' (Contrast the proverb 'Fine feathers make fine birds'.)

52. *motley:* apparel of various colours, which the professional clown normally wore. (Compare 'mottled' – speckled.) The word 'motley' has come to be used to denote professional foolery or humorous entertainment. Feste means that, though he is a fool by profession, that does not mean that his intelligence is in any way inferior.

55. *Dexteriously:* A deliberate mispronunciation?

57. *catechize:* to instruct orally, usually by question and answer (as in the Church Catechism).

57. *mouse.* Regularly used as a term of affection.

the botcher mend him. Anything that's mended is but
patch'd; virtue that transgresses is but patch'd with
sin, and sin that amends is but patch'd with virtue. If
that this simple syllogism will serve, so; if it will not, 45
what remedy? As there is no true cuckold but calamity,
so beauty's a flower. The lady bade take away the fool;
therefore, I say again, take her away.

Olivia

Sir, I bade them take away you.

Clown

Misprision in the highest degree! Lady, 'Cucullus non 50
facit monachum'; that's as much to say as I wear not
motley in my brain. Good Madonna, give me leave to
prove you a fool.

Olivia

Can you do it?

Clown

Dexteriously, good Madonna. 55

Olivia

Make your proof.

Clown

I must catechize you for it, Madonna. Good my mouse
of virtue, answer me.

Olivia

Well, sir, for want of other idleness, I'll bide your
proof. 60

Clown

Good Madonna, why mourn'st thou?

Olivia

Good fool, for my brother's death.

Clown

I think his soul is in hell, Madonna.

Olivia

I know his soul is in heaven, fool.

Clown

The more fool, Madonna, to mourn for your brother's 65
soul being in heaven. Take away the fool, gentlemen.

67. Malvolio is now for the first time brought into the picture. An innocent enough question is put, but his sour reply marks him out for what he is. He is especially bitter towards Feste, and the things he represents, gaiety and lightheartedness; and Feste never really forgives or forgets.

68. *mend:* amend, improve, reform.

69. 'Shall' is used emphatically – it is Malvolio's desire and intention for the moment, that the rest of Feste's life *shall* be one long process of reformation.

70-1. *Infirmity . . . fool.* Infirmity (in this case, advancing age, with its increasing eccentricities) will add to the fool's equipment. This shows clearly what a poor opinion Malvolio has of Feste's brand of humour.

74. *fox:* then, as now, thought of as the embodiment of cunning.

77-83. Malvolio's criticism here, of the professional jester (equivalent to our modern stage comedian) is not without justification. He despises their utter dependence on a suitable 'lead' from someone else, and their lack of spontaneity. Not that Malvolio is much interested in humour for its own sake – he simply resents the popularity enjoyed by such people, who, as he thinks, have far less intelligence than himself.

78. *put down:* silenced, beaten in an argument.

80. *out of his guard:* a fencing term, meaning 'off his guard' not ready to defend himself.

81. *minister:* supply.

82. *crow:* laugh in an empty, unintelligent way.

83. *set kind of fools:* jesters who can be humorous only according to a set pattern. *zanies.* A clown was often accompanied by an assistant ('zany') who would clumsily imitate his antics.

84. *O, you are sick of self-love, Malvolio.* A line to remember, in which Olivia puts her finger on the probable root-cause of Malvolio's unattractiveness.

85. *distemper'd:* diseased, disordered.

86. *free disposition:* more or less repeats the sense of *generous.* Those are the very virtues Malvolio lacks.

86. *bird-bolts:* blunt-headed arrows for shooting birds.

88. *allow'd fool:* recognized jester (that is, of course, the 'professional clown').

88. *rail:* use abusive language.

89-90. *nor no railing . . . reprove.* A not too gentle hint that Malvolio could have expressed his disapproval without growing abusive.

91. *Mercury:* a Roman god, thought of not only as messenger but also as patron of thieves and cheating. *leasing:* telling lies. So, mockseriously, Feste prays that Olivia may receive this reward – a skill in telling lies – to repay her for her kindness in speaking on his behalf. He is saying this against himself – implying that to speak well of fools is dishonesty anyway, and so Mercury will readily reward one of his own disciples!

Olivia

What think you of this fool, Malvolio? Doth he not
mend?

Malvolio

Yes, and shall do, till the pangs of death shake him.
Infirmity, that decays the wise, doth ever make the   70
better fool.

Clown

God send you, sir, a speedy infirmity, for the better
increasing your folly! Sir Toby will be sworn that I am
no fox; but he will not pass his word for twopence
that you are no fool.   75

Olivia

How say you to that, Malvolio?

Malvolio

I marvel your ladyship takes delight in such a barren
rascal; I saw him put down the other day with an
ordinary fool that has no more brain than a stone.
Look you now, he's out of his guard already; unless   80
you laugh and minister occasion to him, he is gagg'd.
I protest I take these wise men that crow so at these
set kind of fools no better than the fools' zanies.

Olivia

O, you are sick of self-love, Malvolio, and taste with a
distemper'd appetite. To be generous, guiltless, and of 85
free disposition, is to take those things for bird-bolts
that you deem cannon bullets. There is no slander in
an allow'd fool, though he do nothing but rail; nor
no railing in a known discreet man, though he do
nothing but reprove.   90

Clown

Now Mercury endue thee with leasing, for thou speak'st
well of fools!

[Re-enter MARIA]

93–4. Maria's announcement focuses all Olivia's attention now on the arrival of Viola with the Duke's latest message for herself. (In modern English we should put the word 'who' between *gentleman* and *much*.)

100–1. *speaks nothing but madman:* speaks entirely like a madman.

103. *what you will to dismiss it:* 'make any excuse you like to get rid of him.'

106–9. There is a certain measure of affection in the relationship between Olivia and Feste. A clown needed to feel secure in his employer's affections, when so much of his time had to be spent saying things that people could find highly offensive, if they so chose.

107–8. *Jove cram with brains:* 'may Jove cram with brains.' Wishes are often thus expressed, by the simple verb without the auxiliary. (Compare 'God *save* the Queen'.)

109. *pia mater:* brain (strictly a medical term for a membrane enclosing the brain).

110. Sir Toby in one of his less impressive moments. When sober, he manages some measure of deference towards Olivia; but at the moment his behaviour leaves much to be desired. There is probably as much resignation as indignation in Olivia's comments – but in any case she has more interesting things to occupy her, just now.

Maria

   Madam, there is at the gate a young gentleman much
   desires to speak with you.

Olivia

   From the Count Orsino, is it?   95

Maria

   I know not, madam; 'tis a fair young man, and well
   attended.

Olivia

   Who of my people hold him in delay?

Maria

   Sir Toby, madam, your kinsman.

Olivia

   Fetch him off, I pray you; he speaks nothing but 100
   madman. Fie on him! *[Exit MARIA]* Go you, Malvolio:
   if it be a suit from the Count, I am sick, or not at home
   – what you will to dismiss it. *[Exit MALVOLIO]* Now you
   see, sir, how your fooling grows old, and people dislike
   it.   105

Clown

   Thou hast spoke for us, Madonna, as if thy eldest son
   should be a fool; whose skull Jove cram with brains!
   For – here he comes – one of thy kin has a most weak
   pia mater.

                    [Enter SIR TOBY]

Olivia

   By mine honour, half drunk! What is he at the gate, 110
   cousin?

Sir Toby

   A gentleman.

Olivia

   A gentleman! What gentleman?

Sir Toby

   'Tis a gentleman here. *[Hiccups]* A plague o' these pickle-
   herring! How now, sot!   115

117–18. 'How have you managed to get so drowsy at this early hour?' (She knows the real reason, of course.) *lethargy:* drowsiness.

119. Sir Toby is so befuddled that he does not hear her properly. Or is he pretending to be stupid or deaf, so as to take the edge off her sarcasm?
120. *what is he?* We would probably say 'who is it?' (see line 110).

123–9. Olivia is genuinely distressed by her uncle's condition, and is becoming agitated at the prospect of a fresh messenger from Orsino. It is largely to settle her own thoughts, and play for time, that she turns to Feste. (We can see how valuable a function the clown could fulfil, in being at hand to provide artificial and irresponsible conversation which could tide people over an embarrassing or painful situation.)
125. *above heat:* above his normal body temperature.

127. *crowner:* coroner. The word means 'of the Crown' and a coroner was originally a King's special representative in legal administration. Olivia is using the word here in its modern sense (the official who investigates possibly suspicious deaths), for Sir Toby is *drown'd* in drink.

132–7. We can well picture such a scene as Malvolio recounts—
'I'm afraid the Countess isn't well.'
'Yes, I know all about that – I'm coming to see her.'
'No, actually she's still asleep.'
'I've heard that before, too – let me in.'

Clown
Good Sir Toby!

Olivia
Cousin, cousin, how have you come so early by this
lethargy?

Sir Toby
Lechery! I defy lechery. There's one at the gate.

Olivia
Ay, marry; what is he? 120

Sir Toby
Let him be the devil an he will, I care not; give me
faith, say I. Well, it's all one.

[Exit]

Olivia
What's a drunken man like, fool?

Clown
Like a drown'd man, a fool, and a madman: one
draught above heat makes him a fool; the second mads 125
him; and a third drowns him.

Olivia
Go thou and seek the crowner, and let him sit o' my
coz; for he's in the third degree of drink, he's drown'd;
go look after him.

Clown
He is but mad yet, Madonna, and the fool shall look 130
to the madman.

[Exit. Re-enter MALVOLIO]

Malvolio
Madam, yond young fellow swears he will speak with
you. I told him you were sick; he takes on him to
understand so much, and therefore comes to speak
with you. I told him you were asleep; he seems to have 135
a foreknowledge of that too, and therefore comes to
speak with you. What is to be said to him, lady? He's
fortified against any denial.

141. *sheriff's post:* probably a post fixed at the Sheriff's door, for the display of public notices, *supporter to a bench:* another necessary piece of wood, not to be lightly shifted!

144. *of mankind:* 'just a human being.'

146–7. *will you or no:* 'whether you want him to, or not.'

150. *squash:* unripe pea pod.
150–1. *codling:* unripe apple.
151–2. *standing water:* the turn of the tide, when the water level is stationary.
152–3. *well-favour'd:* good-looking; *shrewishly:* sharply, impatiently.
154. *mother's milk . . . out of him:* only just weaned (an obvious exaggeration of Viola's youthfulness).

Viola's first encounter with Olivia is highly entertaining. The contrast between the two is excellently brought out. An apparent disparity in age or dignity makes Viola seem ingenuous and impetuous, for she has yet to learn Olivia's sophisticated wiles. (Though these will count for less and less with Olivia as she abandons herself to her new-found romance.) In sheer resolution and astuteness, Viola is more than her match. With none of her people to embarrass her by their presence, Olivia probably gets a perverse satisfaction out of Viola's unceremonious treatment of her. And before she is dismissed, Olivia has begun to fall in love.

Viola knows how to be courteous; her attitude to the Duke earlier was full of deference. What then is the reason for her awkwardness? Is it through loyalty to her master that she resents Olivia's indifference to him – or is it plain jealousy? Olivia could be a formidable rival, whose rare beauty had to be conceded, however grudgingly. Probably both motives are present – nothing has as yet taken final shape in Viola's mind and emotions.

Olivia
  Tell him he shall not speak with me.
Malvolio
  Has been told so; and he says he'll stand at your door 140
  like a sheriff's post, and be the supporter to a bench,
  but he'll speak with you.
Olivia
  What kind o' man is he?
Malvolio
  Why, of mankind.
Olivia
  What manner of man?   145
Malvolio
  Of very ill manner; he'll speak with you, will you or
  no.
Olivia
  Of what personage and years is he?
Malvolio
  Not yet old enough for a man, nor young enough
  for a boy; as a squash is before 'tis a peascod, or a 150
  codling when 'tis almost an apple; 'tis with him in
  standing water, between boy and man. He is very
  well-favour'd, and he speaks very shrewishly; one
  would think his mother's milk were scarce out of
  him.   155
Olivia
  Let him approach. Call in my gentlewoman.
Malvolio
  Gentlewoman, my lady calls.

[Exit. Re-enter MARIA]

Olivia
  Give me my veil; come, throw it o'er my face; We'll
  once more hear Orsino's embassy.

[Enter VIOLA]

161. *Speak to me . . . Your will?* Olivia deliberately dodges the question.

162. Viola starts to reel off the piece she has learned by heart, and then breaks off, still not sure which one is Olivia, and not wanting to feel that all her memorizing has been wasted (see also lines 170–1 and 181–3). This amuses Olivia greatly. Viola herself is not entirely serious either, probably.
165. *penn'd:* written.
166. *con:* learn by heart.
167. *comptible:* susceptible.
168. *least sinister usage:* 'the slightest unkindness.'

170–1. *I can say little more . . . out of my part.* Is there a slight dig here at certain actors who were incapable of improvization?

176. *I am not that I play.* The audience knows what Viola means by this cryptic statement, which, however, only adds to the mystery surrounding Viola, in the mind of Olivia.

181. *from my commission:* 'not included in what I have been sent to convey.'

184–5. *I forgive you the praise:* 'I will let you leave out that part of your message that simply flatters me.'

Viola

The honourable lady of the house, which is she?   160

Olivia

Speak to me; I shall answer for her. Your will?

Viola

Most radiant, exquisite, and unmatchable beauty – I
pray you tell me if this be the lady of the house, for
I never saw her. I would be loath to cast away my
speech; for, besides that it is excellently well penn'd, 165
I have taken great pains to con it. Good beauties, let
me sustain no scorn; I am very comptible, even to the
least sinister usage.

Olivia

Whence came you, sir?

Viola

I can say little more than I have studied, and that 170
question's out of my part. Good gentle one, give me
modest assurance if you be the lady of the house, that
I may proceed in my speech.

Olivia

Are you a comedian?

Viola

No, my profound heart; and yet, by the very fangs of 175
malice I swear, I am not that I play. Are you the lady
of the house?

Olivia

If I do not usurp myself, I am.

Viola

Most certain, if you are she, you do usurp yourself; for
what is yours to bestow is not yours to reserve. But 180
this is from my commission. I will on with my speech
in your praise, and then show you the heart of my
message.

Olivia

Come to what is important in't. I forgive you the
praise.   185

191–2. *to make one in so skipping a dialogue:* 'to take part in such a flippant conversation.'

194. *swabber:* one who scrubs the ship's deck. (A fit reply to Maria, and in the same metaphor.); *hull:* drift to and fro with no sails hoisted.
195. *Some mollification for your giant:* 'Something to pacify this great protector of yours.' Maria is clearly presented as a very small person. (See Act II, Scene v, line 11, and Act III, Scene ii, line 62.) The sight of her, then, adopting this rough, bullying tone, strikes Viola as very funny – hence her comment. We have the amusing spectacle of these two very slight persons trying to outface each other.

199. *Speak your office:* 'Say what you have been instructed to say.'
201. *taxation of homage:* demand for homage. *olive:* olive branch (traditional symbol of peace).
203. *What are you ?* See lines 110 and 120.
206. *from my entertainment:* 'from the way I have been treated since I arrived at your house' – implying that Olivia and her people have 'got what they asked for'.
207. *maidenhead:* virginity.
207–8. *to your ears . . . profanation:* 'it is of such a highly personal (almost sacred) nature that it would be quite out of place for someone else to hear it.' (*Profanation* is the abuse of something sacred.)
209. *Give us the place alone.* Olivia sends everyone else out. *We will hear this divinity.* A touch of gentle irony.
There follows a fairly light dialogue, with typical Elizabethan verbal dexterity. Yet beneath their self-possession we see more than a little of their true emotions. Olivia is very concerned about how Viola will react when she sees her face; and Viola is momentarily taken aback when she sees for herself how beautiful Olivia is. The entire confrontation, with all that it means to both of them, is most delicately handled. At no time is their outward poise effectively disturbed; but the audience, knowing the true situation, is keenly aware of what lies behind each ambiguity.

Viola

Alas, I took great pains to study it, and 'tis poetical.

Olivia

It is the more like to be feigned; I pray you keep it in.
I heard you were saucy at my gates, and allow'd your
approach rather to wonder at you than to hear you.
If you be not mad, be gone; if you have reason, be 190
brief; 'tis not that time of moon with me to make one
in so skipping a dialogue.

Maria

Will you hoist sail, sir? Here lies your way.

Viola

No, good swabber, I am to hull here a little longer.
Some mollification for your giant, sweet lady.   195

Olivia

Tell me your mind.

Viola

I am a messenger.

Olivia

Sure, you have some hideous matter to deliver, when
the courtesy of it is so fearful. Speak your office.

Viola

It alone concerns your ear. I bring no overture of war, 200
no taxation of homage: I hold the olive in my hand;
my words are as full of peace as matter.

Olivia

Yet you began rudely. What are you? What would
you?

Viola

The rudeness that hath appear'd in me have I learn'd 205
from my entertainment. What I am and what I would
are as secret as maidenhead – to your ears, divinity; to
any other's, profanation.

Olivia

Give us the place alone; we will hear this divinity.

[*Exeunt* MARIA *and* ATTENDANTS]

210–18. Olivia purposely plays down the rather pompous setting of Orsino's love message. She finds his attentions increasingly tedious; and she is probably looking for some way to topple the confidence of this persistent 'young man' whom she cannot quite make out. By the use of the word 'divinity' in Viola's piece, Orsino's passion has been invested with a kind of sanctity. Irritated by this, Olivia seeks to deflate his pretentiousness by sustaining the metaphor up to a point, but in fact reducing his hopeful eloquence to the dreary level of a sermon. Hence her use of *text, chapter* and *heresy*.

216. *To answer by the method:* 'to answer in the same kind of metaphor as you are using'.

221. *out of your text:* 'saying something that has nothing to do with your text.' In other words, Olivia suggests – probably by now hopes – that Viola's request to see her face is entirely her own idea.
222. *draw the curtain.* Compare with Act I, Scene iii, line 116.

225. *if God did all:* 'if it is the way God made you' (i.e., with no artificial aid).
226. *'Tis in grain.* 'Dyed in grain' meant 'indelible'. We have the word 'ingrained' meaning much the same.

227. *blent:* blended.
228. *cunning:* skilled. (The word then usually had no sense of underhandedness.)

230–1. 'If you will remain unmarried, and so childless, so that there is no one to inherit your good looks.'
232–4. Though delighted, no doubt, with the praise, Olivia pretends to misunderstand Viola's meaning, and answers flippantly enough: 'I will make sure that all my good looks are carefully listed and published.'
234. *particle:* small part. *utensil:* any article serving a useful purpose. (The modern usage is more limited.)

Now, sir, what is your text? 210

Viola

Most sweet lady—

Olivia

A comfortable doctrine, and much may be said of it.
Where lies your text?

Viola

In Orsino's bosom.

Olivia

In his bosom! In what chapter of his bosom? 215

Viola

To answer by the method: in the first of his heart.

Olivia

O, I have read it; it is heresy. Have you no more to
say?

Viola

Good madam, let me see your face,

Olivia

Have you any commission from your lord to negotiate 220
with my face? You are now out of your text; but we
will draw the curtain and show you the picture.
[Unveiling] Look you, sir, such a one I was this present.
Is't not well done?

Viola

Excellently done, if God did all. 225

Olivia

'Tis in grain, sir; 'twill endure wind and weather.

Viola

'Tis beauty truly blent, whose red and white
Nature's own sweet and cunning hand laid on.
Lady, you are the cruell'st she alive,
If you will lead these graces to the grave, 230
And leave the world no copy.

Olivia

O, sir, I will not be so hard-hearted; I will give out
divers schedules of my beauty. It shall be inventoried,
and every particle and utensil labell'd to my will:

235. *'item':* literally 'likewise'. We use the word 'itemize' today, meaning 'to set out in detail,' or 'make a detailed list'. In Shakespeare, the word 'item' is often used to preface each item in a list – in much the way we would say 'number one', 'number two' and so on.

239. Viola has just blamed Olivia for her hardheartedness; but goes on, 'But however bad you may be, no one can deny that you are beautiful.'

241. *but:* only.

242. *nonpareil:* one who has no equal. Loyal to her master, Viola claims that only if Olivia were the most beautiful lady in the world, could she deserve such love as Orsino has for her.

245. A paradoxical way of describing Orsino's pent-up passion. His 'groaning' is but a faint echo of the 'thunder' of his emotions, and the 'fire' of his passion can only be reflected by mere 'sighs'.

246. *I cannot love him.* Olivia simply means that love is not something that can be forced into existence. It takes possession when it chooses to do so. (A little later Olivia will have become thus possessed – perhaps she is already aware of this.) She is quite willing to admit that Orsino has many excellent qualities (lines 247–51), but these elicit her approval only, not her love. How ironical (but how true to life so often) that she cannot fall for the 'obvious' man, with so much to recommend their union; but instead becomes involved in what is likely to be a comparatively uncertain relationship – even granting that Viola were of the right sex!

249. *In voices well divulg'd:* of good reputation.

250. *shape of nature:* outward appearance.

253. *in my master's flame:* 'with the same burning passion as my master feels.'

254. *such a deadly life:* 'a life so full of love-sickness as to be more like death'. (Compare 'a living death'.)

256. *Why, what would you?* 'Why, what would you do?'

257. *cabin:* hut. The willow tree was traditionally associated with unhappy love.

258. Viola simply means that she would call upon Olivia. Lovers have often referred to the object of their affection as their 'heart' or 'soul'. (Compare perhaps 'losing one's heart' to someone.)

259. *cantons:* poems or sections of poems ('canto' is the more usual form). *contemned:* despised.

261. *reverberate:* reverberant, echoing.

262–3. The very air would echo the sound of Olivia's name. We have to admire the sheer poetry of these lines, whatever our view may be of the sincerity of the emotion behind them. Notice that here Viola is voicing her own ideas, and no longer simply repeating her memorized lines.

as – item, two lips indifferent red; item, two grey eyes   235
with lids to them; item, one neck, one chin, and so
forth. Were you sent hither to praise me?

Viola

I see you what you are: you are too proud;
But, if you were the devil, you are fair.
My lord and master loves you – O, such love   240
Could be but recompens'd though you were
     crown'd
The nonpareil of beauty!

Olivia

How does he love me?

Viola

With adorations, fertile tears,
With groans that thunder love, with sighs of fire.   245

Olivia

Your lord does know my mind; I cannot love him.
Yet I suppose him virtuous, know him noble,
Of great estate, of fresh and stainless youth;
In voices well divulg'd, free, learn'd, and valiant,
And in dimension and the shape of nature   250
A gracious person; but yet I cannot love him.
He might have took his answer long ago.

Viola

If I did love you in my master's flame,
With such a suff'ring, such a deadly life,
In your denial I would find no sense;   255
I would not understand it.

Olivia

                                        Why, what would you?

Viola

Make me a willow cabin at your gate,
And call upon my soul within the house;
Write loyal cantons of contemned love
And sing them loud even in the dead of night;   260
Halloo your name to the reverberate hills,
And make the babbling gossip of the air
Cry out 'Olivia!' O, you should not rest

265. *But you should pity me:* unless (or until) you took pity on me. *You might do much.* Is this spoken as an 'aside'? Olivia is probably 'thinking aloud', as we say, as she has to admit, perhaps in spite of herself, that Viola's pleading, though on Orsino's behalf, is beginning to have an alarmingly potent influence on her.

267–8. It pleases Olivia, no doubt, to have this assurance, however disguised, that Viola comes from a 'good background', and is at least not ineligible on this score.

269–71. A lovely touch here – Olivia is about to say 'Don't come back with any more messages from Orsino', but then realizes that, if so, she will be depriving herself of what she is coming to need desperately – Viola's company. Her reason for Viola's next visit, *to tell me how he takes it,* is feeble in the extreme. But how life-like! She is so infatuated now that she acts less and less rationally.

273. *fee'd post:* paid messenger.
273–7. Viola's indignation is entirely genuine. Loyal devotion to the Duke still comes first. It is the only relationship possible for her anyway – or so she thinks; and so it never occurs to her that Olivia's rejection of Orsino, which she has just been attacking so vehemently, may in the long run be her own gain.

285–7. A description of love-at-first-sight that would be hard to improve upon. *Well, let it be.* Resignation, but of what kind – despairing, or contented?

Between the elements of air and earth
But you should pity me!

Olivia

                    You might do much.   265

What is your parentage?

Viola

Above my fortunes, yet my state is well:
I am a gentleman.

Olivia

             Get you to your lord.
I cannot love him; let him send no more—
Unless perchance you come to me again   270
To tell me how he takes it. Fare you well.
I thank you for your pains; spend this for me.

Viola

I am no fee'd post, lady; keep your purse;
My master, not myself, lacks recompense.
Love make his heart of flint that you shall love;   275
And let your fervour, like my master's, be
Plac'd in contempt! Farewell, fair cruelty.

[Exit]

Olivia

'What is your parentage?'
'Above my fortunes, yet my state is well:
I am a gentleman.' I'll be sworn thou art;   280
Thy tongue, thy face, thy limbs, actions, and spirit,
Do give thee five-fold blazon. Not too fast! Soft, soft!
Unless the master were the man. How now!
Even so quickly may one catch the plague?
Methinks I feel this youth's perfections   285
With an invisible and subtle stealth
To creep in at mine eyes. Well, let it be.
What ho, Malvolio!

[Re-enter MALVOLIO]

Malvolio

             Here, madam, at your service.

289. *peevish messenger*. A familiar subterfuge in the first stages of romance is to show no sign of affection. Olivia must in any case maintain some appearance of propriety, to cover up her next undignified little scheme.

290. *County's man:* Count's man. (It is probably a rendering of *Countes man* a legitimate possessive form in earlier English.)

290–1. She is, of course, going to 'plant' the ring on Viola. It is a foolish thing to do, because Viola will certainly see through it. Or does Olivia half hope that she will, and will then begin to 'put two and two together' and realize what is going on in Olivia's mind?

293–4. Notice the abrupt change. *I am not for him* is immediately followed by *If that the youth will come*. Olivia has to get this second part of her message in at once, before Malvolio goes out, taking with him only the general tone of rejection she started with.

297–8. 'I don't know what I'm doing; and I'm afraid I may have let this young man's looks go to my head.'

299. *owe:* own.

300. Olivia's resignation probably has as much in it of pleasurable anticipation as of fear.

Olivia

    Run after that same peevish messenger,
    The County's man. He left this ring behind him,   290
    Would I or not. Tell him I'll none of it.
    Desire him not to flatter with his lord,
    Nor hold him up with hopes; I am not for him.
    If that the youth will come this way to-morrow,
    I'll give him reasons for't. Hie thee, Malvolio.   295

Malvolio

    Madam, I will.

                [Exit}

Olivia

    I do I know not what, and fear to find
    Mine eye too great a flatterer for my mind.
    Fate, show thy force: ourselves we do not owe;
    What is decreed must be; and be this so!   300

                [Exit]

ACT TWO SCENE I

A short but necessary scene introducing Sebastian, Viola's twin brother, and Antonio. Vital to the main plot is Sebastian's present assumption that Viola is dead. Equally vital is the strong physical likeness between brother and sister, which Sebastian humorously points out. Though not vital, yet helping the play forward convincingly, and contributing much to its excitement and pathos, is the loyal attachment Antonio shows for Sebastian.

Most of this scene uses a dignified prose, not very different in its effect from the verse that ends the scene. The changed form marks the changed atmosphere when Antonio is alone, and 'thinking aloud'. Solitary thoughts are usually better conveyed in verse than in prose.

1–2. *nor will you not that I go with you?* (a double negative) 'Don't you want me to go with you either?'

3. *stars shine darkly.* Refers to the effect, for good or ill, that the stars were thought to have upon people's lives.

4. *malignancy:* bad influence. *distemper:* disturb, blight. Sebastian and Antonio exhibit generous concern for each other's well-being. We are reminded of the earlier coast-scene when Viola's plight is greatly cheered by the loyalty of the Captain.

9. *determinate:* intended.

9–10. *extravagancy:* wandering. 'All I have in mind is simply to wander idly from place to place.' ('Vagrant' is still the legal word for a 'tramp', someone of 'no fixed abode'.)

12. *it charges me in manners:* 'out of politeness, I ought . . .' Antonio has been considerate enough not to press Sebastian for information, and so Sebastian feels that the polite thing to do, in reply, is to tell Antonio about himself.

15. *Roderigo.* Sebastian has adopted a false name, almost automatically, as a security measure. (His predicament, and the remedy he has chosen, remind us of Viola's almost identical situation.)

17–18. *if the heavens had been pleas'd, would we had so ended!* 'I wish we had both drowned together (that is, within the same hour), if that had been God's will.' We may recall Viola's similar grief when she thinks Sebastian has been drowned.

19. *But you, sir, alter'd that.* Antonio has clearly saved Sebastian from drowning, and this, as they both imagine, prevented him from sharing his sister's fate.

ACT TWO
SCENE I

The sea-coast

[Enter ANTONIO and SEBASTIAN]

Antonio

Will you stay no longer; nor will you not that I go
with you?

Sebastian

By your patience, no. My stars shine darkly over me;
the malignancy of my fate might perhaps distemper
yours; therefore I shall crave of you your leave that I   5
may bear my evils alone. It were a bad recompense for
your love to lay any of them on you.

Antonio

Let me yet know of you whither you are bound.

Sebastian

No, sooth, sir; my determinate voyage is mere extravagancy. But I perceive in you so excellent a touch of   10
modesty that you will not extort from me what I am
willing to keep in; therefore it charges me in manners
the rather to express myself. You must know of me
then, Antonio, my name is Sebastian, which I call'd
Roderigo; my father was that Sebastian of Messaline   15
whom I know you have heard of. He left behind him
myself and a sister, both born in an hour; if the
heavens had been pleas'd, would we had so ended!
But you, sir, alter'd that; for some hour before you
took me from the breach of the sea was my sister   20
drown'd.

23–4. *though it was said she much resembled me*. Is it modesty that prompts Sebastian to express surprise at Viola's reputation for beauty, since it will follow that he must share it, being so like her in appearance? Whatever his reason, there is a gentle humour in his comment.

24–6. *though I could not with such estimable wonder overfar believe that*: 'though I couldn't go as far as to share their excessive admiration' (*estimable* means 'esteeming highly'.)

26–7. *she bore a mind that envy could not but call fair*. Sebastian cannot, for reasons of modesty, enlarge upon her outward beauty; but he has no qualms about confirming her inner goodness. Even those who envy her have to admit that.

28–29. *drown her remembrance again with more*. Sebastian speaks of the tears he could easily shed as he calls her to mind.

30. 'I'm sorry I haven't been able to look after you better.' (For this use of 'entertainment', see Act I, Scene v, line 206.)

31. *forgive me your trouble*: 'forgive me the trouble you have been put to (on my behalf).'

32. *If you will not* . . .: 'Unless you wish to . . .' What Antonio means here is that it will be as bad as dying if he is not allowed to stay with Sebastian as his loyal servant.

35. *kill him whom you have recover'd*. Sebastian seems to be exaggerating the effect that Antonio will have if he stays there any longer; he goes on to explain exactly what this effect will be. He is so overwrought that he is likely to break down and weep if Antonio speaks so openly of his affection.

37. *yet so near the manners of my mother*: 'still possessing so many unmanly feelings' – i.e. 'I feel like crying.' There is the further implication that he has not been long enough out in the world to become hardened.

38–9. *mine eyes will tell tales of me*: 'by weeping I shall reveal that I am still not much more than a child.'

39. *I am bound*: 'I am on my way.'

Antonio's affection for Sebastian (which plays a not insignificant part in the play) develops with lightning speed – to judge by the brevity of this conversation and the implied encounter that has preceded it. This 'compression' is sometimes forced upon a playwright. In this instance, it is clearly better to make secondary things happen over-rapidly, than to allow the proper lapse of time, which would then be taking up a disproportionate place in the play.

Antonio

Alas the day!

Sebastian

A lady, sir, though it was said she much resembled
me, was yet of many accounted beautiful; but though
I could not with such estimable wonder overfar believe   25
that, yet thus far I will boldly publish her: she bore a
mind that envy could not but call fair. She is drown'd
already, sir, with salt water, though I seem to drown
her remembrance again with more.

Antonio

Pardon me, sir, your bad entertainment.   30

Sebastian

O good Antonio, forgive me your trouble.

Antonio

If you will not murder me for my love, let me be your
servant.

Sebastian

If you will not undo what you have done – that is,
kill him whom you have recover'd – desire it not.   35
Fare ye well at once; my bosom is full of kindness,
and I am yet so near the manners of my mother that,
upon the least occasion more, mine eyes will tell tales
of me. I am bound to the Count Orsino's court.
Farewell.   40

[Exit]

Antonio

The gentleness of all the gods go with thee!
I have many enemies in Orsino's court,
Else would I very shortly see thee there.
But come what may, I do adore thee so
That danger shall seem sport, and I will go.   45

[Exit]

SCENE II

Simply the sequel to Olivia's dismissal of Viola at the end of Act I. But it becomes an occasion – a most effective one – for Viola to impart, in soliloquy, her growing realization that the worst has happened, and Olivia has, all unwittingly, fallen in love with her.

1. Malvolio's peremptory enquiry (entirely in character) has little effect on Viola, whose reply is completely unruffled.

2. *on a moderate pace:* strolling along.

4–5. *you might have saved me my pains.* Malvolio is clearly annoyed at having been brought into this business. It must seem quite beneath the dignity of his office to have to go running after a young page – especially one so unmoved by these bullying tactics. However, he delivers his message faithfully, though we may detect more of Malvolio than Olivia in his final throwing down of the ring.

11. *I'll none of it:* 'I'll have nothing to do with it.'

14. *be it his that finds it:* 'Whoever finds it is welcome to it.'

15–39. Verse is now used, as it was at the end of the previous scene, to convey more fittingly the profounder thoughts that Viola can share with no one but herself. The whole mood has changed – and with it the language – from outward wrangling, where little of true self needs to be involved, to meditative discussion of deepest needs.

15. It does not take Viola long to see through to the real motive behind the business of the ring. She had noticed Olivia's odd behaviour; and now, with this further bit of evidence, she has no alternative but to believe the worst.

16. A double negative here. We would say 'Heaven (*Fortune*) forbid that my looks (*outside*) should have charmed her.'

17. *She made good view of me:* 'She had a good look at me.'

18–19. This is almost the way Olivia described the experience herself. (Act I, Scene v, lines 297–8). The meaning here is that Olivia's whole attention is so engrossed in simply gazing at Viola that there is no rational control left for her words – and so she speaks *distractedly*.

20. *cunning.* Here the word seems to have more of its modern meaning (unlike its use in Act I, Scene v, line 228). Olivia's emotions are so stirred that she will make use even of this most unlikely go-between to further her purpose, and maintain contact with Viola.

21. *churlish:* ill-mannered.

22. *None of my lord's ring!* 'This is certainly not my lord's ring.'

23. *I am the man.* 'I am the *one*' might have been enough, but Viola deliberately says 'man' because it is her feigned manhood that is being singled out and pursued.

23. . . . *as 'tis* . . . What a wealth of feeling in this parenthesis!

SCENE II

A street

[Enter VIOLA *and* MALVOLIO *at several doors]*

Malvolio
Were you not ev'n now with the Countess Olivia?

Viola
Even now, sir; on a moderate pace I have since arriv'd
but hither.

Malvolio
She returns this ring to you, sir; you might have saved
me my pains, to have taken it away yourself. She adds,   5
moreover, that you should put your lord into a
desperate assurance she will none of him. And one
thing more: that you be never so hardy to come again
in his affairs, unless it be to report your lord's taking
of this. Receive it so.   10

Viola
She took the ring of me; I'll none of it.

Malvolio
Come, sir, you peevishly threw it to her; and her will
is it should be so return'd. If it be worth stooping for,
there it lies in your eye; if not, be it his that finds it.

[Exit]

Viola
I left no ring with her; what means this lady?   15
Fortune forbid my outside have not charm'd her!
She made good view of me; indeed, so much
That methought her eyes had lost her tongue
For she did speak in starts distractedly
She loves me, sure: the cunning of her passion   20
Invites me in this churlish messenger
None of my lord's ring! Why, he sent her none
I am the man. If it be so – as 'tis—

24. She were better love a dream: 'It would be better for her if she loved a dream.' (Clearly, there would be less attachment then than to a real person, and the subsequent moment of disillusionment less painful.)

26. Viola is reminded that all disguise is potentially evil, since it deceives. The **pregnant** (resourceful) **enemy** is the Devil.

27. proper-false: prepossessing outwardly but inwardly false.

28. waxen hearts. 'Waxen' because more easily impressed by false charmers (just as wax receives the imprint of a seal).

29–30. A memorable couplet, almost proverbial, and underlined, as it were, by the use of rhyme (which normally is reserved for the ending of a scene or speech). The point of it is that women are frail by nature, so it is not their fault.

31. fadge: turn out.

32. monster: basically (as here) something that is outside the normal pattern of nature. Viola's double role suggests the title.

34. As I am man: 'As long as I must play the part of man.'

35. 'I have no hope that my love for Orsino can have a happy fulfilment.'

36. As I am woman. If and when she resumes her proper rôle as woman (and she is beginning to wish she had not been born a woman), then it will be Olivia's turn to suffer frustration.

37. thriftless sighs: wasted sighs (since they will be followed by no joy of fulfilment, to make up for their sadness).

38–9. Compare Viola's resignation with Olivia's, when she first recognized her love for Viola. On that occasion there was mostly happy anticipation – however irresponsibly conceived – but with Viola now, heavy despair. (Compare also Act I, Scene ii, line 60.)

SCENE III

Sir Toby and Sir Andrew again, familiarly enough employed, this time abetted by Feste. The significance now of their roistering is that it brings them into head-on collision with Malvolio who has been sent to remonstrate – a duty he finds highly gratifying. It becomes plain that two ways of life are here in conflict, Sir Toby and his cronies representing irresponsible lightheartedness, and Malvolio standing stubbornly alone in opposition. The upshot is that a plan is conceived for Malvolio's humiliation; and so the 'sub-plot', held back till now, is set in motion.

1–2. Not to be abed . . . betimes: 'To be still up after midnight is to be up early.'

2. 'diluculo surgere.' This is the first part of a proverb in Latin – 'To get up early' – the part omitted simply adding 'is most healthful'.

5. an unfill'd can. This, to drink-loving Sir Toby, is frustration indeed; and so he uses it to illustrate **A false conclusion.** Both are to be deplored since neither provides what it seems to promise.

Poor lady, she were better love a dream.
Disguise, I see thou art a wickedness   25
Wherein the pregnant enemy does much.
How easy is it for the proper-false
In women's waxen hearts to set their forms!
Alas, our frailty is the cause, not we!
For such as we are made of, such we be.   30
How will this fadge? My master loves her dearly,
And I, poor monster, fond as much on him;
And she, mistaken, seems to dote on me.
What will become of this? As I am man,
My state is desperate for my master's love;   35
As I am woman – now alas the day!—
What thriftless sighs shall poor Olivia breathe!
O Time, thou must untangle this, not I;
It is too hard a knot for me t' untie!

[Exit]

SCENE III

Olivia's house

[Enter SIR TOBY *and* SIR ANDREW*]*

Sir Toby

Approach, Sir Andrew. Not to be abed after midnight
is to be up betimes; and 'diluculo surgere' thou
know'st—

Sir Andrew

Nay, by my troth, I know not; but I know to be up
late is to be up late.   5

Sir Toby

A false conclusion! I hate it as an unfill'd can. To be
up after midnight and to go to bed then is early; so
that to go to bed after midnight is to go to bed betimes.

9. *the four elements*. The ancient belief, still not discarded entirely in Shakespeare's day, was that all material creation was made up of the four distinct 'elements' – fire, water, earth and air – in varying proportions.

11. *eating and drinking*. This may seem a down-to-earth and quite humorous way to demolish such a theory. But coming from Sir Andrew, we should perhaps take it as a quite serious observation – that life is sustained by food and drink. That he hasn't intentionally made a joke here is borne out by the fact that Sir Toby makes his rejoinder – *let us therefore eat and drink* – as the one who is providing the humorous twist to the conversation.

13. *stoup:* a drinking vessel.

15. *Did you never . . . 'we three'?* Feste, by joining the group, and making the number up to three (probably by popping up between them) recalls an inn-sign, familiar at the time, showing two fools, or logger-heads, with the title 'We Three Loggerheads' – thus implying that the viewer himself becomes the third, as he reads it.

17. *catch:* song sung by three or more people, all of them singing the same piece, but each one starting off a line later than the one before.

18. *breast:* a term frequently used for 'voice'.

22–3. *Pigrogromitus . . . Vapians . . . Queubus*. Clearly Feste has been putting on a very impressive display of learning, though just so much nonsense in actual fact, but it has achieved its purpose – Sir Andrew is positively dazzled by it.

24. *leman:* sweetheart.

25. *impeticos thy gratillity*. More fancy words invented by Feste to impress Sir Andrew. He means that he has put Sir Andrew's gratuity into his pocket.

32. *testril:* a coin (=tester) of the same value as a sixpenny piece (=2½p).

Does not our lives consist of the four elements?

Sir Andrew

Faith, so they say; but I think it rather consists of 10
eating and drinking.

Sir Toby

Th'art a scholar; let us therefore eat and drink.
Marian, I say! a stoup of wine.

[Enter CLOWN*]*

Sir Andrew

Here comes the fool, i' faith.

Clown

How now, my hearts! Did you never see the picture 15
of 'we three'?

Sir Toby

Welcome, ass. Now let's have a catch.

Sir Andrew

By my troth, the fool has an excellent breast. I had
rather than forty shillings I had such a leg, and so
sweet a breath to sing, as the fool has. In sooth, thou 20
wast in very gracious fooling last night, when thou
spok'st of Pigrogromitus, of the Vapians passing the
equinoctial of Queubus; 'twas very good, i' faith. I sent
thee sixpence for thy leman; hadst it?

Clown

I did impeticos thy gratillity; for Malvolio's nose is no 25
whipstock. My lady has a white hand, and the
Myrmidons are no bottle-ale houses.

Sir Andrew

Excellent! Why, this is the best fooling, when all is
done. Now, a song.

Sir Toby

Come on, there is sixpence for you, Let's have a 30
song.

Sir Andrew

There's a testril of me too; if one knight give a—

35. *I care not for good life.* Sir Andrew, as so often, tamely follows Sir Toby's lead. And there is something quite ludicrous in the idea of Sir Andrew playing the hardened cynic.

36–49. The songs in *Twelfth Night* are highly effective, and to be valued in their own right. This one certainly seems to have been in existence before Shakespeare made use of it in his play. Its theme – that pleasure is fleeting, and therefore to be snatched while offered – is one we would expect to find in favour with Sir Toby and his kind.

50. *mellifluous:* literally 'flowing with honey', i.e. 'sweetly flowing.'
51. *A contagious breath.* Sir Toby praises the moving, affecting quality of the singing, in his own peculiar way.
52. Sir Andrew has already made a perfectly apposite comment (*mellifluous voice*), but the moment Sir Toby adds something different, then he seems to distrust his own choice, as if his only hope of social acceptability lies in slavishly copying Sir Toby.
53. *to hear by the nose.* Sir Toby is deliberately mixing words up in a nonsensical way to mock Sir Andrew's strange use of language. *dulcet in contagion:* 'sweetly stinking'.
54. *welkin:* sky.
55–6. *draw three souls out of one weaver.* Weavers, especially perhaps those who were Calvinist refugees from the Continent, seem to have had a reputation for hearty singing (with 'heart' and 'soul') of hymns and psalms. But to move them so deeply in a drinking-song would be a great achievement.

Clown
    Would you have a love-song, or a song of good life?
Sir Toby
    A love-song, a love-song.
Sir Andrew
    Ay, ay; I care not for good life.   35

[CLOWN sings]

    O mistress mine, where are you roaming?
    O, stay and hear; your true love's coming,
        That can sing both high and low.
        Trip no further, pretty sweeting;
        Journeys end in lovers meeting,   40
        Every wise man's son doth know.

Sir Andrew
    Excellent good, i' faith!
Sir Toby
    Good, good!

[CLOWN sings]

    What is love? 'Tis not hereafter;
    Present mirth hath present laughter;   45
        What's to come is still unsure.
    In delay there lies no plenty,
    Then come kiss me, sweet and twenty;
        Youth's a stuff will not endure.

Sir Andrew
    A mellifluous voice, as I am true knight.   50
Sir Toby
    A contagious breath.
Sir Andrew
    Very sweet and contagious, i' faith.
Sir Toby
    To hear by the nose, it is dulcet in contagion. But shall
    we make the welkin dance indeed? Shall we rouse the
    night-owl in a catch that will draw three souls out of   55
    one weaver? Shall we do that?

57. *dog at a catch.* To be 'dog' at anything simply meant to be good at it.

58. *some dogs will catch well.* Feste, as so often, takes the literal meaning of 'dog' and 'catch', suggesting a dog biting someone.

60. *Hold thy peace:* keep quiet.

62–3. *'Tis not the first time . . . call me knave.* What a pathetic delight Sir Andrew gets if he can at all convince anyone (including himself) of some instance of roguishness in his life! (Compare line 35.)

66. Maria does her best to forewarn them of Malvolio's approach, by hurrying to them, ahead of Malvolio, whom she knows to be on his way. Though when she arrives and catches them at the height of their rowdiness, her instinctive reaction is as disapproving as Malvolio's. *caterwauling:* the noise cats make at mating time. *keep:* make.

69. Sir Toby is now more than a little drunk, but, as drunkards often do, concentrates a great deal of colourful vehemence into his choice of language. *Cataian:* someone from Cathay, i.e. China. Used thus in Elizabethan times, this would mean 'cheat'. *Peg-a-Ramsey:* There was a contemporary song of this name. It may mean something like 'scarecrow' here.

70. *Three merry men be we:* another contemporary song.

71. *consanguineous.* This is explained in the next sentence, *of her blood*, related to her. Sir Toby is resentful that his own niece should feel she has to call in a servant, even if her steward, to reprimand him, her uncle.

72. *Tilly-vally:* a term of scorn and reproof – 'nonsense!'

73. *There dwelt a man in Babylon.* A line from a contemporary ballad.

75. *Beshrew me:* a plague on me. *in admirable fooling:* 'playing the fool most successfully.'

76–7. *so do I too.* Sir Andrew does so want to share, if only a little, in Sir Toby's success.

77–8. *more natural.* He means this as in such a modern expression as 'a natural games-player'; but a regular Elizabethan meaning was 'idiotic' or 'half-witted'.

Sir Andrew

    An you love me, let's do't. I am dog at a catch.

Clown

    By'r lady, sir, and some dogs will catch well.

Sir Andrew

    Most certain. Let our catch be 'Thou knave'.

Clown

    'Hold thy peace, thou knave' knight? I shall be   60
    constrain'd in't to call thee knave, knight.

Sir Andrew

    'Tis not the first time I have constrained one to call
    me knave. Begin, fool: it begins 'Hold thy peace'.

Clown

    I shall never begin if I hold my peace.

Sir Andrew

    Good, i' faith! Come, begin.   65

        [Catch sung. Enter MARIA]

Maria

    What a caterwauling do you keep here! If my lady have
    not call'd up her steward Malvolio, and bid him turn
    you out of doors, never trust me.

Sir Toby

    My lady's a Cataian, we are politicians, Malvolio's a
    Peg-a-Ramsey, and *[Sings]*
                     Three merry men be we.   70
    Am not I consanguineous? Am I not of her blood?
    Tilly-vally, lady. *[Sings]*
             There dwelt a man in Babylon,
             Lady, lady.

Clown

    Beshrew me, the knight's in admirable fooling.   75

Sir Andrew

    Ay, he does well enough if he be dispos'd, and so do
    I too; he does it with a better grace, but I do it more
    natural.

79. O' the twelfth day of December: another ballad, probably.

81. We have to admit that Malvolio's protest is entirely justified – in any case, he has to voice his mistress's opinion. Yet the four are convinced that he is putting into it far too much of his own kill-joy attitude. It is as if they have been waiting for just such an occasion, to make a stand against him. But they have to wait for Sir Toby to shake himself clear of his drunkenness sufficiently to rally them to the cause of gaiety and good humour, before they discover their solidarity.

82. wit: good sense. honesty: decency.

83. tinkers. These wandering, gipsy-like people had a reputation for drunken chattering.

85. cozier's catches: cobblers' songs.

85–6. without any mitigation or remorse of voice: 'at the top of your voices, without stopping'.

88. We did keep time. The other meaning of 'time' – rhythm. Sneck up! 'be hanged!'

89. round: outspoken.

91. she's nothing allied to your disorders: 'she entirely dissociates herself from your unruly conduct.'

92. separate yourself and your misdemeanours: 'separate yourself from your bad deeds.'

96. The next bit of dialogue, interspersed with snatches of songs, is most effective. This oblique way of answering has an insolence about it more intolerable than a plain statement of opposition. Sir Toby and Feste are ignoring Malvolio, by simply conversing, however unsoberly, with each other, but they are talking *about* him. Their very flippancy is meant to show how little they care for his reproof. (The lines they sing are taken, but altered somewhat, from a contemporary ballad.)

Sir Toby [Sings]
 O' the twelfth day of December—
Maria
 For the love o' God, peace! 80

[Enter MALVOLIO]

Malvolio
 My masters, are you mad? Or what are you? Have
 you no wit, manners, nor honesty, but to gabble like
 tinkers at this time of night? Do ye make an ale-house
 of my lady's house, that ye squeak out your coziers'
 catches without any mitigation or remorse of voice? 85
 Is there no respect of place, persons, nor time, in
 you?
Sir Toby
 We did keep time, sir, in our catches. Sneck up!
Malvolio
 Sir Toby, I must be round with you. My lady bade me
 tell you that, though she harbours you as her kinsman, 90
 she's nothing allied to your disorders. If you can
 separate yourself and your misdemeanours, you are
 welcome to the house; if not, and it would please you
 to take leave of her, she is very willing to bid you
 farewell. 95
Sir Toby [Sings]
 Farewell, dear heart, since I must needs be gone.
Maria
 Nay, good Sir Toby.
Clown [Sings]
 His eyes do show his days are almost done.
Malvolio
 Is't even so?
Sir Toby [Sings]
 But I will never die. 100

[Falls down]

107–13. Drunkenness may accentuate views already held, but it slows down the reactions; and Sir Toby's mind seems up to now to have done little to cope with the crisis. Even now it is Malvolio's earlier remark (line 87), and then not correctly remembered – Malvolio spoke of 'time' but to Sir Toby it has become 'tune' – that finally 'needles' him. It has taken till now to penetrate. But when he does turn and address Malvolio, it is as though he had, all through the small-talk, been simply priming himself for it. As he rises to his feet, however unsteadily, his whole person seems in that instant to overtop Malvolio. We could hardly imagine a more telling line of confrontation.

107. *Art any more than a steward?* Even at his drunken worst, Sir Toby is what Malvolio can never be – blood-relation to the Countess – and at this moment he intends that Malvolio shall have that fact thrust down his throat.

108–9. That other half of Malvolio – his intolerance of all merry-making – is equally hateful to Sir Toby. In lines perhaps more memorable than any others in the whole play, he demolishes the entire case for censoriousness. Malvolio's virtue (even if it has a valid existence), cannot possibly justify his dictating how the rest of the world shall amuse itself. 'Cakes and ale' (typical Elizabethan holiday fare) neatly suggests the simple pleasures of simple folk, especially during the 'twelve days of Christmas'. Feasting at that time was particularly opposed by the Puritans.

110–11. *ginger shall be hot i' th' mouth, too.* Feste is quick to side with Sir Toby in his stand against Malvolio, but we may feel that his enthusiasm at this moment is stimulated more by the taste he recalls of good fare, than by any principle involved. (Ginger was often used to add flavour to ale.)

112–13. *rub your chain with crumbs.* Malvolio's chain of office would normally be cleaned by being rubbed with breadcrumbs. By asking Maria for yet more wine, Sir Toby gives the finishing touch to his scornful defiance of Malvolio.

114–17. By addressing his parting remarks to Maria, Malvolio is virtually accepting temporary defeat. His invective against Sir Toby has bounced back upon himself, and he recognizes that he can get no further in that direction in the present encounter. All he can do is turn and blame Maria for supplying them with intoxicants, and thus enencouraging their drunken rowdiness.

115–16. *give means for this uncivil rule:* 'provide opportunity for this uncivilized behaviour.'

118. An expression of contempt, possibly addressed usually to a dog. Maria is careful to keep back her comment till Malvolio is out of hearing.

119. *as good a deed . . . ahungry.* Sir Andrew means that the device he is about to suggest would exasperate Malvolio as much as offering a man drink when he was hungry for solid food.

Clown [Sings]
   Sir Toby, there you lie.
Malvolio
   This is much credit to you.
Sir Toby [Sings]
   Shall I bid him go?
Clown [Sings]
   What an if you do?
Sir Toby [Sings]
   Shall I bid him go, and spare not?   105
Clown [Sings]
   O, no, no, no, no, you dare not.
Sir Toby [Rising]
   Out o' tune, sir! Ye lie. Art any more than a steward?
   Dost thou think, because thou art virtuous, there shall
   be no more cakes and ale?
Clown
   Yes, by Saint Anne; and ginger shall be hot i' th' mouth 110
   too.
Sir Toby
   Th'art i' th' right. Go, sir, rub your chain with crumbs.
   A stoup of wine, Maria!
Malvolio
   Mistress Mary, if you priz'd my lady's favour at
   anything more than contempt, you would not give 115
   means for this uncivil rule; she shall know of it, by
   this hand.

                            [Exit]

Maria
   Go shake your ears.
Sir Andrew
   'Twere as good a deed as to drink when a man's
   ahungry, to challenge him the field, and then to break 120
   promise with him and make a fool of him.
Sir Toby
   Do't, knight. I'll write thee a challenge; or I'll deliver
   thy indignation to him by word of mouth.

124–30. Maria has a better plan, and urges them to delay or abandon any other ideas.

126. *out of quiet:* restless.

127. *gull:* trick. ('Gullible' means 'easy to trick', 'easily deceived'.) *nayword:* byword; so *gull him into a nayword* means 'go on fooling him until he becomes a famous ass'.

128. *common recreation:* a figure of fun, laughed at by everybody.

131. *Possess us:* inform us. *Tell us something of him.* Sir Toby isn't just asking for general information about Malvolio, but for that particular point on which he imagines she will be basing her plan.

132. *Puritan.* The word then included all that it still does, of opposition to ordinary human joys and jollity. Originally this attitude was but part of a larger religious attitude – the Puritans were a substantial party in the contemporary Church. But it seems that when Maria uses it of Malvolio she is thinking only of the kill-joy aspect of Puritanism. (We must not see in her remark any sort of crusade by Shakespeare against the Puritans as such.)

133–5. When Sir Andrew seems to be making this very mistake, and to vow vengeance on Malvolio for being one of the Puritan party – this is what he thinks Maria is saying – then Sir Toby at once checks him. He knows that he is simply echoing popular sentiment, with never a thought for what is really at stake; and Sir Toby has no time for that.

134. *exquisite:* ingeniously devised.

138–9. *The devil a Puritan . . . time-pleaser:* 'He's no Puritan (in the regular, religious sense), or anything else that requires selfless loyalty to a cause. He is simply one who judges every situation by its potential advantage to himself.'

139. *affection'd:* affected. *cons state:* learns matters of state, theories of state-craft.

140. *without book:* by heart (as actors in a play, who have to dispense with their written lines). *swarths.* A swath, or swarth, is that quantity of grass or hay cut by a mower with one sweep of his sickle.

140–1. *the best persuaded of himself:* always thinking most favourably about himself; having the highest opinion of himself.

142. *his grounds of faith.* This certainty about his own attractiveness is as fundamental to Malvolio's whole character as a religious person's faith is.

143. *that vice in him:* his conviction that people cannot help admiring him.

146. *epistles:* letters.

148. *expressure:* expression.

150. *feelingly:* accurately. *personated:* described. By including descriptions that so obviously must refer to himself, Maria will convince Malvolio that the letter is intended for him, but from one who is at present unable to name himself, or herself, openly and in writing. The subtlety of the letter, with many more such hints of identity, is that it is Malvolio's vanity that is played upon every time. He can identify himself progressively as the addressee only by entertaining more and more outrageous notions of his own charms.

151. *forgotten:* unimportant.

Maria

Sweet Sir Toby, be patient for to-night; since the youth
of the Count's was to-day with my lady, she is much 125
out of quiet. For Monsieur Malvolio, let me alone
with him; if I do not gull him into a nayword, and
make him a common recreation, do not think I have
wit enough to lie straight in my bed. I know I can
do it. 130

Sir Toby

Possess us, possess us; tell us something of him.

Maria

Marry, sir, sometimes he is a kind of Puritan.

Sir Andrew

O, if I thought that, I'd beat him like a dog.

Sir Toby

What, for being a Puritan? Thy exquisite reason, dear
knight? 135

Sir Andrew

I have no exquisite reason for't, but I have reason good
enough.

Maria

The devil a Puritan that he is, or anything constantly
but a time-pleaser; an affection'd ass that cons state
without book and utters it by great swarths; the best 140
persuaded of himself, so cramm'd, as he thinks, with
excellencies that it is his grounds of faith that all that
look on him love him; and on that vice in him will
my revenge find notable cause to work.

Sir Toby

What wilt thou do? 145

Maria

I will drop in his way some obscure epistles of love;
wherein, by the colour of his beard, the shape of his
leg, the manner of his gait, the expressure of his eye,
forehead, and complexion, he shall find himself most
feelingly personated. I can write very like my lady, 150
your niece; on a forgotten matter we can hardly make

153. *I smell a device.* An unusual way of describing the detecting of a plot, but just as logical in fact as to speak of 'seeing' it. (We have the saying 'to smell a rat' – to detect something deceptive or unfavourable.)

154. Once again, Sir Andrew feels he must echo the very metaphor Sir Toby has used.

158. *a horse of that colour:* 'something like that.'

159. *your horse . . . an ass.* Rather unexpected, perhaps, from Sir Andrew, but we must not begrudge h m his occasional small joke.

162. *Sport royal:* first-rate entertainment.

164–5. *observe his cons ruction of it:* 'watch what he makes of it.

166. *event:* outcome.

167. *Penthesilea:* Queen of the Amazons (a legendary race of warlike females). The thought of the tiny Maria having conceived this impressive strategy no doubt prompts Sir Toby to make his humorous comparison.

169. *beagle:* a small type of hunting dog. Here the term is used affectionately, and with reference to Maria's size.

171. Sir Andrew is again feebly imitative, but on this occasion there is something quite pathetic about his timid reminiscence. It certainly forms a contrast to what we see in Sir Toby in a moment – a side usually obscured by his outward good humour – when he callously presses Sir Andrew for more money, promising him a success in his wooing of Olivia which he knows to be out of the question.

distinction of our hands.

Sir Toby

Excellent! I smell a device.

Sir Andrew

I have't in my nose too.

Sir Toby

He shall think, by the letters that thou wilt drop, that 155
they come from my niece, and that she's in love with
him.

Maria

My purpose is, indeed, a horse of that colour.

Sir Andrew

And your horse now would make him an ass.

Maria

Ass, I doubt not. 160

Sir Andrew

O, 'twill be admirable!

Maria

Sport royal, I warrant you. I know my physic will work
with him. I will plant you two, and let the fool make
a third, where he shall find the letter; observe his
construction of it. For this night, to bed, and dream 165
on the event. Farewell.

[Exit]

Sir Toby

Good night, Penthesilea.

Sir Andrew

Before me, she's a good wench.

Sir Toby

She's a beagle true-bred, and one that adores me.
What o' that? 170

Sir Andrew

I was ador'd once too.

Sir Toby

Let's to bed, knight. Thou hadst need send for more
money.

174. *a foul way out:* in a desperate state.

176. *Cut:* a common name for a working horse. The phrase *call me Cut* here simply means that Sir Toby will accept blame and insult if he is proved wrong about Sir Andrew and Olivia.

178. *burn some sack.* Sack was a white wine from Spain or the Canary Islands which was sometimes heated.

SCENE IV

The lapse of time needed for the maturing of the plot against Malvolio is put to good use on the stage. We are now for a while to be more subtly entertained by the shifting fortunes of Viola and the Duke, whom we find in characteristic setting, with appropriate music and discourse to soothe – or more likely stimulate – his love-sick mood. (There is the added interest that the singing now is provided by Feste.)

1. *Give me some music.* This is exactly how the play began; and we may well feel that nothing that has happened since to the Duke has had the slightest effect on him. There is something very affected about his 'loveliking'. Here, we feel, is a love-sick noble, attentive primarily to his own emotional state. It is only incidentally that Olivia has been singled out as the object of his desire – it could just as easily have been any other lady of noble birth.

3. *old and antique song.* An interesting comparison follows, between the merits of old-fashioned, 'nostalgic' music, and contemporary compositions. Orsino prefers the former, finding the modern pieces too contrived.

5. *recollected terms:* suggests unnatural striving after effect.

Sir Andrew

If I cannot recover your niece, I am a foul way out.

Sir Toby

Send for money, knight; if thou hast her not i' th' end, 175
call me Cut.

Sir Andrew

If I do not, never trust me; take it how you will.

Sir Toby

Come, come, I'll go burn some sack; 'tis too late to go
to bed now. Come, knight; come, knight.

[Exeunt]

SCENE IV

The Duke's palace

[Enter DUKE, VIOLA, CURIO and OTHERS]

Duke

Give me some music. Now, good morrow, friends,
Now, good Cesario, but that piece of song
That old and antique song we heard last night,
Methought it did relieve my passion much
More than light airs and recollected terms   5
Of these most brisk and giddy-paced times
Come, but one verse.

Curio

He is not here, so please your lordship, that should
sing it.

Duke   10

Who was it?

Curio

Feste, the jester, my lord; a fool that the Lady Olivia's
father took much delight in. He is about the house

Duke

Seek him out, and play the tune the while

[Exit CURIO. Music plays]

14. *Come hither, boy*. Viola is brought into the Duke's reverie with little thought at first for her own independent existence. It is not long, however, before Orsino finds himself taking note of her as a person in her own right, whose forthrightness involves him soon in discussion with her on equal terms. His own emotional problems, till now filling all his thoughts, are pushed into the background, as his curiosity about Viola grows. At the end of the scene (line 122) he has forgotten all about Olivia; and it is only when Viola asks him, practically enough – or mischievously – *shall I to this lady?*, that he brings himself to a not very convincing *Ay, that's the theme*. (Almost, 'that's the general idea'.)

17. *skittish:* fickle. ***motions:*** emotions.

18. *Save in the constant image:* except in the unchanging picture I have in my mind.

20–1. We are to think of Viola as speaking these lines with deep feeling. She has good reason now to be as moved as Orsino by evocative music.

22. *My life upon't:* 'I'll stake my life on it.'

23. *stay'd upon some favour:* 'gazed for a long time at the face of someone.'

24. *by your favour:* 'with your permission.' A mere convention of politeness. (We often insert the phrase 'if you please' into a simple narrative, in much the same way.) But there is a play on the two meanings of 'favour'. Orsino will have taken it to mean 'permission' – the simple convention. Viola knows this, but also has in mind Orsino's face (the other meaning of *favour* he himself has just used), on which she has gazed many times.

25. *Of your complexion:* 'like you in appearance.'

26. *worth:* good enough for.

27. *About your years*. Here again, note the delicate humour inherent in this false encounter. The audience knows why Viola describes the person she loves, in this way – Orsino's features are thus singled out because Orsino *is* the man! But he has no idea of this, and pursues the discussion deliberately, pointing out what would be in fact sensible advice if Viola *were* a young man with his heart set on a woman with Orsino's looks and age.

28. *still:* always.

29. *so wears she to him:* 'in this way she grows to him.'

30. *So sways she level:* 'in this way she maintains a steady course.'

31–4. Orsino's argument seems to be that, since men are more likely to be unfaithful, they should not put undue strain on the relationship by union with not-so-young women who have lost their earlier charms.

34. *I think it well, my lord*. Another fine touch of irony. Orsino has been speaking, though not over-discreetly, against his own sex, with which Viola can heartily agree – which may well surprise Orsino.

36. *hold the bent:* stand the strain (as of a bow-string).

39. Viola can regret this quite properly in her male role, but how much more feelingly when she identifies – as of course she must – with womanly frailty! The sudden deepening of emotion is brought out most effectively by the second half of the line – using virtually the same words as in the first half, but neatly rearranged.

Come hither, boy. If ever thou shalt love,
In the sweet pangs of it remember me; 15
For such as I am all true lovers are,
Unstaid and skittish in all motions else
Save in the constant image of the creature
That is belov'd. How dost thou like this tune?

Viola
It gives a very echo to the seat 20
Where Love is thron'd.

Duke
      Thou dost speak masterly.
My life upon't, young though thou art, thine eye
Hath stay'd upon some favour that it loves;
Hath it not, boy?

Viola
     A little, by your favour.

Duke
What kind of woman is't?

Viola
      Of your complexion, 25

Duke
She is not worth thee, then. What years, i' faith?

Viola
About your years, my lord.

Duke
Too old, by heaven! Let still the woman take
An elder than herself; so wears she to him
So sways she level in her husband's heart. 30
For, boy, however we do praise ourselves,
Our fancies are more giddy and unfirm,
More longing, wavering, sooner lost and won,
Than women's are.

Viola
    I think it well, my lord.

Duke
Then let thy love be younger than thyself,
Or they affection cannot hold the bent; 35
For women are as roses, whose fair flow'r
Being once display'd doth fall that very hour.

Viola
And so they are; alas, that they are so!

43. *spinsters.* This is simply the feminine of 'spinners'.

44. *bones:* bobbins made of bone, used often in spinning.

45. *silly sooth:* simple truth.

46. *dallies:* deals lightly. It is easy to see why Feste's song, with its theme of broken-heartedness, has made such an appeal to Orsino. He can perfectly identify – so he persuades himself – with the betrayed lover who welcomes death.

51. *cypress.* The wood of the cypress tree was used for coffins.

54. *shroud:* sheet in which a corpse was wrapped before burial. *stuck all with yew:* with sprigs of yew fastened on it. (The yew tree was for centuries associated with funerals, and is still often found in churchyards.)

60. *greet:* weep for.

To die, even when they to perfection grow!   40

[Re-enter CURIO *and* CLOWN*]*

Duke

O, fellow, come, the song we had last night.
Mark it, Cesario; it is old and plain;
The spinsters and the knitters in the sun,
And the free maids that weave their thread with
      bones,
Do use to chant it; it is silly sooth,   45
And dallies with the innocence of love,
Like the old age.

Clown

Are you ready, sir?

Duke

Ay; prithee, sing.

[Music. FESTE'S *song]*

Come away, come away, death;   50
And in sad cypress let me be laid;
   Fly away, fly away, breath,
I am slain by a fair cruel maid.
My shroud of white, stuck all with yew,
               O, prepare it!   55
My part of death no one so true
               Did share it.
   Not a flower, not a flower sweet,
On my black coffin let there be strown;
   Not a friend, not a friend greet   60
My poor corpse where my bones shall be thrown;
A thousand thousand sighs to save,
               Lay me, O, where
Sad true lover never find my grave,
               To weep there!   65

69–70. *pleasure will be paid one time or another*. This time, Feste means it in the sense, rather regretfully, that we have to pay for our pleasure, sooner or later – that a life of self-indulgence eventually brings its own discomfiture.

71. *Give me now leave* (permission) *to leave you:* a courteous form of dismissal – the Duke is telling Feste to go.

73. *changeable taffeta*. Taffeta is a thin silk which changes colour when looked at from another angle; as it is *changeable*, it suits the moody Orsino. This is the point also of *opal* (line 74), a precious stone that seems to have shades of all the other jewels in itself. Feste sees Orsino as someone who is so 'beside himself' with love-sickness that all manner of thoughts and moods light upon his mind, and as quickly leave. His use, then, of *constancy* (line 74) is in gentle irony – he means just the opposite.

77. *makes a good voyage of nothing*. Such a person's imagination is so active that the smallest thing is given a disproportionate significance. (The clown is the only one who would be allowed to speak so frankly to the Duke.)

80. *sovereign cruelty*. Olivia is thus described because her 'cruelty' is 'sovereign' (all-powerful) – she will allow nothing to soften her attitude towards Orsino.

80–5. Orsino here insists that he loves her for herself, and not for any of her material possessions.

82. *dirty:* contemptible.

83. 'Those possessions that happen to be hers through no virtue of her own.'

84. *giddily:* inconstantly (in this case, with complete indifference to their material value). *as Fortune*. Because Fortune is equally indifferent in the way she distributes her blessings.

86. *pranks:* dresses up. The 'miracle' that Orsino is attracted by is Olivia's real self.

87. This is Viola's way of gradually bringing Orsino to face the truth she knows he will sooner or later have to accept.

88. *I cannot be so answer'd:* 'I refuse to accept this explanation.'

Duke

There's for thy pains.

Clown

No pains, sir; I take pleasure in singing, sir.

Duke

I'll pay thy pleasure, then.

Clown

Truly, sir, and pleasure will be paid one time or another. 70

Duke

Give me now leave to leave thee.

Clown

Now the melancholy god protect thee; and the tailor make thy doublet of changeable taffeta, for thy mind is a very opal. I would have men of such constancy put to sea, that their business might be everything, 75 and their intent everywhere: for that's it that always makes a good voyage of nothing. Farewell.

[Exit CLOWN]

Duke

Let all the rest give place.

[Exeunt CURIO and ATTENDANTS]

Once more, Cesario,
Get thee to yond same sovereign cruelty. 80
Tell her my love, more noble than the world,
Prizes not quantity of dirty lands;
The parts that fortune hath bestow'd upon her,
Tell her I hold as giddily as Fortune;
But 'tis that miracle and queen of gems 85
That Nature pranks her in attracts my soul.

Viola

But if she cannot love you, sir?

Duke

I cannot be so answer'd.

88–92. Viola suggests that the Duke should picture a parallel situation, in which he might have to tell someone who was desperately in love with him, but for whom he felt no affection, that he couldn't love her. When Viola speaks of *some lady, as perhaps there is*, she is, as we know, meaning herself. She is, in this oblique way, going as far as she dares, in declaring her love for the Duke. Even this slight emotional release is better for her than nothing.

93–103. But Viola's comparison is unacceptable, for Orsino insists that women love far less intensely than men. (He is inconsistent: he said men were fickle in lines 32–4; now it is women who have no stability). It is ironic that he says this as one who is completely confident that his hearer will of necessity share his masculine view-point. Viola cannot ignore this attack upon her own sex. But see how neatly she refutes him, without in any way disclosing her identity! (lines 103–9).

94. *bide:* endure.

98. *liver.* It was popularly believed that the liver was the seat of love. Orsino, seeking to discredit the love felt by women, says that it doesn't originate in the liver (where true love should) but in the *palate*, simply as a 'taste'.

99. *surfeit* and *cloyment* are synonymous, both meaning 'excess'. *revolt:* revulsion of appetite.

100–101. Compare what Orsino says in Act I, Scene i, lines 10–11.

101. *compare:* comparison. (We sometimes use the phrase 'beyond compare'.)

104. Notice how quick Orsino is here. What might he be thinking Viola is about to say?

105. All that Viola says now has double meaning – Orsino takes the one superficial sense of her description of her supposed sister's love; but we, the audience, know she is describing her own affections. In lines 107–9 the second meaning almost breaks through to the surface. We may wonder why Orsino doesn't detect the heightened emotion which must surely be apparent in Viola as she says this.

107–9. 'My father had a daughter who loved a man in the same way that I might love you, if I were a woman.'

109. *what's her history?* 'What happened to her?'

110. *A blank:* nothing.

111. *concealment:* the keeping to herself of her true feelings.

112. *damask:* rose-coloured. The comparison between the disfiguring effect of wrongly concealed emotion, and the grub eating away the rose-bud, from inside, is very effective. *pin'd in thought:* grieved secretly.

113. *green and yellow:* sickly (as the colours suggest).

114. *Patience on a monument.* It is not known whether any particular statue of Patience is here recollected.

115. *Smiling at grief:* enduring it cheerfully.

117. *Our shows are more than will:* 'We lack the determination to put our good intentions into effect.' *still: always.*

Viola

               Sooth, but you must.
Say that some lady, as perhaps there is,
Hath for your love as great a pang of heart   90
As you have for Olivia. You cannot love her;
You tell her so. Must she not then be answer'd?

Duke

There is no woman's sides
Can bide the beating of so strong a passion
As love doth give my heart; no woman's heart   95
So big to hold so much; they lack retention.
Alas, their love may be call'd appetite—
No motion of the liver, but the palate—
That suffer surfeit, cloyment, and revolt;
But mine is all as hungry as the sea,   100
And can digest as much. Make no compare
Between that love a woman can bear me
And that I owe Olivia.

Viola

              Ay, but I know—

Duke

What dost thou know?

Viola

Too well what love women to men may owe.   105
In faith, they are as true of heart as we.
My father had a daughter lov'd a man,
As it might be perhaps, were I a woman,
I should your lordship.

Duke

           And what's her history?

Viola

A blank, my lord. She never told her love,   110
But let concealment, like a worm i' th' bud,
Feed on her damask cheek. She pin'd in thought;
And with a green and yellow melancholy
She sat like Patience on a monument,
Smiling at grief. Was not this love indeed?   115
We men may say more, swear more, but indeed
Our shows are more than will; for still we prove
Much in our vows, but little in our love.

119. This is perhaps the first point at which we feel that the Duke is becoming sufficiently forgetful of himself to feel genuine concern for the imaginary sister's fate.

120. *I am all the daughters.* Viola knows this to be true, and can affirm it without betraying her secret.

121. *And all the brothers, too.* She still thinks that Sebastian is probably dead . . . ; *and yet I know not.* But she is not certain; she retains some hope.

124. *can give no place:* will not surrender; *denay:* denial, refusal.

SCENE V

This scene provides what many people regard as the funniest episode in the play. It is probably the most ingenious. The plot to humiliate Malvolio has not yet matured – this happens later when he has outraged his mistress with his new mood of confidence, and is put in custody for it – but it is here at its most entertaining stage. For, thinking himself to be alone, Malvolio displays the whole range of his conceitedness. (Maria's carefully-worded letter sees to it that no single trait is overlooked.) Every soliloquy gives to the audience this 'unfair advantage' – of seeing without being seen, and of prying unobserved into secret thoughts. But this particular one we share with some of the players – hidden viewers of the results of their plot – and our own amusement is increased by theirs. The group of Malvolio-baiters is joined by Fabian, another of Olivia's household, who from now on associates himself with them.

2. *scruple:* a very small part.

4. *niggardly:* mean.

5. *sheep-biter:* a term of abuse, literally a dog that worries sheep, and metaphorically, perhaps, a man who chases women. *notable:* public.

6. Fabian has the same cause, basically, as the others, for wanting to 'get his own back' on Malvolio. He has been faulted by him for indulging in disreputable pastimes. (Bear-baiting, like theatre-going, was frowned upon by the Puritan element in England.)

11. *little villain.* We have already been reminded of Maria's small stature, some of the jokes depending upon the fact (e.g., Act I, Scene v, line 195). *metal:* precious metal, gold.

Duke

But died thy sister of her love, my boy?

Viola

I am all the daughters of my father's house,   120
And all the brothers too – and yet I know not.
Sir, shall I to this lady?

Duke

                  Ay, that's the theme.
To her in haste. Give her this jewel; say.
My love can give no place, bide no denay.

[Exeunt.]

SCENE V

Olivia's garden

[Enter SIR TOBY, SIR ANDREW, *and* FABIAN]

Sir Toby

Come thy ways, Signior Fabian.

Fabian

Nay, I'll come; if I lose a scruple of this sport let me
be boil'd to death with melancholy.

Sir Toby

Wouldst thou not be glad to have the niggardly rascally
sheep-biter come by some notable shame?   5

Fabian

I would exult, man; you know he brought me out o'
favour with my lady about a bear-baiting here.

Sir Toby

To anger him we'll have the bear again; and we will
fool him black and blue – shall we not, Sir Andrew?

Sir Andrew

And we do not, it is pity of our lives.   10

[Enter MARIA]

Sir Toby

Here comes the little villain. How now, my metal of
India!

14–15. *practising behaviour to his own shadow this half-hour.* It is not the letter that turns Malvolio into such a conceited ass – he is this already. The letter simply accentuates the characteristic. So Maria's observation serves as one more reminder that his vanity is unrelieved and inexcusable; the blame cannot be laid at anyone else's door. •

17. *a contemplative idiot.* His foolishness will become the more apparent, as the letter prompts him to indulge his imagination further and further. *Close:* 'Be still.' (We often describe a person as 'close' when he shows a tendency to 'keep himself to himself', and not talk freely.)

19–20. *trout that must be caught with tickling.* This is an actual method of catching fish in shallow water. What Maria means is that Malvolio's humiliation will be best effected by subtle means.

21. *'Tis but fortune; all is fortune.* Malvolio seems to be ascribing his growing success with Olivia (so he regards it) to pure chance, where we might have expected him to accept it as a quite natural result of his own charm. How should we interpret his comment – how will he say it? Malvolio is already highly optimistic about his chances with Olivia. Even before he sees the letter, he discloses enough of his conceitedness to warrant a pretty severe reprimand from somebody. Nowhere else in the play are his thoughts and motives laid quite so bare as in this scene. There is a degree of concentration here upon his innate character – his 'humour' – that occurs with no one else. Thus when Viola, for example, speaks her thoughts aloud in soliloquy, or half-disguises them before Olivia or the Duke, the focus is not upon her character as something already formulated, but upon her reactions to the present situation. We are never required to assume anything about her – only to take in what she is at that moment experiencing. She will no doubt emerge as an entirely credible person at the end. But the picture is initially blank; and all that there is, virtually, of Viola, has come into being during the course of the play. But with Malvolio, the process is just the opposite. His character is never in question, having been completely defined from the start. The interest this time is what happens to such a character when it meets determined opposition. It is the sheer spectacle of collision that provides the entertainment. This sort of thing takes up only part of Shakespeare's play, whereas it forms the chief theme in that other type of comedy, called 'Comedy of Humours', for which Ben Jonson is famous.

22. *affect:* feel affection for.

24. *complexion:* appearance (see Scene iv, line 25); *uses:* treats.

27. *overweening:* thinking too highly of himself.

28. *O, peace!* Throughout the ensuing dialogue, one or other of the hidden observers has the job of keeping the others quiet, in case Malvolio should notice them, and the whole plot be ruined. This is simply a dramatic convention. They will in fact be speaking loud enough all the time for Malvolio to have heard every word. But to preserve some semblance of realism or to make the ridiculous situation even funnier, there are these frequent requests for silence. *Contemplation:* see note on line 17. *turkey-cock.* The male turkey, like most male birds, makes a great and colourful display with its feathers, to attract the hen, or frighten off rival males.

Maria

Get ye all three into the box-tree. Malvolio's coming
down this walk. He has been yonder i' the sun practising behaviour to his own shadow this half hour. 15
Observe him, for the love of mockery, for I know this
letter will make a contemplative idiot of him. Close,
in the name of jesting! *[As the men hide she drops a
letter]* Lie thou there; for here comes the trout that
must be caught with tickling. 20

[Exit. Enter MALVOLIO]

Malvolio

'Tis but fortune; all is fortune. Maria once told me she
did affect me; and I have heard herself come thus near,
that, should she fancy, it should be one of my
complexion. Besides, she uses me with a more exalted
respect than any one else that follows her. What should 25
I think on't?

Sir Toby

Here's an overweening rogue!

Fabian

O, peace! Contemplation makes a rare turkey-cock

29. *jets:* struts pompously. ***advanc'd:*** raised. Malvolio's self-confidence grows noticeably, the more he dwells upon what seems to him clear evidence of Olivia's favour. The turkey-cock description would, then, come readily to mind.

30. *'Slight:* 'By God's light.'

32. *Count Malvolio:* his title, as Olivia's husband. Even Malvolio needs some slight reassurance before he can hold out this hope! So he recalls an instance of a notable lady who married a member of her household staff. (There is no clear evidence of any actual lady of this name, but there was a story in existence, on which Webster's *Duchess of Malfi* was based, of a noble lady who married her steward.)

38. *Jezebel:* wife of Ahab, an Israelite King. She has become proverbial for shamelessness – in women, however, not men.

39. *he's deeply in:* 'he has succeeded in deceiving himself completely.'

40. *blows him:* inflates him. (We still sometimes describe a self-opinionated person as 'puffed-up'.)

42. *state* –. Malvolio is probably about to say 'state-chair' (but the word *state* by itself could mean 'throne').

43. *stone-bow:* a cross-bow using stones as missiles.

44. *branch'd:* decorated with a branch-like pattern.

45. *day-bed:* sofa.

49. *humour:* disposition. ***state:*** power. The whole phrase *humour of state* means 'whim of a man of authority'.

49–50. *after a demure travel of regard:* 'after gazing gravely round.'

of him; how he jets under his advanc'd plumes!

Sir Andrew
'Slight, I could so beat the rogue—   30

Sir Toby
Peace, I say.

Malvolio
To be Count Malvolio!

Sir Toby
Ah, rogue!

Sir Andrew
Pistol him, pistol him.

Sir Toby
Peace, peace!   35

Malvolio
There is example for't: the Lady of the Strachy married
the yeoman of the wardrobe.

Sir Andrew
Fie on him, Jezebel!

Fabian
O, peace! Now he's deeply in; look how imagination
blows him.   40

Malvolio
Having been three months married to her, sitting in
my state—

Sir Toby
O, for a stone-bow to hit him in the eye!

Malvolio
Calling my officers about me, in my branch'd velvet
gown, having come from a day-bed – where I have left   45
Olivia sleeping—

Sir Toby
Fire and brimstone!

Fabian
O, peace, peace!

Malvolio
And then to have the humour of state; and after a
demure travel of regard, telling them I know my   50

52. kinsman. If he married Olivia, he would become Sir Toby's relative. But Sir Toby clearly doesn't relish the idea, nor the omission of 'Sir'.

53. Bolts and shackles! Both mean 'fetters', used to chain up offenders; together they make an effective exclamation.

55. Seven of my people. Malvolio's new dignity would call for no fewer than seven servants to carry out his wishes.

57. play with my . . . some rich jewel. Malvolio is about to say 'chain of office', as his hand lights upon it, but then recalls that, in his new exalted state, it will no longer be there, to remind him of his subordinate status, but will be replaced by 'some rich jewel'.

58. curtsies. The word is the same as 'courtesy' and means 'to show proper respect by bowing'. It applied to either sex, and not just to women, as it does today.

60. cars: carts, or other horse-drawn vehicles. The sense is that their silence will be as painful as if it was having to be dragged forcibly out, yet they must maintain it. (We have the expression, 'wild horses won't drag it out of him', to indicate someone's determination not to divulge information – though there the pressure is to produce words, whereas in Fabian's image, the pressure is for silence.)

62. extend my hand: i.e., to be kissed (a regal gesture of condescension).

62–3. familiar smile. If Malvolio is miming all this – and he almost certainly has to – then how do we picture this 'familiar smile'?

63. austere regard of control: 'stern look of authority.'

66. give me this prerogative of speech: 'give me leave to address you in this way.' (How significant, that Sir Toby's drunkenness is the first thing to be reproved!)

69. scab: contemptible fellow.

place as I would they should do theirs, to ask for my
kinsman Toby—

Sir Toby

Bolts and shackles!

Fabian

O, peace, peace, peace! Now, now.

Malvolio

Seven of my people, with an obedient start, make out 55
for him. I frown the while, and perchance wind up
my watch, or play with my – some rich jewel. Toby
approaches; curtsies there to me—

Sir Toby

Shall this fellow live?

Fabian

Though our silence be drawn from us with cars, yet 60
peace.

Malvolio

I extend my hand to him thus, quenching my familiar
smile with an austere regard of control—

Sir Toby

And does not Toby take you a blow o' the lips then?

Malvolio

Saying 'Cousin Toby, my fortunes having cast me on 65
your niece give me this prerogative of speech'—

Sir Toby

What, what?

Malvolio

'You must amend your drunkenness'—

Sir Toby

Out, scab!

Fabian

Nay, patience, or we break the sinews of our plot. 70

Malvolio

'Besides, you waste the treasure of your time with a
foolish knight'—

Sir Andrew

That's me, I warrant you.

75. *many do call me fool*. How different Sir Andrew's reaction is from Sir Toby's, to Malvolio's insults! He has been just as outspoken as the others against Malvolio's presumptuousness; and he has forgotten about himself in his enthusiasm. But the moment Malvolio slights him personally, all the fight is knocked out of him. Instead of countering insult with insult, as Sir Toby has done, he becomes once again his old, diffident self, and meekly accepts Malvolio's low opinion of him.

76. 'What's this business?'

77. *woodcock*: a game-bird that is supposed to be stupid; *gin*: a bird snare.

78–9. *the spirit of humours . . . to him!* Sir Toby fondly hopes that Malvolio will be moved to read the letter aloud – so that they may miss none of the fun. *Intimate* is a verb expressing a wish: *'may* the spirit of humours (his inclination) suggest to him that he read it aloud.'

82. *in contempt of question*: beyond question. ***hand*:** handwriting The careful wording of the letter is so devised as to seem exactly the kind of message Olivia would compose, if she wished to tell him of her love, but at the same time preserve just that degree of anonymity that modesty and security might demand. She would not be expected, in such a rare situation, to commit openly to writing, with her own plain signature, such strong feelings for her steward – not in the opening stages, anyway, when she would need first to ascertain *his* feelings in the matter. Lovers have commonly used a kind of code in the early stages of contact; and so, to Malvolio now, it seems the most likely thing in the world that Olivia would choose to compose her first love-letter to him in such riddles.

84. *this*: that is, the letter itself.

85. *By your leave, wax*. In exaggerated politeness – or quite genuine homage – Malvolio asks the wax seal on the letter for permission to open it. *Soft!* Normally this is a request for silence. Here, it indicates more of the hushed mood of intense concentration Malvolio now adopts – he is saying it to himself.

85–6. *the impressure her Lucrece*: the impression (on the wax) is of her seal (or brooch) with an engraving of Lucretia upon it. (Lucretia was the wife of one of the Tarquins of legendary Rome, who took her own life after having been raped by another Tarquin. Her modesty was legendary) ***with which she uses to seal*:** with which she normally seals.

88. *liver*: thought of as the seat of love, in the human anatomy.

94–5. *The numbers alter'd*. This probably refers to the changed length of line in the next four verses of the letter.

96. *brock*: a badger. Used as a term of contempt (possibly on account of its strong smell).

Malvolio
  'One Sir Andrew.'
Sir Andrew
  I knew 'twas I; for many do call me fool.   75
Malvolio
  What employment have we here? *[Taking up the letter]*
Fabian
  Now is the woodcock near the gin.
Sir Toby
  O, peace! And the spirit of humours intimate reading
  aloud to him!
Malvolio
  By my life, this is my lady's hand: these be her very 80
  C's, her U's, and her T's; and thus makes she her great
  P's. It is, in contempt of question, her hand.
Sir Andrew
  Her C's, her U's, and her T's. Why that?
Malvolio [Reads]
  'To the unknown belov'd, this, and my good wishes.'
  Her very phrases! By your leave, wax. Soft! And the 85
  impressure her Lucrece with which she uses to seal;
  'tis my lady. To whom should this be?
Fabian
  This wins him, liver and all.
Malvolio [Reads]

> 'Jove knows I love,
>   But who?   90
> Lips, do not move;
> No man must know.'

  'No man must know.' What follows? The numbers
  alter'd! 'No man must know.' If this should be thee,
  Malvolio?   95
Sir Toby
  Marry, hang thee, brock!

98–9. Having to keep silent, up to now, about her love has been as painful as the knife-wound with which Lucretia committed suicide, only in this case there has been no ensuing death to end the suffering.

100. Maria's choice of these letters from Malvolio's name gives rise to much amusement, not least because Malvolio seems slow to apply the 'code' to himself. Thus the others can laugh at him for his lack of astuteness, as well as for his vanity. (Though there is no suggestion elsewhere in the play that Malvolio is, in normal circumstances, at all lacking in intelligence.)

101. *fustian:* ridiculously pompous. (Literally, fustian was a coarse kind of cloth.)

104. Malvolio's agitation is well brought out here.

105. *dress'd him:* prepared for him. Maria's bogus letter is likened to an attractive-looking meal which, in fact, contains deadly poison.

106. *staniel:* an inferior kind of hawk. *checks:* a hawking term. When a hawk 'checks', it turns from pursuing the quarry it is meant to follow, and instead goes after some other bird that chances to cross its path. So here is Malvolio, simply not reacting the way he should have done, to the suggestion of his own name in the four letters. There would have been (and will in a few moments be) ample satisfaction for them, in the way they have anticipated, when he succeeds in identifying himself with the 'code'. But his apparent stupidity at first is something they have not anticipated – but find amusing enough, nevertheless. They watch fascinated, as we do, as Malvolio laboriously works his way through the puzzle.

109. *formal capacity:* logical reasoning.

109–10. *obstruction:* difficulty.

110. *the end:* the end of the verses.

111–12. *If I could make that resemble something in me.* It is hard perhaps here, not to feel a momentary pity for Malvolio. He would dearly love to believe that Olivia does care for him, and the entire plot leads him on, subtly but inevitably, to feel convinced that she does. Yet all the while we know how desperately mistaken he is, and how ludicrous he will be made to appear in the end. We can enjoy the situation only if we regard him more as the stereotyped villain of melodrama or pantomime, for whom no sort of compassion is seriously expected.

113. *O, ay.* We may imagine Sir Toby emphasising this, as a pun on the letters 'O' and 'I' that Malvolio has just repeated. *cold scent.* The metaphor is now of hounds following the scent of the creature they are trying to catch. A 'cold' scent is one that is hard to find, because time has gone by since the animal passed.

114. *Sowter:* cobbler, or clumsy workman – but here, simply the name of a hound. Fabian means that Malvolio will 'give tongue', or *cry upon* the false scent when he finds it – which, being a not very good hound, he will – even though it is as strong, and therefore as utterly distinctive, as a fox's scent. (It is to be assumed that this imagined hound is supposed to be hunting something else!)

118. *faults:* wrong trails. (Though, in fact, of course, Malvolio is beginning to get on to the right trail.)

119. *consonancy:* agreement; *the sequel:* the end bit (of the 'code').

120. *suffers under probation:* 'doesn't fit in when put to the test.'

Malvolio [Reads]

> 'I may command where I adore;
>> But silence, like a Lucrece knife,
> With bloodless stroke my heart doth gore;
>> M. O. A. I. doth sway my life.'   100

Fabian
A fustian riddle!

Sir Toby
Excellent wench, say I.

Malvolio
'M. O. A. I. doth sway my life.'
Nay, but first let me see, let me see, let me see.

Fabian
What dish o' poison has she dress'd him!   105

Sir Toby
And with what wing the staniel checks at it!

Malvolio
'I may command where I adore.' Why, she may
command me: I serve her; she is my lady. Why, this
is evident to any formal capacity; there is no obstruction in this. And the end – what should that alphabetical 110
position portend? If I could make that resemble something in me. Softly! M. O. A. I.—

Sir Toby
O, ay, make up that! He is now at a cold scent.

Fabian
Sowter will cry upon't for all this, though it be as rank
as a fox.   115

Malvolio
M – Malvolio; M – why, that begins my name.

Fabian
Did not I say he would work it out? The cur is excellent at faults.

Malvolio
M – But then there is no consonancy in the sequel;
that suffers under probation: A should follow, but O 120
does.

122.Fabian's pun – if it is such – on 'O' is not obvious (like Sir Toby's in the next line). In the Book of Revelation in the Bible, God is described as 'Alpha and Omega' (the first and last letters of the Greek alphabet), because He is the 'Beginning and the End'. Perhaps Fabian simply hopes that this is going to be the end of Malvolio's riddle-solving.

125. Fabian is clearly punning here, however. The *I . . . behind* becomes the 'eye', and the *detraction* it would see means the loss of reputation that will shortly overtake Malvolio. Fabian probably also refers to the threatening antics going on behind Malvolio's back, or at least out of his sight.

128. *This simulation is not as the former:* 'This disguise is not the same as the one used before' – that is, the actual words which seemed to describe, so unmistakably to Malvolio, Olivia's situation and his own.

129. *to crush this a little:* 'to force things a bit,' meaning to change the order of the letters in the 'code'. *bow to me:* 'fit in with my needs,' 'do what I want it to do.'

132. *revolve:* consider.

132–3. *In my stars I am above thee:* 'Fortune has made me superior to you.'

135. *open their hands:* 'make a generous offer' ('open-handed' means 'generous').

137. *inure:* accustom. *like:* likely.

137–8. *cast . . . slough.* A snake 'casts its slough' when it gets rid of its old skin, to make way for the new skin underneath. Malvolio's *humble* slough is the subordinate rôle he has up to now filled, as her steward.

138. *Be opposite:* 'be unfriendly.'

139. *kinsman:* meaning, of course, Sir Toby; *tang:* clang (sound like a bell).

140–1. *put thyself into the trick of singularity:* 'start behaving in an eccentric way.'

142–3. *Remember who commended . . . cross-garter'd.* From Malvolio's comment, a little later, on this part of the letter, it is clear that there was an occasion when his mistress had apparently spoken favourably about this leg-wear. But Maria makes it clear, at the end of the scene, that any such remark by Olivia could have been no more than a polite gesture to cover up her very strong dislike of this mode of dress, which was probably old-fashioned at that time.

144. *thou art made:* 'your success is assured'

147. *alter services with thee* 'Olivia' would gladly change places with him, and offer willing service to him, because she loves him so helplessly. *Fortunate-Unhappy.* A love-sick person is both elated and despairing, almost in the same moment.

148. *champain:* flat, open country; *discovers:* reveals.

150. *baffle:* publicly disgrace; *wash off gross acquaintance:* 'break off acquaintance with unworthy people'

151. *point-devise:* correct in every detail.

152. *jade:* deceive.

Fabian
And O shall end, I hope.

Sir Toby
Ay, or I'll cudgel him, and make him cry 'O!'

Malvolio
And then I comes behind.

Fabian
Ay, an you had any eye behind you, you might see 125
more detraction at your heels than fortunes before
you.

Malvolio
M. O. A. I. This simulation is not as the former; and
yet, to crush this a little, it would bow to me, for every
one of these letters are in my name. Soft! here follows 130
prose.

[Reads] 'If this fall into thy hand, revolve. In my stars I
am above thee; but be not afraid of greatness. Some
are born great, some achieve greatness, and some have
greatness thrust upon 'em. Thy Fates open their hands; 135
let thy blood and spirit embrace them; and, to inure
thyself to what thou art like to be, cast thy humble
slough and appear fresh. Be opposite with a kinsman,
surly with servants; let thy tongue tang arguments of
state; put thyself into the trick of singularity. She thus 140
advises thee that sighs for thee. Remember who
commended thy yellow stockings, and wish'd to see
thee ever cross-garter'd. I say, remember. Go to, thou
art made, if thou desir'st to be so; if not, let me see
thee a steward still, the fellow of servants, and not 145
worthy to touch Fortune's fingers. Farewell. She that
would alter services with thee,
                    THE FORTUNATE-UNHAPPY.'
Daylight and champain discovers not more. This is
open. I will be proud, I will read politic authors, I will
baffle Sir Toby, I will wash off gross acquaintance, I 150
will be point-devise the very man. I do not now fool
myself to let imagination jade me; for every reason

153. *excites to this:* 'drives me to this conclusion.

156-7. *with a kind of injunction . . . of her liking:* 'almost commands me to adopt this way of dress that she so much admires.'

158. *strange:* aloof; *stout:* haughty.

159-60. *even with the swiftness of putting on:* 'and I'll be no longer than it takes just to put them on.'

163. *let it appear in thy smiling.* Believing that Olivia is thus inviting him to show his feelings for her by smiling continuously, Malvolio is tricked into what will be perhaps his most ludicrous exhibition.
165. *still:* all the time.

169. *Sophy:* Shah of Persia.

171. *So could I too.* Sir Andrew has been so overawed by the brilliance of Maria's trick, that he is reduced to a tame kind of repetition of each of Sir Toby's remarks – he does it four more times before the end of this scene. This is a characteristic we have noticed before, but it has never been quite so pronounced. Any independent Sir Andrew there may have been has now been frightened out of sight, and we are simply left with feeble echoes of Sir Toby.

175. *gull-catcher.* This was a recognised term for a cheat or someone who preyed on fools. (In this instance, to cheat Malvolio is regarded by Fabian as something commendable.)
176. *set thy foot o' my neck.* The victor in a combat would, by tradition, place his foot on the neck of his vanquished opponent, as a sign of his supremacy. By asking Maria to do this to himself, Sir Toby is signifying that her success with the letter has been outstanding.

excites to this, that my lady loves me. She did
commend my yellow stockings of late, she did praise
my leg being cross-garter'd; and in this she manifests 155
herself to my love, and with a kind of injunction
drives me to these habits of her liking. I thank my
stars I am happy. I will be strange, stout, in yellow
stockings, and cross-garter'd, even with the swiftness
of putting on. Jove and my stars be praised! Here is 160
yet a postscript.

[Reads] 'Thou canst not choose but know who I am. If
thou entertain'st my love, let it appear in thy smiling;
thy smiles become thee well. Therefore in my presence
still smile, dear my sweet, I prithee.' 165
Jove, I thank thee. I will smile; I will do everything
that thou wilt have me.

[Exit]

Fabian
I will not give my part of this sport for a pension of
thousands to be paid from the Sophy.
Sir Toby
I could marry this wench for this device. 170
Sir Andrew
So could I too.
Sir Toby
And ask no other dowry with her but such another
jest.

[Enter MARIA]

Sir Andrew
Nor I neither.
Fabian
Here comes my noble gull-catcher. 175
Sir Toby
Wilt thou set thy foot o' my neck?
Sir Andrew
Or o' mine either?

178. *tray-trip:* a game with dice, in which the winner had to throw a 'three' (*tray*). Sir Toby means that he would willingly wager his *freedom* in such a game, and very cheerfully lose it, to become Maria's bond-slave, so impressed is he by her cleverness.

181–2. Sir Toby has summed it up well – this is the very essence of the 'torture' Maria has devised; *dream* and *image* in fact both mean the same thing, namely, the false notion (of Olivia's love for him) that Maria has so successfully implanted in Malvolio's mind. (This notion does keep him going for a long time, in the face of pretty solid evidence to the contrary, making the moment of disenchantment the more painful when it comes.)

183. *Nay, but say true:* 'No, but honestly now . . .'

184. *aqua-vitae:* alcoholic stimulant; spirits. This probably refers to a reputation midwives had for functioning efficiently only when supplied with intoxicants.

187–8. *abhors . . . detests.* See note on line 142.

190. *melancholy.* Not the original mood of grief for her brother, but her recent love-sickness for Viola.

191–2. *notable contempt:* a laughing-stock.

193. *Tartar:* hell, the right place for a devil!

Sir Toby

    Shall I play my freedom at tray-trip, and become thy
    bond-slave?

Sir Andrew

    I' faith, or I either?   180

Sir Toby

    Why, thou hast put him in such a dream that when
    the image of it leaves him he must run mad.

Maria

    Nay, but say true; does it work upon him?

Sir Toby

    Like aqua-vitae with a midwife.

Maria

    If you will then see the fruits of the sport, mark his 185
    first approach before my lady. He will come to her in
    yellow stockings, and 'tis a colour she abhors, and
    cross-garter'd, a fashion she detests; and he will smile
    upon her, which will now be so unsuitable to her
    disposition, being addicted to a melancholy as she is, 190
    that it cannot but turn him into a notable contempt.
    If you will see it, follow me.

Sir Toby

    To the gates of Tartar, thou most excellent devil of
    wit!

Sir Andrew

    I'll make one too.   195

[Exeunt]

ACT THREE SCENE I

This scene shows us, for the first time, how Viola handles Feste, Sir Toby and Sir Andrew. She 'holds her own' admirably, and answers them in their own language – resiliently enough but not unkindly. Then, with Olivia, she has a much more serious part to play. Olivia's love for her, at first hinted, then almost defiantly affirmed, presents her with perhaps the greatest challenge yet, to her self-possession. Fortunately she is primed for this, having already diagnosed Olivia's feelings accurately (Act II, Scene ii). More than anyone else in the play, Viola seems unsubdued by her circumstances, acutely distressing though they are. She is able to remain detached sufficiently to greet each new face and situation freshly and with genuine interest.

1. *Save thee:* 'God save thee.' Viola's greeting, and her appreciation of his music, are warm and sincere.

2. *tabor:* a small drum, often used by professional jesters.

3. A simple enough pun on the two meanings of *'live by'* – 'to make a living out of', and 'to live near to'.

11. *To see this age.* Feste professes admiration – but does he mean it for 'the present day' (and the wonderful things that are happening), or for the 'youthfulness' of Viola, whose wit Feste pretends, or really believes, to be a challenge to his own? This kind of ironical praise, by the professional for the amateur, is a familar comic device – though the irony is not always as gentle as on this occasion.

11–12. *A sentence is . . . a good wit.* A cheveril glove is one made of kid-leather which can easily be turned inside out. Feste means that a witty person can easily find a double meaning in the simplest of sentences.

14. Viola enjoys this 'sharpening of wits' with Feste. *dally:* 'trifle,' and also 'to play amorously'. *nicely:* with close attention to the finer points of meaning. (This is the proper meaning of the word 'nice' – much more than its modern use, indicating vague approval.)

15. *wanton:* 'going beyond the bounds of convention', and also 'lascivious'. Viola had pointed out cleverly that, if you play with words, you'll land yourself in dubious meanings

ACT THREE
SCENE I

Olivia's garden

[Enter VIOLA, and CLOWN with a tabor]

Viola
Save thee, friend, and thy music!
Dost thou live by thy tabor?

Clown
No, sir, I live by the church.

Viola
Art thou a churchman?

Clown
No such matter, sir: I do live by the church; for I do   5
live at my house, and my house doth stand by the
church.

Viola
So thou mayst say the king lies by a beggar, if a beggar
dwell near him; or the church stands by thy tabor, if
thy tabor stand by the church.   10

Clown
You have said, sir. To see this age! A sentence is but a
chev'ril glove to a good wit. How quickly the wrong
side may be turn'd outward!

Viola
Nay, that's certain; they that dally nicely with words
may quickly make them wanton.   15

Clown
I would, therefore, my sister had had no name, sir.

Viola
Why, man?

Clown
Why, sir, her name's a word; and to dally with that

19–20. *words are . . . disgrac'd them.* Feste pretends to deplore the corrupting effect which the writing down of a word (as in a legal agreement) has upon its meaning. There is a pun on the word 'bond' – a person is disgraced by imprisonment, and probably remains lawless at heart ever after; and words, having been 'disciplined' by formal writing, never again recover their intrinsic liveliness – which was their best guarantee of integrity.

22–4. Another quibble – Feste protesting that he cannot explain his reason, since he would have to use discredited words. He then uses **reason** in a more basic sense, where **false** words would be even further out of place.

32–6. Another play on the two meanings of *fool* – 'professional jester' and 'foolish person'.

34. *pilchers:* another spelling, then, of 'pilchards' – fish not unlike a small herring.

38. *orb:* world.

39–41. Feste is suggesting, not over-politely, that there is as much scope for his work with Orsino as with his own mistress.

41. *your wisdom.* A playful irony at Viola's expense, for having matched her wits against his. (See note on line 11.)

42. *an thou pass upon me:* 'if you are getting the better of me.'

43. *expenses:* pay (for having entertained her with his wit).

44. *commodity:* consignment. Feste may quite seriously think that Viola ought to have a beard and look more manly; for her actual manner, towards himself and everyone else, is much too self-assertive and poised for any young man who looks as smooth-faced and immature physically as she does. The fact that the sexes mature physically and psychologically at different ages, and how this expresses itself, is made great use of in the play, and provides much of its subtler humour.

word might make my sister wanton. But indeed words
are very rascals since bonds disgrac'd them.   20

Viola

Thy reason, man?

Clown

Troth, sir, I can yield you none without words, and
words are grown so false I am loath to prove reason
with them.

Viola

I warrant thou art a merry fellow and car'st for   25
nothing.

Clown

Not so, sir; I do care for something; but in my
conscience, sir, I do not care for you. If that be to care
for nothing, sir, I would it would make you
invisible.   30

Viola

Art not thou the Lady Olivia's fool?

Clown

No, indeed, sir; the Lady Olivia has no folly; she will
keep no fool, sir, till she be married; and fools are as
like husbands as pilchers are to herrings – the husband's
the bigger. I am indeed not her fool, but her corrupter   35
of words.

Viola

I saw thee late at the Count Orsino's.

Clown

Foolery, sir, does walk about the orb like the sun – it
shines everywhere. I would be sorry, sir, but the fool
should be as oft with your master as with my mistress: 40
I think I saw your wisdom there.

Viola

Nay, an thou pass upon me, I'll no more with thee.
Hold, there's expenses for thee.   *[Giving a coin]*

Clown

Now Jove, in his next commodity of hair, send thee a
beard!   45

46–8. Viola's reply has a double meaning: for Feste, she simply endorses his wish, but for herself, she is expressing her longing for the bearded Orsino.

49. Before Feste will answer Viola's question, he holds out his hand for another coin – with the saucy excuse that two coins (he already has the one she has just given him) will be able to breed, and so make more money.

51–2. *Pandarus . . . Cressida . . . Troilus.* These are characters from the ancient legend of the Trojan War. Pandarus has been developed in literature as a 'Go-between', who brought Troilus and Cressida together and assisted their love. (He has given his name to the word 'pander', which means to encourage a low desire.) Superficially, Feste calls the coin in his hand, *Troilus*, and the one he hopes to add to it, *Cressida*. But he may well also be thinking of Viola as *this Troilus*, and wondering what sort of a *Cressida* he could be introducing to her.

53. *'tis well begg'd.* Feste's 'begging' has been effective.

54. *The matter:* the thing he has begged for.

55. *Cressida was a beggar.* In one version of the legend Cressida became a leper and begged from door to door.

57. *welkin:* usually means 'sky'; here something like 'world'. Perhaps Feste is humorously suggesting that Viola is 'above and beyond' him.

59–67. Viola, now alone, gives us a fairly general observation on professional jesting, which she can do after such a first-hand experience. She speaks in blank verse, appropriately, for her comment is meant to stand out from the haphazard exchanges that precede and follow it. (See note, Act I, Scene v, lines 32–3.)

59. This line sums up the whole case, which clearly sides with the clown, and appreciates the insight and shrewdness he must possess.

60. *craves:* demands.

62. *time:* appropriate moment, occasion.

63. *haggard:* a wild female hawk caught when adult and therefore difficult to train properly to concentrate on its quarry; it *check* (s), or turns aside, to follow every *feather* (or bird) that comes into its view. The idea is that a clown should be quick enough to change his tactics from moment to moment. He must not decide beforehand on the person or subject to mock.

66. 'His jesting, if it is introduced tactfully, and with real understanding of his audience, is most valuable and acceptable.'

67. *folly-fall'n:* fallen into folly. (Here meaning foolishness in its general sense, and not as in the previous line.) Note the rhyme in the last two lines, to mark the ending of the passage.

Viola

By my troth, I'll tell thee, I am almost sick for one;
[Aside] though I would not have it grow on my chin.
– Is thy lady within?

Clown

Would not a pair of these have bred, sir?

Viola

Yes, being kept together and put to use.   50

Clown

I would play Lord Pandarus of Phrygia, sir, to bring a
Cressida to this Troilus.

Viola

I understand you, sir; 'tis well begg'd. *[Giving another
coin]*

Clown

The matter, I hope, is not great, sir, begging but a
beggar: Cressida was a beggar. My lady is within, sir.   55
I will construe to them whence you come; who you
are and what you would are out of my welkin – I might
say 'element' but the word is overworn.

[Exit]

Viola

This fellow is wise enough to play the fool;
And to do that well craves a kind of wit.   60
He must observe their mood on whom he jests,
The quality of persons, and the time;
And, like the haggard, check at every feather
That comes before his eye. This is a practice
As full of labour as a wise man's art;   65
For folly that he wisely shows is fit;
But wise men, folly-fall'n, quite taint their wit.

[Enter SIR TOBY *and* SIR ANDREW*]*

Sir Toby

Save you, gentleman!

70. Sir Andrew's greeting is the same as Sir Toby's but in French. It might surprise us that he has now mastered enough of the language to conduct at least this bit of conversation, in view of his earlier confession of ignorance (Act I, Scene iii, line 85). But it seems that he has been busy with phrase-book and pencil since then, picking up whatever scraps of sophistication he can, in English or French. (See lines 85 and 88.)

73. encounter the house: a deliberately pompous way of saying, simply, 'go in'. (*taste your legs*, in line 77 meaning 'put them to the test', 'try them out', and so simply 'go', is in the same exaggerated style.)

74. trade: business.

75. bound to: on my way to. (See Act II, Scene i, line 39.)

75–6. list of my voyage: limit of my journey (and therefore, 'destination'.) The word *voyage* was not restricted to a journey by sea

78–9. understand . . . understand. When Viola says this first, she means 'understand' or 'stand underneath', – which is, of course, what one's legs do! The second meaning she gives is the normal one, 'to comprehend'.

81. gait and entrance. The first ('way of walking') answers Sir Toby's *go*, the second answers his *enter*.

82. prevented: forestalled. (This was a common meaning of the word.)

87. pregnant: receptive, **vouchsafed.** To vouchsafe means to 'allow', usually with some idea of condescension. So here, Viola means that her message is for Olivia alone, if she will be gracious enough to listen to it.

88–9. See note on line 70, **get 'em all three all ready.** Sir Andrew is going to learn the words so that he can use them later on as his own

Viola
And you, sir.

Sir Andrew
Dieu vous garde, monsieur.   70

Viola
Et vous aussi; votre serviteur.

Sir Andrew
I hope, sir, you are; and I am yours.

Sir Toby
Will you encounter the house? My niece is desirous
you should enter, if your trade be to her.

Viola
I am bound to your niece, sir; I mean, she is the list   75
of my voyage.

Sir Toby
Taste your legs, sir; put them to motion.

Viola
My legs do better understand me, sir, than I understand
what you mean by bidding me taste my legs.

Sir Toby
I mean, to go, sir, to enter.   80

Viola
I will answer you with gait and entrance. But we are
prevented.

[Enter OLIVIA *and* MARIA*]*

Most excellent accomplish'd lady, the heavens rain
odours on you!

Sir Andrew
That youth's a rare courtier – 'Rain odours' well!   85

Viola
My matter hath no voice, lady, but to your own most
pregnant and vouchsafed ear.

Sir Andrew
'Odours', 'pregnant', and 'vouchsafed' – I'll get 'em all
three all ready.

93. This is pointedly formal. The last thing Viola wants is that Olivia shall imagine that she is in the slightest degree identifying herself with the Duke's enthusiasm. She is still trying, almost instinctively, to keep Olivia at arm's length; and she is virtually saying to her, 'I am speaking and acting like this solely out of duty to my master; but nothing could be further from my own personal inclinations.'

96. *My servant, sir.* Olivia is clearly riled by Viola's behaviour. She can at least see that, whatever her purpose, Viola is not being 'straight' with her. The fact that she is being so effusive, but clearly means none of it, is particularly hard for Olivia to accept or understand, when she so desperately needs to be treated sincerely. *'Twas never merry world:* 'Things have never been happy and right.'

97. *Lowly feigning* is better put as 'feigned lowliness', meaning 'false humility', which Olivia hates to see made use of in the paying of compliments. Not that she imagines that Viola is trying to compliment her! (If she did think so, then Olivia would be the last person to criticise her method!) But she detects an unmistakable opposition in Viola's present tactics, and she cannot disguise her feeling of injury. We can imagine how infuriating Olivia will find this 'clever' talk, not least because it studiously avoids any indication of Viola's personal feelings, which alone are what Olivia is now concerned about. Notice the changed motive behind her protestation of indifference to Orsino. Earlier, this could have been a simple statement of fact, which would, she hoped, have ended further courtship from that quarter. But now she has a far more pressing reason for disclaiming any fondness for the Duke; for as long as there appears even a slight chance of winning her for her master, Viola can entertain no thought that Olivia may have set her heart on someone else. (At least, this is how Olivia sees it, for she can have no idea yet that Viola both knows of her feelings for her, and is in no position ever to reciprocate them.) Viola started out on her 'mission' with little to inspire her except loyalty to the Duke. But she is now beginning to warm to her task, if only to 'draw Olivia off' from pursuing her. So she must indeed hope to succeed in 'whetting' Olivia's thoughts towards Orsino, to give them greater keenness. (*to whet* is to sharpen.)

104. Olivia's irritated *'O, by your leave, I pray you'* is almost our modern 'Oh, for goodness sake, shut up!'

106. *another suit.* The look on Olivia's face, perhaps more than her voice, will make it clear that she wishes to be courted by Viola, and not by the Duke.

108. *music from the spheres.* There was a theory that the movement of the stars in the sky was accompanied by a heavenly music normally beyond the hearing of human beings, because of their imperfection. To hear 'the music of the spheres' (transparent globes, each with a star fixed in it) was thus regarded as a privilege indeed.

109. Olivia again cuts Viola short.

110. *enchantment.* An over-expressive word, if simply to describe Orsino's love-messages dutifully presented by Viola. But by her use of it Olivia is betraying her own reaction to Viola, whose visits have, quite irrespective of the Duke's addresses, cast a kind of spell upon her.

Olivia

Let the garden door be shut, and leave me to my 90
hearing. *[Exeunt all but* OLIVIA *and* VIOLA*]* Give me your
hand, sir.

Viola

My duty, madam, and most humble service.

Olivia

What is your name?

Viola

Cesario is your servant's name, fair Princess. 95

Olivia

My servant, sir! 'Twas never merry world
Since lowly feigning was call'd compliment.
Y'are servant to the Count Orsino, youth.

Viola

And he is yours, and his must needs be yours:
Your servant's servant is your servant, madam. 100

Olivia

For him, I think not on him; for his thoughts,
Would they were blanks rather than fill'd with me!

Viola

Madam, I come to whet your gentle thoughts
On his behalf.

Olivia

O, by your leave, I pray you:
I bade you never speak again of him; 105
But, would you undertake another suit,
I had rather hear you to solicit that
Than music from the spheres.

Viola

Dear lady—

Olivia

Give me leave, beseech you. I did send,
After the last enchantment you did here, 110

111–20. Olivia now has the painful task of admitting her foolish in discretion over the ring. She appears entirely conscience-stricken. Is it perhaps, that her very genuine love (however misguided) for Viola has begun to drive out the inferior motives of deception and pride?

111. *abuse:* treat badly.

113. *construction:* judgment.

115. *Which you knew none of yours:* 'which you knew didn't belong to you.' *What might you think?* 'What must you have thought?'

116–17. *stake . . . baited . . . unmuzzled.* The image Olivia is using is from bear-baiting (a contemporary entertainment in which a bear was fastened to a *stake*, and *baited* or teased by dogs using their fangs and teeth to harass the bear). It seems to her a very appropriate way to describe what she is convinced Viola must have been thinking about her and her *honour*, ever since the ring was 'planted' for her to take up. The savagery of the illustration indicates more of Olivia's vexation with herself than with Viola.

118. *To one of your receiving:* 'to someone as receptive, and as hard to deceive, as you are.' There is little left now of Olivia's self-possession. Viola certainly does have these characteristics; but it is resentment that makes Olivia refer to them now. She feels cruelly humiliated, and wants to put the blame, irrationally, on Viola, for having seen through her trick. (In her embarrassment, she feels certain that Viola has seen through it, though Viola has said nothing to suggest this.)

119–20. *a cypress, not a bosom, Hides my heart.* In fine imagery, she makes some amends for her unfair bitterness, by admitting that her love-sickness must be obvious not only to Viola but to everyone else – just as someone wearing cypress (the black mourning crepe-cloth, rather than part of the tree) could not expect to keep his grief secret from other people.

120. *So, let me hear you speak.* What reply does Olivia expect? Her question almost implies that she is prepared for the worst, and thinks she has ruined all her chances with Viola.

121. Viola replies in all sincerity – in contrast to her deliberate uninvolvement up to this point. Olivia notes the compassion in her voice, and takes it as a step in the right direction (*degree to love*). She has no idea that it is the sheer hopelessness of her quest that excites Viola's pity.

122. *grize:* step; *vulgar proof:* common experience. Viola really pities Olivia; but to save herself from Olivia's eagerness, which refuses to be checked, she has to 'pass it off' now as a kind of scorn. But even this is gladly accepted by Olivia.

125. *poor.* Olivia sees herself as *poor,* in begging for Viola's affection, and so she is really reminding herself not to be too proud to submit to Viola's scorn.

126–7. If she is to be treated cruelly, she would rather it were at the hands of Viola than anyone else. Viola, in her present imperious mood, suggests a *lion* to Olivia, any other suitor seeming a *wolf* by contrast.

128. *upbraids:* blames. The chiming clock gives her the chance, which she seizes, of recovering some shred of dignity. She attempts to dissociate herself from what has just taken place, dismissing it as a *waste of time.*

A ring in chase of you; so did I abuse
Myself, my servant, and, I fear me, you.
Under your hard construction must I sit,
To force that on you in a shameful cunning
Which you knew none of yours. What might you
    think?   115
Have you not set mine honour at the stake,
And baited it with all th' unmuzzled thoughts
That tyrannous heart can think? To one of your
    receiving
Enough is shown: a cypress, not a bosom,
Hides my heart. So, let me hear you speak.   120

Viola

  I pity you.

Olivia

               That's a degree to love.

Viola

  No, not a grize; for 'tis a vulgar proof
That very oft we pity enemies.

Olivia

  Why, then, methinks 'tis time to smile again.
O world, how apt the poor are to be proud!   125
If one should be a prey, how much the better
To fall before the lion than the wolf! *[Clock strikes]*
The clock upbraids me with the waste of time.

129. This is said patronisingly; and the subsequent reference to Viola's youthfulness is in the same vein. It is as if Olivia is trying to detach herself from the whole affair without 'losing face'. She would like to convince Viola momentarily – herself even – that she couldn't possibly have had any serious thoughts about anyone so young.

130. But she can't keep this up, nor refrain from further personal involvements. *when wit and youth is come to harvest:* 'when you have reached maturity, in years and wisdom.' (The use of the singular verb *is* after the double subject, is quite common in Shakespeare.)

131. *like:* likely. *reap.* The word is used to keep up the harvest image. *proper:* with all the appropriate qualities of a man.

132. The moment Olivia suggests leaving, Viola almost leaps to it, heartily relieved to escape from her ordeal. Her leave-taking is entirely formal, and Orsino is mentioned only as an afterthought.

135–6. Seeing her go is too much for Olivia. She puts the question she has been longing to ask ever since they were alone together – for this may be her last chance.

137. Nothing could be more to the point – yet Viola manages to dodge the issue once again. Instead of giving, as one might expect, a straight-forward opinion of Olivia's womanly qualities, Viola simply says that Olivia is not being honest with herself, or is deluding herself. (It is only through hints like this that Viola can come anywhere near the plain truth. Olivia is hopelessly mistaken in thinking that she can ever be in love with Viola; but to explain why would mean divulging the whole secret.)

138. 'If I am not being honest with myself, then no more are you.'

139. With this, Viola can heartily agree – she knows only too well how self-contradictory her own position is.

142. *I am your fool:* 'I am being used simply to provide your entertainment (as a Clown).' There is a note of peevishness here, as if Viola's self-control suddenly breaks down. But whatever her motive, it becomes, for Olivia, yet one more side of Viola's character for her to idolize. And so, however hard Viola tries to alienate Olivia, she simply increases her own attractiveness in Olivia's eyes. Olivia believes that Viola's display of vexation is simply a 'cover-up' for her love, which she cannot, however, conceal, any more than a murderer can hide his guilt.

146 *love's night is noon.* An excellent example of how, in few words, poetry can say so much more, and with far greater effectiveness, than prose. 'The most secret thoughts (*night*) of those in love are as conspicuous as the noonday sun.'

147 *roses of the spring.* Why does Olivia think of roses? Perhaps because the rare beauty of roses, like youthful love, is both exquisite and brief. (See Act II Scene iv, lines 37–8.)

148 *maidhood:* virginity

149 *maugre:* in spite of

150 *wit* and *reason.* Olivia has just tried both of these, but has had to come out at last with the truth.

151–2 'Do not try to justify yourself (*extort thy reasons*) on the grounds that (*from this clause*), because (*For that*) I have made the first move, there is no need for you to do anything in response.'

Be not afraid, good youth; I will not have you;
And yet, when wit and youth is come to harvest,   130
Your wife is like to reap a proper man.
There lies your way, due west.

Viola

                     Then westward-ho!
Grace and good disposition attend your ladyship!
You'll nothing, madam, to my lord by me?

Olivia

Stay.   135
I prithee tell me what thou think'st of me.

Viola

That you do think you are not what you are.

Olivia

If I think so, I think the same of you.

Viola

Then think you right: I am not what I am.

Olivia

I would you were as I would have you be!   140

Viola

Would it be better, madam, than I am?
I wish it might, for now I am your fool.

Olivia

O, what a deal of scorn looks beautiful
In the contempt and anger of his lip!
A murd'rous guilt shows not itself more soon   145
Than love that would seem hid: love's night is noon.
Cesario, by the roses of the spring,
By maidhood, honour, truth, and every thing,
I love thee so that, maugre all thy pride,
Nor wit nor reason can my passion hide.   150
Do not extort thy reasons from this clause,
For that I woo, thou therefore hast no cause;

153. *fetter* is the verb here. Viola is to control (*fetter*) one reason (namely, the false argument that Olivia has just rejected) with another (namely, the one she gives in the next line).

154. Olivia is trying to convince Viola that the conventional kind of wooing – when the man takes the initiative (*love sought*) – has less to commend it than when the lady actually offers herself first (*given unsought*).

155–8. Equally earnest now, it is Viola's turn for solemn oaths.

156. *truth:* loyalty. By great dexterity, as on previous occasions, she manages to speak truthfully – and therefore with obvious sincerity – but without in any way revealing her secret. (Compare Act II, Scene iv, lines 105–9.)

157. *no woman has:* 'no woman possesses these things of mine' (as a lover).

157. *nor never none.* We often find double negatives in Elizabethan English, for extra emphasis (they do not, as today, 'cancel out'); but a triple negative, again for emphasis, is rare. This is dramatic irony at its most effective. The audience knows what Viola means. No other woman can ever be in love with her – her own womanhood precludes it – but Olivia thinks she is stubbornly protesting that she will 'have nothing to do with the opposite sex'.

160. *deplore:* tell, with grief.

162. *That heart.* Namely, Olivia's own. *abhors to like his love:* 'shrinks from responding to his (the Duke's) love.'

SCENE II

This scene brings a kind of progress report, from Maria, of the plot against Malvolio. But before this, Sir Toby and Fabian begin to hatch a second plot, a slightly gentler version, against Sir Andrew (and involving Viola), this time with no justification except to provide themselves (and the audience) with a good laugh. As before, the humour consists in talking Sir Andrew into a course of action that is entirely out of character. (It is almost as if, with Malvolio satisfactorily disposed of, they cast about for a second victim.)

1. *jot:* a moment, 'jot' is from the Greek letter 'i' (iota), the smallest in the alphabet, and hence refers to the smallest part of anything.

2. *dear venom.* A playful touch of irony. Sir Andrew is showing more spirit than is his custom, but nothing that could seriously be described as *venom* (the poison of a snake). (Compare Feste's *your wisdom* in Scene i, lines 39–41.)

9. *a great argument:* clear evidence.

But rather reason thus with reason fetter:
Love sought is good, but given unsought is better.

Viola

By innocence I swear, and by my youth,   155
I have one heart, one bosom, and one truth,
And that no woman has; nor never none
Shall mistress be of it, save I alone.
And so adieu, good madam; never more
Will I my master's tears to you deplore.   160

Olivia

Yet come again; for thou perhaps mayst move
That heart which now abhors to like his love.

[Exeunt]

SCENE II

Olivia's house

[Enter SIR TOBY, SIR ANDREW, *and* FABIAN*]*

Sir Andrew

No, faith, I'll not stay a jot longer.

Sir Toby

Thy reason, dear venom, give thy reason.

Fabian

You must needs yield your reason, Sir Andrew.

Sir Andrew

Marry, I saw your niece do more favours to the Count's
serving man than ever she bestow'd upon me; I saw't   5
i' th' orchard.

Sir Toby

Did she see thee the while, old boy? Tell me that.

Sir Andrew

As plain as I see you now.

Fabian

This was a great argument of love in her toward you.

Sir Andrew

'Slight! will you make an ass o' me?   10

11. *prove it legitimate:* 'show that I am right.'

13–14. Sir Toby says this sarcastically, implying that people have regularly appealed to good sense and reason even when their cause was undeserving.

14. *Noah . . . sailor.* Refers to the Biblical story of the Flood, from which Noah and his family escaped by building the Ark. Here it simply means 'from earliest times'.

16. *dormouse valour.* A most expressive description of Sir Andrew's timidity. The dormouse is one of the tiniest animals – when asleep, virtually invisible, and, when awake, hardly ferocious!

17. *liver.* See note, Act II, Scene iv, line 98.

18. *accosted.* How well did Sir Andrew understand this word previously?

19. *fire-new from the mint:* original, like genuine coins that have just been made. (Unoriginal jests would be like counterfeit coins.)

20. *bang'd:* thumped, or beaten.

20–1. *look'd for:* expected. *baulk'd:* avoided.

21. *gilt:* gold paint.

23. *north:* the colder, and therefore less friendly part.

26. *policy:* diplomacy.

27. *An't:* if it.

28. *had as lief be:* would as willingly be. *Brownist.* Brownists were followers of Robert Brown, a Puritan. (We have already seen how strongly Sir Andrew disapproved of Puritans – Act II, Scene iii, lines 132–7.)

29–30. *build me thy fortunes . . . Challenge me the Count's youth.* The word *me* here is an old grammatical form which adds little to the meaning.

32. *love-broker:* someone who acts as an agent between lovers; a match-maker.

33–4. *man's commendation with woman:* 'man's reputation in the eyes of woman.'

37. *curst:* sharp.

39. *with the licence of ink.* One is much less inhibited writing things, than saying them to a person's face.

Fabian

I will prove it legitimate, sir, upon the oaths of judgment and reason.

Sir Toby

And they have been grand-jurymen since before
Noah was a sailor.

Fabian

She did show favour to the youth in your sight only   15
to exasperate you, to awake your dormouse valour, to
put fire in your heart and brimstone in your liver. You
should then have accosted her; and with some excellent jests, fire-new from the mint, you should have
bang'd the youth into dumbness. This was look'd for   20
at your hand, and this was baulk'd. The double gilt of
this opportunity you let time wash off, and you are
now sail'd into the north of my lady's opinion; where
you will hang like an icicle on a Dutchman's beard,
unless you do redeem it by some laudable attempt   25
either of valour or policy.

Sir Andrew

An't be any way, it must be with valour, for policy I
hate; I had as lief be a Brownist as a politician.

Sir Toby

Why, then, build me thy fortunes upon the basis of
valour. Challenge me the Count's youth to fight with   30
him; hurt him in eleven places. My niece shall take
note of it; and assure thyself there is no love-broker
in the world can more prevail in man's commendation
with woman than report of valour.

Fabian

There is no way but this, Sir Andrew.   35

Sir Andrew

Will either of you bear me a challenge to him?

Sir Toby

Go, write it in a martial hand; be curst and brief; it is
no matter how witty, so it be eloquent and full of
invention. Taunt him with the license of ink; if thou

40. *thou'st.* To 'thou' a person meant to address him as 'thou', which was taken as a sign of contempt. (It still is, sometimes, in modern French).

42. *bed of Ware.* An actual bed, reputed to be the biggest in existence, formerly housed at the Saracen's Head Inn, in Ware, Hertfordshire, and now in the Victoria and Albert Museum, in London. It could accommodate twelve people.

43. *gall:* bitterness.

44–5. *goose-pen.* Goose-feathers were used for pens (a 'pen-knife' was originally so called because it was used to shape the end of the feather, or quill, for writing.) A goose was proverbial for its cowardice.

47. *cubiculo:* a small room. *Go:* a simple dramatic convenience, to have Sir Andrew out of the way now, so that the others can be more explicit (for our benefit) about their plan to fool Sir Andrew and Viola.

48. *manakin:* little man. Fabian uses the term derisively rather than with affection.

49. A pun on *dear.* Sir Toby has cost him two thousand ducats or so, by living off Sir Andrew's generosity.

53. *Never trust me then:* 'Never trust me again if I don't.' (Though in fact Sir Toby has second thoughts, and in the end thinks it better to deliver the challenge verbally, and in his own words.)

54. *oxen.* Still used to pull loads. *wainropes:* wagon-ropes. (Compare Act II, Scene v, line 60, and Note.)

55. *hale:* pull.

55–7. The liver was thought to be the source of blood, and the seat of courage (compare the expression 'lily-livered', i.e. with a bloodless liver, meaning cowardly).

58. *opposite:* opponent.

59. *presage:* indication.

60. *youngest wren of nine:* refers to Maria's slight stature. The wren is one of the smallest birds, and the ninth or last chick to be hatched could be expected to be the weakest and smallest of the whole brood.

61. *spleen.* This organ was thought to be associated with laughter, and to become enlarged through too much mirth. 'To have the spleen' here means to suffer from an enlarged spleen.

62. *Yond:* yonder, over there. (Here the word virtually adds no meaning.)

thou'st him some thrice, it shall not be amiss; and as   40
many lies as will lie in thy sheet of paper, although
the sheet were big enough for the bed of Ware in
England, set 'em down; go about it. Let there be gall
enough in thy ink, though thou write with a goose-
pen, no matter. About it.   45

Sir Andrew

Where shall I find you?

Sir Toby

We'll call thee at the cubiculo. Go.

[Exit SIR ANDREW*]*

Fabian

This is a dear manakin to you, Sir Toby.

Sir Toby

I have been dear to him, lad – some two thousand
strong, or so.   50

Fabian

We shall have a rare letter from him; but you'll not
deliver't?

Sir Toby

Never trust me then; and by all means stir on the
youth to an answer. I think oxen and wainropes cannot
hale them together. For Andrew, if he were open'd and   55
you find so much blood in his liver as will clog the
foot of a flea, I'll eat the rest of th' anatomy.

Fabian

And his opposite, the youth, bears in his visage no
great presage of cruelty.

[Enter MARIA*]*

Sir Toby

Look where the youngest wren of nine comes.   60

Maria

If you desire the spleen, and will laugh yourselves into
stitches, follow me. Yond gull Malvolio is turned

63. renegado: renegade – one who gives up one religion and adopts another. No one, thinks Maria, could go on being a Christian (where right belief is essential) and at the same time believe the outrageous nonsense that Malvolio now entertains.

68. villainously. This means little more than 'in shocking taste', **pedant:** teacher.
68–9. school i' the church. A not unusual practice at the time.
69. dogg'd: followed closely (as a dog follows its master).

72. new map with the augmentation of the Indies. A new map had been published in 1600, on new principles of projection, which made the Indies look much bigger than on previous maps. (This reference has been used by some scholars to help in dating *Twelfth Night*.)

SCENE III

A short but useful scene, to explain why Sebastian and Antonio, though still devoted friends, agree to separate for a few hours, and why Sebastian is persuaded to borrow Antonio's purse of money. Both these factors contribute significantly to the plot. The scene is useful, too, in not allowing us to forget about Sebastian, and his close resemblance to his sister – though this will, in a stage production, have to be conveyed chiefly by their wearing of identical attire. They must never be so alike that we, the audience, become confused.
1. by my will: intentionally.
2. make your pleasure of: enjoy, **pains:** hardships.
3. chide: reprove – for following him, as the next line makes clear.

6–7. not all love to see you . . . voyage: 'not simply because I love to see you, though that in itself would make a much longer journey worth while.'
8. jealousy: anxiety.
9. skilless: inexperienced.

136

heathen, a very renegado; for there is no Christian that
means to be saved by believing rightly can ever believe
such impossible passages of grossness. He's in yellow   65
stockings.

Sir Toby

And cross-garter'd?

Maria

Most villainously; like a pedant that keeps a school i'
th' church. I have dogg'd him like his murderer. He
does obey every point of the letter that I dropp'd to   70
betray him. He does smile his face into more lines than
is in the new map with the augmentation of the Indies.
You have not seen such a thing as 'tis; I can hardly
forbear hurling things at him. I know my lady will
strike him; if she do, he'll smile and take't for a great   75
favour.

Sir Toby

Come, bring us, bring us where he is.

[Exeunt]

SCENE III

A street

[Enter SEBASTIAN *and* ANTONIO*]*

Sebastian

I would not by my will have troubled you;
But since you make your pleasure of your pains,
I will no further chide you.

Antonio

I could not stay behind you: my desire,
More sharp than filed steel, did spur me forth;   5
And not all love to see you – though so much
As might have drawn one to a longer voyage—
But jealousy what might befall your travel,
Being skilless in these parts; which to a stranger,

10. *unfriended:* friendless. (We have 'befriended' today.)

11. *willing:* freely given.

12. *arguments of:* causes for.

14. Being shipwrecked, and therefore penniless, he is in no position to do otherwise.

16. *shuffl'd off:* unfairly rewarded. *uncurrent:* not valid as coinage. (There is no 'cash value' in thanks.)

17. 'But if my actual wealth matched my sincere intentions.'

18. *What's to do?* 'What is there for us to do?'

19. *reliques:* objects (buildings chiefly) of interest because of their age.

21. *'tis long to night:* 'it is a long time till night.'

23. *memorials:* sights worth remembering.

24. *Would you'd pardon me:* 'I wish you would excuse me (from accompanying you).'

26. *the Count his galleys:* the Count's galleys (the old form of the possessive).

27. *of such note.* Antonio's part in the battle was so conspicuous.

28. *ta'en:* arrested. *it would scarce be answer'd:* 'it would be extremely difficult to answer their charges against me.'

29. *Belike:* Probably.

31–2. 'Though we had occasion enough for fierce fighting.'

33. *It might have since been answer'd:* 'We might have made amends.'

34. *for traffic's sake:* 'to re-establish normal relationships.'

36. *lapsed:* arrested.

37. *too open:* too openly.

Unguided and unfriended, often prove   10
Rough and unhospitable. My willing love,
The rather by these arguments of fear,
Set forth in your pursuit.
Sebastian
                My kind Antonio,
I can no other answer make but thanks,
And thanks, and ever thanks; and oft good turns   15
Are shuffl'd off with such uncurrent pay;
But were my worth as is my conscience firm,
You should find better dealing. What's to do?
Shall we go see the reliques of this town?
Antonio
To-morrow, sir; best first go see your lodging.   20
Sebastian
I am not weary, and 'tis long to night;
I pray you, let us satisfy our eyes
With the memorials and the things of fame
That do renown this city.
Antonio
                 Would you'd pardon me.
I do not without danger walk these streets: 25
Once in a sea-fight 'gainst the Count his galleys
I did some service; of such note, indeed,
That, were I ta'en here, it would scarce be answer'd.
Sebastian
Belike you slew great number of his people.
Antonio
Th' offence is not of such a bloody nature;   30
Albeit the quality of the time and quarrel
Might well have given us bloody argument.
It might have since been answer'd in repaying
What we took from them; which, for traffic's sake,
Most of our city did. Only myself stood out;   35
For which, if I be lapsed in this place,
I shall pay dear.
Sebastian
          Do not then walk too open.
Antonio
It doth not fit me. Hold, sir, here's my purse;

40. *bespeak our diet:* 'order what meals we shall require.'

41. *beguile the time:* 'pass the time pleasantly.'

42. *have me:* find me.

44. *Haply:* Perhaps. *toy:* ornament.

45. *have desire:* would like.

45–6. *your store, I think, is not for idle markets:* 'what you have, of your own, won't go very far in shopping for luxuries.' So they part – Antonio, a 'marked man' already in considerable jeopardy through his strong loyalty to his friend; and Sebastian, greatly indebted to Antonio, and warmly appreciative. What does this scene gain from being spoken in blank verse? (The previous one with Sebastian and Antonio was chiefly in prose.) Is it to contrast with the comic scenes that precede and follow it? Or because their friendship is to be seen always as a thing of dignity and depth?

SCENE IV

A long and highly exciting scene, in which the plots against Malvolio and Sir Andrew come to a head. (Whatever happens to either, after this, is bound to seem something of an anti-climax – their mocking has reached saturation-point.) Viola, too, involved in the contrived duel, has to face further embarrassment, and – something new for her – a completely undeserved charge of treachery, which, however, brings with it new hope of her brother's survival.

2. *bestow of:* confer as a gift upon.

3. Does Olivia really feel as cynical towards young people?

4. *I speak too loud.* This suggests that Olivia's opening remarks are really addressed to herself. She has managed to persuade Viola to visit her again, but she doesn't want anyone, not even Maria, to witness her agitation as she considers how best to win her over.

5. *sad:* serious. *civil:* well-mannered (not speaking out of turn).

6. *with my fortunes:* 'who has to share my fortunes.'

In the south suburbs, at the Elephant,
Is best to lodge. I will bespeak our diet,   40
Whiles you beguile the time and feed your
    knowledge
With viewing of the town; there shall you have me.

Sebastian
Why I your purse?

Antonio
Haply your eye shall light upon some toy
You have desire to purchase; and your store,   45
I think, is not for idle markets, sir.

Sebastian
I'll be your purse-bearer, and leave you for
An hour.

Antonio
To th' Elephant.

Sebastian
                I do remember.

                [Exeunt]

SCENE IV

***

Olivia's garden

[Enter OLIVIA and MARIA]

Olivia
I have sent after him; he says he'll come.
How shall I feast him? What bestow of him?
For youth is bought more oft than begg'd or
    borrow'd.
I speak too loud.
Where's Malvolio? He is sad and civil,   5
And suits well for a servant with my fortunes.
Where is Malvolio?

8–9. Either Maria is 'acting' very convincingly, or else she is genuinely alarmed at the extent to which Malvolio has responded to their 'treatment', and feels that the whole thing has got out of hand.

11–13. This concern for Olivia's personal safety suggests that Maria is really convinced. As the scene progresses, Maria's misgivings increase. Much as she hates Malvolio – perhaps more than all the others do – the thought of him in the power of the Devil is something she has not bargained for, and she begins to panic. She may be feeling more than a little guilty for her own major part in the affair. (A deranged mind was then popularly ascribed to devil-possession.)
13. *tainted:* impaired.

15. Malvolio's madness is *merry*, since he keeps smiling; and Olivia's is *sad* in the sense that she is distraught with grief.

19. *upon a sad occasion:* for a serious purpose.

22. *please the eye of one.* Malvolio is referring to Olivia, of course.

26. *black in my mind:* without understanding.
27. *to his hands.* Malvolio speaks of himself, but with a coy indirectness.
28. *Roman hand:* a sloping Italian-style handwriting, much imitated at the time.
29. Olivia suggests bed for Malvolio as a sick man; but to Malvolio it is an invitation to go to bed with her!

Maria

    He's coming, madam; but in very strange manner.

    He is sure possess'd, madam.

Olivia

    Why, what's the matter? Does he rave?   10

Maria

    No, madam, he does nothing but smile. Your ladyship

    were best to have some guard about you if he come;

    for sure the man is tainted in's wits.

Olivia

    Go call him hither.

[Exit MARIA]

                I am as mad as he,

    If sad and merry madness equal be.   15

[Re-enter MARIA with MALVOLIO]

    How now, Malvolio!

Malvolio

    Sweet lady, ho, ho.

Olivia

    Smil'st thou?

    I sent for thee upon a sad occasion.

Malvolio

    Sad, lady? I could be sad. This does make some obstruc-   20

    tion in the blood, this cross-gartering; but what of

    that? If it please the eye of one, it is with me as the

    very true sonnet is: 'Please one and please all'.

Olivia

    Why, how dost thou, man? What is the matter with

    thee?   25

Malvolio

    Not black in my mind, though yellow in my legs. It

    did come to his hands, and commands shall be

    executed. I think we do know the sweet Roman hand.

Olivia

    Wilt thou go to bed, Malvolio?

33. How do you? 'How are you feeling?'

34 At your request? '(Why should I answer simply) because you ask me?' **nightingales answer daws!** Malvolio is the 'nightingale', Maria the 'daw' (jackdaw), a mischievous 'undignified' bird; and so, like the nightingale, Malvolio will condescend to reply.

35–52. Now follows a succession of quick exchanges – a well-tried comic device – between Malvolio and Olivia, with Malvolio so convinced of the genuineness of the letter, and of Olivia's eager affection, that none of her protestations deters him. Being Malvolio, he will take longer anyway to give up his delusions of greatness, and to recognise that she has no idea what he is talking about. One by one, her attempts to deflate him are surmounted, by quotations – her own heartfelt sentiments, he believes – from the letter.

Malvolio
　To bed? Ay, sweetheart, and I'll come to thee.　　30
Olivia
　God comfort thee! Why dost thou smile so, and kiss
　thy hand so oft?
Maria
　How do you, Malvolio?
Malvolio
　At your request? Yes, nightingales answer daws!
Maria
　Why appear you with this ridiculous boldness before　35
　my lady?
Malvolio
　'Be not afraid of greatness.' 'Twas well writ.
Olivia
　What mean'st thou by that, Malvolio?
Malvolio
　'Some are born great,'—
Olivia
　Ha?　　40
Malvolio
　'Some achieve greatness,'—
Olivia
　What say'st thou?
Malvolio
　'And some have greatness thrust upon them.'
Olivia
　Heaven restore thee!
Malvolio
　'Remember who commended thy yellow stockings,'—　45
Olivia
　'Thy yellow stockings'?
Malvolio
　'And wish'd to see thee cross-garter'd.'
Olivia
　'Cross-garter'd'?

50. *Am I made?* Olivia, not knowing, of course, that his strange remarks are quotations from the letter, assumes that they are meant for her. In this instance, she may well be taking the word as 'maid', which would have some bearing upon herself.

52. *midsummer madness.* Midsummer was popularly thought to be a season in which all manner of strange behaviour ran riot.

56. How relieved Olivia must be to have something to 'break the spell'! Yet, eager as she must be to escape from this present painful encounter, and be with Viola again, she cares enough about Malvolio to give instructions for his welfare.

58–9. *I would not have him miscarry.* For all his irritating ways, Malvolio must hold a high place in Olivia's regard, even in her affection. (Maria confirms this a little later, in line 101.)

61. Malvolio now has the stage to himself – his last opportunity in fact, to speak to us direct. It is, therefore, perhaps as well that he should still be exulting in his supposed success. If we regard this as his last free utterance before the doors of 'justice' close upon him, then we have to admit that he still needs further 'remedial treatment'. His self-confidence shows no signs of weakening – indeed, thanks to Maria's thoroughness, it is more firmly established than ever. The entire conception of his 'one-track' personality, and the ruthlessness that has still to be used to oppose it, would be called into question if we saw signs in him now of normal human affection, to arouse our pity at least. All that has been done to him already, probably, and all that is still to be done, certainly, would begin to strike us as altogether too inhuman. (Is Olivia's concern, then, an inconsistency on Shakespeare's part?) So well has Maria done her work on the letter – too well, she may now think – that even Olivia's desperate request for Sir Toby to look after him in his distraction, is seen by Malvolio as simply confirming what she has already indicated in writing!

61. *do you come near me now?* 'You're beginning to understand me now, aren't you?'

62. *look to:* look after.

69. *reverend carriage:* way of movement that will inspire respect.

71. *lim'd:* caught. (Lime was used to catch birds.) *Jove's doing.* Jove was the pagan equivalent of 'God'. (It probably replaces the 'God' of the original text, to comply with regulations, in James I's reign, prohibiting the use of the name of God on the stage.) It is interesting to note Malvolio's attitude here. To thank God is normally a sign of humble trust; but in this instance it more likely indicates an all-too-willing assumption that his fortunes are of over-riding concern to God. (Understood rightly, this can argue a commendable faith in Divine Providence. But in Malvolio's case, it is his own greatness, probably, rather than God's, that is uppermost in his mind.) See also lines 79–80.

Malvolio
'Go to, thou art made, if thou desir'st to be so;'—
Olivia
Am I made? 50
Malvolio
'If not, let me see thee a servant still.'
Olivia
Why, this is very midsummer madness.

[Enter SERVANT]

Servant
Madam, the young gentleman of the Count Orsino's
is return'd; I could hardly entreat him back; he attends
your ladyship's pleasure. 55
Olivia
I'll come to him. *[Exit SERVANT]* Good Maria,
let this fellow be look'd to. Where's my cousin Toby?
Let some of my people have a special care of him; I
would not have him miscarry for the half of my
dowry. 60

[Exeunt OLIVIA and MARIA]

Malvolio
O, ho! do you come near me now? No worse man than
Sir Toby to look to me! This concurs directly with the
letter: she sends him on purpose, that I may appear
stubborn to him; for she incites me to that in the
letter. 'Cast thy humble slough' says she. 'Be opposite 65
with a kinsman, surly with servants; let thy tongue
tang with arguments of state; put thyself into the
trick of singularity' and consequently sets down the
manner how, as: a sad face, a reverend carriage, a
slow tongue, in the habit of some sir of note, and so 70
forth. I have lim'd her; but it is Jove's doing, and Jove
make me thankful! And when she went away now
– 'Let this fellow be look'd to'. 'Fellow' not 'Malvolio'

74. *'fellow.'* This can have two meanings. Olivia used it condescendingly, as to an inferior. It can also denote equality of status, even intimacy. Malvolio in his present mood will have extracted only this second meaning.

75. *dram of a scruple.* Both are, literally, units of apothecaries' weight; the dram is one eighth of an ounce, the scruple one third of a dram.

76. *incredulous:* incredible.

76–7. *no incredulous or unsafe circumstance:* 'nothing that could conceivably go wrong.'

78–9. *full prospect of my hopes:* 'the fulfilment of all my hopes.'

Malvolio is from now on presented to us virtually through the reactions of the other three. He has never really come near to us, as the others have, however much we have been able to see inside his mind. The character he has been given has, by its very self-centredness, precluded our affection. But at this point he seems to recede to the very edge of things, and to detach from the human scene. The others have, from the start, been united by their detestation of his unloving ways. But now, regarding him as a lunatic – one who, in the common view, had passed beyond the reach of normal human contacts – they are banded together even more instinctively against him, as the herd is when faced with an intruder it wishes to isolate and expel. Insanity in those days, and for a long time after, still belonged to the realm of the unknown. Lunatics stood outside the reach of normal human relationships, largely because they seemed to be so un-human themselves. We should bear this in mind, and not expect a modern, enlightened compassion and understanding in their attitude to Malvolio.

81. *Which way is he . . . ?* 'How is he?'

82. *in little:* on a small scale, in miniature. *Legion.* The name of a man 'possessed by many devils' who was cured by Jesus.

86. *Go off:* Go away. *discard:* have nothing more to do with. *private:* privacy.

88. *hollow:* falsely. *fiend:* devil (under whose control Maria thinks he is).

91. *Ah, ha! does she so?* Still quite convinced that Olivia loves him, and quite deaf to their insistence upon his derangement, Malvolio is quick to interpret Olivia's instructions as signs of amorousness.

93. *Let me alone.* Sir Toby would like to handle this alone. This is not surprising, for the other two don't seem to be offering much effective help – Maria is by now almost hysterical with alarm, while Fabian's concern is at best mixed with amusement. Sir Toby himself shakes off his habitual carelessness, and at least tries, boldly and with conviction, to grapple with the problem. (The distinctive reactions of all three to this present emergency are well brought out.) How ironic that Malvolio, the suspected lunatic, should be finding the remarks of the others so fantastic – and we can hardly blame him for this!

97. *La you:* Simply an exclamation of surprise.

98. *at heart:* to heart. Maria, quite genuinely (as throughout this scene) sees in Malvolio's 'touchiness' at mention of the devil, a sign that he is in league with the devil, and resents any opposition to his master.

nor after my degree, but 'fellow'. Why, everything
adheres together, that no dram of a scruple, no scruple   75
of a scruple, no obstacle, no incredulous or unsafe
circumstance – What can be said? Nothing that can
be can come between me and the full prospect of my
hopes. Well, Jove, not I, is the doer of this, and he is
to be thanked.   80

[Re-enter MARIA, with SIR TOBY and FABIAN]

Sir Toby
Which way is he, in the name of sanctity? If all the
devils of hell be drawn in little, and Legion himself
possess'd him, yet I'll speak to him.

Fabian
Here he is, here he is. How is't with you, sir?

Sir Toby
How is't with you, man?   85

Malvolio
Go off; I discard you. Let me enjoy my private; go
off.

Maria
Lo, how hollow the fiend speaks within him! Did not
I tell you? Sir Toby, my lady prays you to have a care
of him.   90

Malvolio
Ah, ha! does she so?

Sir Toby
Go to, go to; peace, peace; we must deal gently with
him. Let me alone. How do you, Malvolio? How is't
with you? What, man, defy the devil; consider, he's
an enemy to mankind.   95

Malvolio
Do you know what you say?

Maria
La you, an you speak ill of the devil, how he takes it
at heart! Pray God he be not bewitch'd.

99. *wise woman:* one who was skilled in folk-medicine. The practice referred to, of inspecting a patient's urine, so as to diagnose his illness, was not in favour among qualified doctors.

100. Whether Fabian means this seriously or not, Maria gladly seizes on the suggestion, as at least offering some hope of a cure.

103. *How now, mistress!* As before (line 91), Malvolio reacts at once, and optimistically, to any mention of Olivia's concern for his welfare. And, to judge by Maria's comment (*O Lord!*) of alarm, or pity, or both, we may suppose that his sudden interest has been accompanied by equally sudden gestures in her direction. We know why he reacts in this way; but to Maria it is one more sign of a deranged mind. Maria's present distress has, if only temporarily, made her forget the letter – *her* letter – and the way it was bound to stimulate Malvolio's desires in Olivia's direction. Malvolio is 'running true to form' in all this, and she should have been prepared for just this reaction from him.

105. *this is not the way.* This is said to Maria. Sir Toby is beginning to have the situation weighed up, and to assert some kind of control. He may not have the full solution, but at least realises that Maria's hysteria is going to excite Malvolio even more.

108. *us'd:* treated.

109. *bawcock:* (from the French 'beau coq') fine fellow.

110. *chuck:* a term of affection (the same as 'chick', which is still used today as an endearment).

111. *Sir!* Malvolio is carrying out what he believes to be Olivia's injunctions, in reproving Sir Toby for his familiarity.

112. *Biddy:* another name for 'chicken' (and so in the same vein as *bawcock* and *chuck*).

112–13. *for gravity:* dignified.

113. *cherrypit:* a children's game in which cherry-stones were thrown into a small hole; so the expression *to play at cherrypit* would mean 'to be on friendly terms with.'

113–14. *Hang him, foul collier!* A miner and the Devil were both black and worked in a pit. Sir Toby, as with a child, is trying to coax Malvolio into renouncing the Devil. ('Don't have anything to do with the Devil, that nasty old thing!')

117. *My prayers, minx!* Malvolio is right in thinking that Maria wants him to pray because she believes that he is in desperate need of spiritual help. It is her reason that he is indignant about, not the idea of praying in itself. (*minx* = wanton woman.)

118. *he will not hear of godliness.* Maria, however, misunderstands him; in her view, he is so possessed by evil, that he instinctively repudiates 'godliness'.

120. *I am not of your element:* 'I live in a different world from you.'

Fabian

Carry his water to th' wise woman.

Maria

Marry, and it shall be done to-morrow morning, if I 100
live. My lady would not lose him for more than I'll
say.

Malvolio

How now, mistress!

Maria

O Lord!

Sir Toby

Prithee hold thy peace; this is not the way. Do you 105
not see you move him? Let me alone with him.

Fabian

No way but gentleness – gently, gently. The fiend is
rough, and will not be roughly us'd.

Sir Toby

Why, how now, my bawcock!
How dost thou, chuck?   110

Malvolio

Sir!

Sir Toby

Ay, Biddy, come with me. What, man, 'tis not for
gravity to play at cherrypit with Satan. Hang him, foul
collier!

Maria

Get him to say his prayers, good Sir Toby, get him to 115
pray.

Malvolio

My prayers, minx!

Maria

No, I warrant you, he will not hear of godliness.

Malvolio

Go, hang yourselves all! You are idle shallow things; I
am not of your element; you shall know more 120
hereafter.

[*Exit*]

122. *Is't possible?* and **124. *improbable fiction.*** The conspirators have really surprised themselves by their success – they can hardly believe their eyes, and ears. Fabian's remark has an additional point, a sort of dramatic irony. Shakespeare is in a way putting himself and his play into our hands, and mischievously inviting our criticism of himself, for devising and handling such an ingenious plot.

125. *His very genius:* His essential self. ***taken the infection of:*** been infected by. Sir Toby is emphasizing the completeness of the deception – Malvolio is beside himself.

127–8. *take air and taint:* grow stale. An odd line for Maria, in face of her recent distress on Malvolio's account. Together with her next observation – *The house will be the quieter* – it suggests that she is now 'back to normal' and as eager as the others to see the matter through to the end. Perhaps, with Malvolio out of sight, she can put out of her mind the harrowing side of his humiliation, and dwell only on the 'justice' of it.

131–7. Sir Toby's closing remarks perhaps come nearest to summing up their common attitude. His words serve, in addition, as a kind of justification – perhaps Shakespeare's own – of the entire Malvolio plot, on moral and dramatic grounds. On moral grounds, the treatment Malvolio is receiving, is designed as a *penance* – to make some amends for his errors. On dramatic grounds, it has given them, and us, *pleasure*. (How significant is it, that they will stop tormenting him only when they are tired of their fun, and not for any reason of compassion?)

136. *to the bar:* to be judged. ***finder of madmen.*** In the sense probably of 'certifying' them as insane.

Sir Andrew's arrival, with his challenge for Viola, is most salutary. It smoothes away any misgivings about Malvolio's fate that may still exist, and brings us at once into a fresh situation, where the humour taxes our susceptibilities less.

138. *May morning:* morning of May 1st, one of the happiest popular feast-days, on which all manner of entertainment took place to celebrate the coming of spring. Fabian sees Sir Andrew's arrival as providing such entertainment for them.

140. *vinegar and pepper.* It will need no 'seasoning' to bring out the flavour, which will be piquant enough as it stands.

Sir Toby

Is't possible?

Fabian

If this were play'd upon a stage now, I could condemn
it as an improbable fiction.

Sir Toby

His very genius hath taken the infection of the device, 125
man.

Maria

Nay, pursue him now, lest the device take air and
taint.

Fabian

Why, we shall make him mad indeed.

Maria

The house will be the quieter.   130

Sir Toby

Come, we'll have him in a dark room and bound. My
niece is already in the belief that he's mad. We may
carry it thus, for our pleasure and his penance, till our
very pastime, tired out of breath, prompt us to have
mercy on him; at which time we will bring the device 135
to the bar and crown thee for a finder of madmen,
But see, but see.

[Enter SIR ANDREW]

Fabian

More matter for a May morning.

Sir Andrew

Here's the challenge; read it. I warrant there's vinegar
and pepper in't.   140

Fabian

Is't so saucy?

Sir Andrew

Ay, is't, I warrant him; do but read.

Sir Toby

Give me. *[Reads]* 'Youth, whatsoever thou art, thou art
but a scurvy fellow.'

145. *Good and valiant.* Fabian and Sir Toby are making fun of Sir Andrew, in their customary style, by pretending that they think he is fierce and aggressive. Sir Andrew doesn't disappoint them – he drinks in their flattery with never a second thought.

146. *admire:* wonder. ***nor . . . not.*** A double negative. Only one of these is needed in modern English.

148. *keeps you from the blow of the law.* By not making specific charges against Viola, Sir Andrew avoids prosecution for libel.

151. *thou liest in thy throat.* What lying does Sir Andrew refer to – her persistent denial of love for Olivia, or when she says (as Sir Andrew assumes she will) that she is being challenged solely because of her attachment to Olivia?

153. *to exceeding good sense:* according to very good sense. Fabian's addition of *less* at the end (making 'senseless') will be spoken 'aside', a little game that children often get up to.

158. *th' windy side of the law:* the right side of the law. (The metaphor is a nautical one – for a sailing ship, the best side was the one on which it could catch the wind, to propel it over the water, and thus escape from an enemy.)

160–1. *He may have mercy . . . hope is better:* an unintentional piece of humour. It sounds as if Sir Andrew hopes for something better than God's mercy! What he actually means, of course, is that he hopes he won't be the loser and die in the forthcoming duel, and thus be needing the mercy of God in the specific way a dead man needs it.

161. *Thy friend.* One of many conventional ways of ending a letter; whereas *thy sworn enemy* (line 162) expresses Sir Andrew's 'real' sentiments at this moment. The humour is in the juxtaposition of the two opposites.

163. *If this letter . . . legs cannot.* Another way of saying that the letter cannot fail to move Viola, any more than her legs can fail to carry her.

165. *fit occasion:* favourable opportunity.

165–6. *in some commerce:* on some business.

168. *scout:* keep a look out. ***me.*** This cannot be directly rendered in Modern English. It is the same usage as in Scene ii, lines 29–30.

Fabian

Good and valiant. 145

Sir Toby [Reads]

'Wonder not, nor admire not in thy mind, why I do
call thee so, for I will show thee no reason for't.'

Fabian

A good note; that keeps you from the blow of the
law.

Sir Toby [Reads]

'Thou com'st to the Lady Olivia, and in my sight she 150
uses thee kindly; but thou liest in thy throat; that is
not the matter I challenge thee for.'

Fabian

Very brief, and to exceeding good sense – less.

Sir Toby [Reads]

'I will waylay thee going home; where if it be thy
chance to kill me'— 155

Fabian

Good.

Sir Toby

'Thou kill's me like a rogue and a villain.'

Fabian

Still you keep o' th' windy side of the law. Good!

Sir Toby [Reads]

'Fare thee well; and God have mercy upon one of
our souls! He may have mercy upon mine; but my 160
hope is better, and so look to thyself. Thy friend, as
thou usest him, and thy sworn enemy,

                    ANDREW AGUECHEEK.'

If this letter move him not, his legs cannot. I'll give't
him.

Maria

You may have very fit occasion for't; he is now in 165
some commerce with my lady, and will by and by
depart.

Sir Toby

Go, Sir Andrew; scout me for him at the corner of

169. *bum-bailey:* sheriff's officer (who would be adept at knowing where to find law-breakers who were trying to escape detection).

172–4. *gives manhood . . . earn'd him:* 'is a better way of showing one's manliness than by trying to act courageously.' This is a cynicism that probably passes over Sir Andrew's head. All that comes through to him is that he must swear ferociously, which he claims he can do better than anyone else – *let me alone for swearing* (line 175). This might equally mean that Sir Andrew's oaths will be too terrifying for them, or anyone else, to listen to.

176–88. Sir Toby is right in surmising that Viola will be far more effectively panicked – and we better entertained – if he personally draws the picture of Sir Andrew's 'ferocity'. Sir Toby is in his element telling tall stories, and he does it superbly. Nothing puts him off his stride, once he has decided on his line of approach, and even this he seems to do with more success, and less effort, than anyone else. It is difficult to imagine a more hilarious scene than the one they are now engineering, between Sir Andrew and Viola. Yet it has cost them virtually no trouble – a few well-chosen untruths are planted in the right places, and all they have to do then is 'sit back' and enjoy the outcome.

177. *gives him out:* shows him.

178. *capacity:* ability.

180. *excellently:* exceedingly. (We tend to limit the word to things that are good.)

182. *clodpole:* person without intelligence. It may jolt us a little to see just how much Sir Andrew is despised by his 'friend'. But there have been signs before (Scene ii, line 49) and will be later (Act v, Scene i, lines 200–1) of Sir Toby's essential callousness towards him.

183. *set upon Aguecheek . . . valour:* 'invent for Aguecheek an outstanding reputation for courage.'

184. *as I know his youth will aptly receive it:* 'which, being young, and inexperienced in fighting, he will be only too ready to believe.'

185. *hideous:* shocking.

188. *cockatrices.* A cockatrice was a fabulous reptile, half serpent and half cockerel, thought to kill by its look and breath. (It was also called a basilisk.)

189. *give them way:* 'let them alone.'

190. *presently after him:* 'follow him at once.'

193–209. This short interlude, in dignified verse, carries us back to the highly-strung atmosphere of the main plot. The Viola who is shortly to step straight into the duelling trap, has to be seen as coming, as it were, straight from her other ordeal, with no time to adjust resourcefully to the new situation.

Viola and Olivia are still at the same impasse as when they last appeared, Olivia having abandoned all attempts to disguise her love for Viola, and Viola still trying to 'redirect' it towards her master.

194. *too unchary:* too rashly.

the orchard, like a bum-baily; so soon as ever thou
seest him, draw; and as thou draw'st, swear horrible; 170
for it comes to pass oft that a terrible oath, with a
swaggering accent sharply twang'd off, gives manhood
more approbation than ever proof itself would have
earn'd him. Away.

Sir Andrew
Nay, let me alone for swearing. 175

[Exit]

Sir Toby
Now will not I deliver his letter; for the behaviour of
the young gentleman gives him out to be of good
capacity and breeding; his employment between his
lord and my niece confirms no less. Therefore this
letter, being so excellently ignorant, will breed no terror 180
in the youth; he will find it comes from a clodpole.
But, sir, I will deliver his challenge by word of mouth,
set upon Aguecheek a notable report of valour, and
drive the gentleman – as I know his youth will aptly
receive it – into a most hideous opinion of his rage, 185
skill, fury, and impetuosity, This will so fright them
both that they will kill one another by the look, like
cockatrices.

[Re-enter OLIVIA, with VIOLA]

Fabian
Here he comes with your niece; give them way till he
take leave, and presently after him. 190

Sir Toby
I will meditate the while upon some horrid message
for a challenge.

[Exeunt SIR TOBY, FABIAN, and MARIA]

Olivia
I have said too much unto a heart of stone,
And laid mine honour too unchary out;

195. *reproves my fault.* The fault, that is, of allowing herself to fall for Viola, and of telling her about it.

196–7. But her love is so overpowering that any conscience she has about it has little effect.

198. *haviour:* behaviour. The order is: My master's griefs go(es) on with the same (be)haviour as your passions bear – 'My master's suffering in love expresses itself in the same way as yours.' (Note the quite common Shakespearian usage of singular verb with plural subject.)

201. *no tongue to vex you.* It will be a reminder of her love, but a silent one.

203–4. 'Whatever you ask me for, I'll give you, if I can do so honourably.'

205. '(I ask for) nothing but this.'

207. *I will acquit you:* 'I will release you (from any obligation to go on loving me).'

209. Another memorable 'aside' to conclude the encounter. Olivia means that she could quite willingly go to hell if the devil who carried her off there was like Viola. (This has a profounder implication – she is prepared to lose her place in heaven as long as she can have Viola.)

212–17. Notice how, in order to carry off the deception more successfully, Sir Toby plunges straight into the business of the challenge. He pretends to assume that Viola knows what he is referring to. This will also make Viola feel that she is caught up in something that is too far advanced to be halted by her, or anyone else.

212. *That defence thou hast, betake thee to't:* 'Be ready to defend yourself, as best you can.'

214. *intercepter:* adversary. (Literally, the one who stands in your way.) ***despite:*** malice.

215–16. *Dismount thy tuck:* draw your rapier from its sheath.

216. *be yare in:* be quick about.

218–20. This present confrontation is probably Viola's most testing experience. In her previous encounters, with Olivia and Orsino, she usually recovers some degree of composure, and even takes the initiative. But here she seems to be nearer the point of feminine panic at the thought of naked steel and bloodshed.

218–19. *quarrel to:* quarrel with.

There's something in me that reproves my fault;   195
But such a headstrong potent fault it is
That it but mocks reproof.

Viola

With the same haviour that your passion bears
Goes on my master's griefs.

Olivia

Here, wear this jewel for me; 'tis my picture.   200
Refuse it not; it hath no tongue to vex you.
And I beseech you come again to-morrow.
What shall you ask of me that I'll deny,
That honour sav'd may upon asking give?

Viola

Nothing but this – your true love for my master.   205

Olivia

How with mine honour may I give him that
Which I have given to you?

Viola

                    I will acquit you.

Olivia

Well, come again to-morrow. Fare thee well;
A fiend like thee might bear my soul to hell.

[Exit. Re-enter SIR TOBY *and* FABIAN*]*

Sir Toby

Gentleman, God save thee.   210

Viola

And you, sir.

Sir Toby

That defence thou hast, betake thee to't. Of what nature
the wrongs are thou hast done him, I know not; but
thy intercepter, full of despite, bloody as the hunter,
attends thee at the orchard end. Dismount thy tuck, 215
be yare in thy preparation, for thy assailant is quick,
skilful, and deadly.

Viola

You mistake, sir; I am sure no man hath any quarrel
to me; my remembrance is very free and clear from

223. *opposite:* opponent. (as in Scene ii, line 58.)

223–4. *youth, strength, skill, and wrath*. This is the sort of outrageous lie that Sir Toby loves to slip into the conversation without turning a hair. ***withal:*** with.

225. *what is he?* 'who is it?'

226. *dubb'd*. To dub a man was to confer knighthood upon him. ***unhatch'd:*** not hacked or blunted in battle. A man's own blade was laid upon him in the ceremony of knighting. Sir Toby, therefore, implies that Sir Andrew had seen no fighting when he became a knight.

226–7. *on carpet consideration:* a knight dubbed when kneeling on a carpet, not on the ground of a battle-field.

228. *divorc'd:* separated – by killing three people. (In death, the soul was thought to be separated from the body.)

229. *incensement:* rage.

230–1. *satisfaction can . . . death and sepulchre:* 'he will be satisfied with nothing less than a fight to the death.' (*Sepulchre* is a burial-place.)

231. *Hob-nob:* another rendering of 'hab-nab' (a corruption from Latin) meaning 'have or have not', almost in the same sense as *give't or take't*. Sir Andrew is prepared (says Sir Toby) to gain or lose all in the ensuing fight.

232–3. *desire some conduct of the lady:* 'ask the Countess for someone to escort me.' (We speak today of granting someone a 'safe conduct'.) What humiliation for Viola if she had ever gone to Olivia with this request!

236. *quirk:* odd trick of behaviour.

237–43. Sir Toby at once blocks this line of escape. We must imagine him doing this literally, barring the way physically himself.

238. *competent:* that calls for redress.

238–9. *give him his desire:* do what he wants.

239. *Back you shall not to the house:* 'You shall not go back to the house.'

239–40. *unless you undertake . . . answer him:* 'unless you are prepared to accept the same challenge from me – and it will involve you in no less violence.' In other words, Sir Toby makes it painfully clear that Viola is expected to fight one or the other!

242. *meddle:* join battle.

243. *forswear to wear iron about you:* 'renounce the right to wear a sword.'

244. *uncivil*. Normally this would mean 'impolite', but it seems here to be used in a stronger sense, almost like our modern 'uncivilised'. ***strange:*** aloof, reserved.

244–5. *do me this courteous office:* 'do me the favour'; ***as to know of the knight:*** 'of finding out from the knight.'

246–7. *something of my negligence, nothing of my purpose:* 'caused by some carelessness on my part, and in no way intentional.'

any image of offence done to any man.   220

Sir Toby
You'll find it otherwise, I assure you; therefore, if you
hold your life at any price, betake you to your guard;
for your opposite hath in him what youth, strength,
skill, and wrath, can furnish man withal.

Viola   225
I pray you, sir, what is he?

Sir Toby
He is knight, dubb'd with unhatch'd rapier and on
carpet consideration; but he is a devil in private brawl.
Souls and bodies hath he divorc'd three; and his
incensement at this moment is so implacable that
satisfaction can be none but by pangs of death and 230
sepulchre. Hob-nob is his word – give't or take't.

Viola
I will return again into the house and desire some
conduct of the lady. I am no fighter. I have heard of
some kind of men that put quarrels purposely on
others to taste their valour; belike this is a man of 235
that quirk.

Sir Toby
Sir, no; his indignation derives itself out of a very
competent injury; therefore, get you on and give him
his desire. Back you shall not to the house, unless you
undertake that with me which with as much safety 240
you might answer him; therefore on, or strip your
sword stark naked; for meddle you must, that's certain,
or forswear to wear iron about you.

Viola
This is as uncivil as strange. I beseech you do me this
courteous office as to know of the knight what my 245
offence to him is: it is something of my negligence,
nothing of my purpose.

Sir Toby
I will do so. Signior Fabian, stay you by this gentleman
till my return.

251. even to a mortal arbitrement: 'to the point of deciding the matter in mortal combat.' (**Arbitrement** means settlement of a dispute.) Can we detect any difference between Fabian's treatment here of Viola, and Sir Toby's?

252–3. but nothing of the circumstance more: 'but no further details.'

255–7. 'There is nothing that you can deduce (**read**) from his appearance (**form**) that suggests what you will discover when his valour is put to the test (**in the proof of his valour**).'

261. bound: obliged.

262. with sir priest than sir knight. Does Viola imply more than a general contrast between a non-violent way of life, and a warlike one?

262–3. I care not who knows. Said in defiance, or desperation?

263. mettle: basic quality. (Of a man, it would normally denote his courage.)

264–9. Alone now with Sir Andrew, Sir Toby subjects him to the same treatment as he dealt to Viola, thus building up to the crowning situation where the two unwilling 'combatants', each terrified of the other, each expecting the roughest handling, are gradually coaxed together, into some kind of duelling stance.

265. firago: (usually virago) a violent, fierce woman. (Sir Toby is simply describing the only kind of ferocity he can imagine in connection with Viola.) **pass:** bout (of fencing).

266. stuck in: a term from fencing, no doubt used by Sir Toby with some relish.

266–7. mortal motion: deadly action.

267. is inevitable: cannot be avoided. (We rarely use the word today in its physical sense.)

267–8. on the answer, he pays you: 'he makes his return stroke.'

269. Sophy: Shah of Persia.

As Sir Toby enlarges upon Viola's swordsmanship, he will almost certainly be miming it, over-emphatically, to make quite sure that Sir Andrew has a clear picture of what could be in store for him.

270. But Sir Andrew reacts too thoroughly, and tries to call the whole thing off, so that Sir Toby has to do some quick thinking, or their joke will 'misfire'.

2736–. Sir Andrew is refreshingly honest – he is quite prepared to bribe Viola to drop the matter, and he doesn't mind who knows about it. (What ingenious excuses would Sir Toby have invented, if he had been caught in a similar dilemma?)

[Exit SIR TOBY*]*

Viola
> Pray you, sir, do you know of this matter? 250

Fabian
> I know the knight is incens'd against you, even to a
> mortal arbitrement; but nothing of the circumstance
> more.

Viola
> I beseech you, what manner of man is he?

Fabian
> Nothing of that wonderful promise, to read him by 255
> his form, as you are like to find him in the proof of
> his valour. He is indeed, sir, the most skilful, bloody,
> and fatal opposite that you could possibly have found
> in any part of Illyria. Will you walk towards him? I
> will make your peace with him if I can. 260

Viola
> I shall be much bound to you for't. I am one that
> would rather go with sir priest than sir knight. I care
> not who knows so much of my mettle.

[Exeunt. Re-enter SIR TOBY *with* SIR ANDREW*]*

Sir Toby
> Why, man, he's a very devil; I have not seen such a
> firago. I had a pass with him, rapier, scabbard, and all, 265
> and he gives me the stuck in with such a mortal motion
> that it is inevitable; and on the answer, he pays you
> as surely as your feet hit the ground they step on. They
> say he has been fencer to the Sophy.

Sir Andrew
> Pox on't, I'll not meddle with him. 270

Sir Toby
> Ay, but he will not now be pacified; Fabian can scarce
> hold him yonder.

Sir Andrew
> Plague on't; an I thought he had been valiant, and so
> cunning in fence, I'd have seen him damn'd ere I'd

277. *I'll make the motion:* 'I'll pass on your proposal' (about the horse)

278. *this shall end without the perdition of souls.* This is put as an assurance, by Sir Toby, that no lives will be lost.

279–80. *as well as I ride you.* Sir Toby is boasting about the way he has Sir Andrew completely under his control (as a rider has his horse).

281. *I have his horse to take up the quarrel. I have* simply implies Sir Toby's part in the arrangement – the offer was put to him as the intermediary.

283. *as horribly conceited:* 'has an equally horrible impression.' (To be 'conceited' here means to have a conceit, or idea, about someone or something.)

286. *better bethought him:* thought better.

288–9. *for the supportance of his vow:* 'to enable him to discharge his vow.'

289. *protests:* declares.

291. *how much I lack of a man:* 'how little manliness I really possess.

293–7. Notice the neat way in which Sir Toby repeats to Sir Andrew what he has just said, by way of explanation, to Viola. The words are almost identical, except that with Sir Andrew, it was an 'oath' to be kept, whereas, in Viola's case, it is 'honour' to be observed. The humour of this, and the barefaced trickery, is for our benefit, and Fabian's, not theirs.

295. *the duello:* the laws of duelling.

297. The antics of Fabian and Sir Toby at this point must be imagined, as they try to get the other two into effective swordplay with each other. (This is a good example of how little the simple text, and stage directions, may indicate of the actual goings-on on the stage.)

have challeng'd him. Let him let the matter slip, and 275
I'll give him my horse, grey Capilet.

Sir Toby
I'll make the motion. Stand here, make a good show
on't; this shall end without the perdition of souls.
[Aside] Marry, I'll ride your horse as well as I ride
you. 280

[Re-enter FABIAN and VIOLA]

[To FABIAN] I have his horse to take up the quarrel; I
have persuaded him the youth's a devil.

Fabian [To SIR TOBY]
He is as horribly conceited of him; and pants and looks
pale, as if a bear were at his heels.

Sir Toby [To VIOLA]
There's no remedy, sir: he will fight with you for's oath 285
sake. Marry, he hath better bethought him of his
quarrel, and he finds that now scarce to be worth
talking of. Therefore draw for the supportance of his
vow; he protests he will not hurt you.

Viola [Aside]
Pray God defend me! A little thing would make me 290
tell them how much I lack of a man.

Fabian
Give ground if you see him furious.

Sir Toby
Come, Sir Andrew, there's no remedy; the gentleman
will, for his honour's sake, have one bout with you;
he cannot by the duello avoid it; but he has promis'd 295
me, as he is a gentleman and a soldier, he will not
hurt you. Come on; to't.

Sir Andrew
Pray God he keep his oath!

[They draw. Enter ANTONIO]

Viola
I do assure you 'tis against my will.

300. Here the confusions start, between Viola and Sebastian – both humorous and distressing (as this one is). Antonio at once rushes to the defence of Viola, thinking her to be his friend Sebastian.

306. *undertaker:* one who takes upon himself a task. (Here it is used rather scathingly, implying that Antonio should 'mind his own business'.)

308. *anon:* presently, i.e. in a little while. ('Anon', like 'presently', originally meant 'at once'.) Notice that Sir Toby, normally a great talker, says nothing from now until the departure of the law officers. Probably he is afraid of being arrested for debt.

310. *for that I promis'd you:* 'as regards the promise I made you' – namely, the gift of Sir Andrew's horse, Capilet.

313. *office:* duty.

314. *at the suit:* on the instruction.

315. *You do mistake me:* 'You are confusing me with someone else.'

316. *favour:* face. (Compare Act II, Scene iv, lines 23–4.)

319. *This comes with seeking you.* This will not be said resentfully. It is only later, when Viola claims complete ignorance of his meaning, that Antonio gives way to bitter reproach.

320. *answer it:* answer their charge.

Antonio
    Put up your sword. If this young gentleman   300
    Have done offence, I take the fault on me:
    If you offend him, I for him defy you.

Sir Toby
    You, sir! Why, what are you?

Antonio
    One, sir, that for his love dares yet do more
    Than you have heard him brag to you he will.   305

Sir Toby
    Nay, if you be an undertaker, I am for you.

        [They draw. Enter OFFICERS*]*

Fabian
    O good Sir Toby, hold! Here come the officers.

Sir Toby [To ANTONIO*]*
    I'll be with you anon.

Viola
    Pray, sir, put your sword up, if you please.

Sir Andrew
    Marry, will I, sir; and for that I promis'd you, I'll be 310
    as good as my word. He will bear you easily and reins
    well.

First Officer
    This is the man; do thy office.

Second Officer
    Antonio, I arrest thee at the suit
    Of Count Orsino.

Antonio
              You do mistake me, sir.   315

First Officer
    No, sir, no jot; I know your favour well,
    Though now you have no sea-cap on your head.
    Take him away; he knows I know him well.

Antonio
    I must obey. *[To* VIOLA*]* This comes with seeking
        you;
    But there's no remedy; I shall answer it.   320

321. *necessity:* need. (In his present situation, he will need money, and he has already lent it to his friend.)

322–4. This is characteristic of Antonio – he is more concerned about having to deprive his friend of material help (by asking for the return of his purse) than about his own fate.

324. *You stand amaz'd.* Antonio imagines that Viola is amazed at his sudden arrest – he has no idea of the true reason.

327. *entreat of you:* 'beg you to give me.'

Viola's spontaneous offer of help is quite moving, and helps to bring out the tragic element in the ensuing encounter. If she had not been so generously motivated, the injustice of her fate at Antonio's hands would not weigh so heavily.

329. Viola refers to his rescue of her from the duelling.

330. *part:* partly. Either reason – her gratitude or his need – is cogent enough to solicit her willing help.

331. *my lean and low ability:* 'the little that I possess.' (Probably no more than she would have received up to now in her service to the Duke.)

332. *My having:* 'what I have.'

333. *my present:* 'all that I have with me.'

334. *coffer:* treasure-chest. Viola is being ironical. *deny:* refuse.

335–6. 'Can you possibly be unmoved by your obligations to me?' (*my deserts to you:* 'what I deserve of you.')

336. *tempt:* 'put too much strain upon.'

337–9. Antonio is afraid that it will sour their entire relationship. To *upbraid* with the *kindnesses* done means to remind 'him' of them, and to point out that 'he' has not been duly grateful – and Antonio has taken his friendship with Sebastian far too seriously to do this sort of thing except as a last desperate remedy.

341–4. Viola's attitude towards ingratitude seems to have been Shakespeare's own. It is worth noting that the 'lesser' faults she lists, by comparison, are the very ones that the play was written ostensibly to expose.

343–4. *vice . . . our frail blood.* This looks like a reference to 'Original Sin', a theological doctrine that all members of the human race inherit a tendency to evil (*strong corruption*) which they are too weak to master (*frail blood*) without the help of God. Viola's list, then, represents some of the ways in which this basic tendency shows itself.

344. We can well sympathize with Antonio's bewilderment – how could anyone so guilty of ingratitude (as he believes 'Sebastian' to be) speak so feelingly against it?

347. *one half out of the jaws of death:* already half-dead.

349. *image:* what Antonio believed to be Sebastian's true nature, but he now thinks he was mistaken.

What will you do, now my necessity
Makes me to ask you for my purse? It grieves me
Much more for what I cannot do for you
Than what befalls myself. You stand amaz'd;
But be of comfort.   325

Second Officer
　Come, sir, away.

Antonio
　I must entreat of you some of that money.

Viola
　What money, sir?
For the fair kindness you have show'd me here,
And part being prompted by your present trouble,   330
Out of my lean and low ability
I'll lend you something. My having is not much;
I'll make division of my present with you;
Hold, there's half my coffer.

Antonio
　　　　　　　　　Will you deny me now?
Is't possible that my deserts to you   335
Can lack persuasion? Do not tempt my misery,
Lest that it make me so unsound a man
As to upbraid you with those kindnesses
That I have done for you.

Viola
　　　　　　　　　I know of none,
Nor know I you by voice or any feature,
I hate ingratitude more in a man   340
Than lying, vainness, babbling drunkenness,
Or any taint of vice whose strong corruption
Inhabits our frail blood.

Antonio
　　　　　　　　O heavens themselves!

Second Officer   345
　Come, sir, I pray you go,

Antonio
　Let me speak a little. This youth that you see here
I snatch'd one half out of the jaws of death,
Reliev'd him with such sanctity of love,
And to his image, which methought did promise   169

350. did I devotion: 'I gave my devoted service.' The use of **sanctity, image, venerable** and **devotion** – all of them having a religious flavour – brings out the essence of Antonio's earlier attitude to Sebastian. We may disapprove of the intensity of his affection, we may even call it an obsession, perhaps, but its singlemindedness and sincerity are undeniable. It is his excessive devotion which is hurt the more deeply by what is seen as a betrayal, and recoils more bitterly from it.

351. Quite understandably, the Officer is not interested in all this – his job is to arrest Antonio. **The time goes by:** 'We're wasting time.'

352–7. But Antonio is so consumed with indignation that he hardly hears him.

352. vile: of no value.

353. good feature: outward appearance of goodness. Antonio means that 'Sebastian' has, by his conduct, discredited the whole concept of beauty.

354. Antonio himself now proceeds to reject outward beauty – it has lost all value for him. The only ugliness (**blemish**) he now considers is that of the mind, or character.

356. Virtue is beauty. Compare 'Beauty is truth, truth beauty,' from Keats' **Ode on a Grecian Urn.**

356–7. the beauteous evil . . . by the devil: 'wicked people with beautiful looks are like hollow trees, overgrown (**o'erflourished**) with another plant, or weed, which may look nice, but is in fact deadly.'

360. When Antonio does finally consent to go along with them, we can well imagine that his arrest has become a matter of little concern to him, compared with his present mental distress.

361–4. It is now Viola's turn to be nonplussed. But Antonio's very sincerity leads her to think that he must believe that there is someone – obviously (to her) not herself – who has treated him like this. So she goes on to hope (**Prove true, imagination**) that Antonio has in fact mistaken her for her brother (which would be strong evidence that he was still alive).

365–6. The approach of the other three passes without notice.

367–8. I my brother know Yet living in my glass. Every time Viola looks at herself in a mirror she can imagine that she is looking at her brother.

369. favour: looks.

369–71. he went still . . . I imitate: 'the clothes he was wearing were like those I now have on – for I chose them in imitation.' Sebastian and Viola have to be in the same attire (a simple enough matter for the wardrobe mistress), if their being mistaken for each other is to be at all credible on the stage. To make their faces look alike is a much less simple business, one which will have to depend virtually upon the audience's imagination.

Most venerable worth, did I devotion,   350

First Officer

What's that to us? The times goes by; away.

Antonio

But, O, how vile an idol proves this god!
Thou hast, Sebastian, done good feature shame.
In nature there's no blemish but the mind:
None can be call'd deform'd but the unkind.   355
Virtue is beauty; but the beauteous evil
Are empty trunks, o'erflourish'd by the devil.

First Officer

The man grows mad. Away with him. Come, come,
sir.

Antonio

Lead me on.   360

[Exit with officers]

Viola

Methinks his words do from such passion fly
That he believes himself; so do not I.
Prove true, imagination, O, prove true,
That I, dear brother, be now ta'en for you!

Sir Toby

Come hither, knight; come hither, Fabian; we'll whisper 365
o'er a couplet or two of most sage saws.

Viola

He nam'd Sebastian. I my brother know
Yet living in my glass; even such and so
In favour was my brother; and he went
Still in this fashion, colour, ornament,   370

371. *if it prove:* if it proves true.

372. 'Storms and waves (like the ones that nearly drowned them both) will have shown themselves to be entirely friendly.'

There is something appropriate in the use of prose to end the scene. It suits the detached, unemotional, almost callous attitude of the three as they 'dissect' Viola's character – just as the verse she has just used was the best way to express her intense emotion. Sir Toby and the others have no sympathy now for Viola, and are conscious only of her cowardice and apparent disloyalty. It is part of the irony of Viola's present situation that she should be suspected of such faithlessness, when in fact she is the most loyal of creatures.

373–4. *more a coward than a hare:* 'a greater coward than a hare' (noted for its timorousness).

377. *devout coward, religious in it.* An obvious contradiction, and laughable for that reason. We can, however, understand why Fabian describes her attitude thus. He is emphasising her preoccupation with her fear; it fills all her thoughts, as one's religion should, and produces a state of intense emotion.

378. What can one think of Sir Andrew for suggesting this now? ***Slid:*** 'By God's lid' (eye-lid); a contemporary oath, like "sblood' (God's blood) and 'zounds' (God's wounds).

381. *event:* outcome.

For him I imitate. O, if it prove,
Tempests are kind, and salt waves fresh in love!

[Exit]

Sir Toby
A very dishonest paltry boy, and more a coward than
a hare. His dishonesty appears in leaving his friend here
in necessity and denying him; and for his cowardship, 375
ask Fabian.
Fabian
A coward, a most devout coward, religious in it.
Sir Andrew
'Slid, I'll after him again and beat him.
Sir Toby
Do; cuff him soundly, but never draw thy sword.
Sir Andrew
An I do not—   380

[Exit]

Fabian
Come, let's see the event.
Sir Toby
I dare lay any money 'twill be nothing yet.

[Exeunt]

ACT FOUR SCENE I

This scene is virtually a continuation of the previous one. The confusion over the identity of Sebastian and Viola, which produced harrowing effects before, is the subject once again, only this time the outcome is entirely laughable. The main humour of the scene (to us) is prefaced by some typical 'clown-wit' – perhaps as a kind of appetiser. The source is still the same – Sebastian is mistaken for Viola – but this is the first occasion on which he is made aware of the confusion, and is touched personally by it. Unlike his sister, who could only wonder and suffer, he is able to fight back, and at the end of it all there is a prize for him that he can gladly accept.

So in this first encounter, it is Feste really who is thrown on to the defensive, having to justify himself, and prove to Sebastian that he is talking sense, and that his request is genuine – both of which he fails to do.

1. 'How can you possibly convince me that I have not been sent to fetch you?'

4. *Well held out, i'faith:* (ironically) 'that's a fine show you're putting up.' The rest of Feste's speech is also ironical – he quotes all the things that to him are plain facts (at least they would be if Sebastian were in fact 'Cesario', and Feste believes he is), and says that they are all untrue.

7. *nor this is not my nose neither.* A triple negative. We only need a single one!

9. *vent:* discharge. This use of the word was still probably somewhat unfamiliar. Feste picks upon it and repeats it mockingly. (Is Feste beginning to lose his customary self-possession? We could hardly blame him in the circumstances.)

13. *lubber:* loutish person.
14. *cockney:* foppish, effeminate person. Sebastian's use of such language makes Feste begin to wonder whether the whole world, for all its roughness, will soon be adopting similar affectations of speech (**will prove a cockney**). *ungird thy strangeness:* 'stop pretending not to know me.'

17. *Greek.* Often used then to describe a merry person.

ACT FOUR

SCENE I

Before Olivia's house

[Enter SEBASTIAN and CLOWN]

Clown
Will you make me believe that I am not sent for you?

Sebastian
Go to, go to, thou art a foolish fellow; let me be clear
of thee.

Clown
Well held out, i' faith! No, I do not know you;
nor I am not sent to you by my lady, to bid you come   5
speak with her; nor your name is not Master Cesario;
nor this is not my nose neither. Nothing that is so is
so.

Sebastian
I prithee vent thy folly somewhere else. Thou know'st
not me.   10

Clown
Vent my folly! He has heard that word of some great
man, and now applies it to a fool. Vent my folly! I am
afraid this great lubber, the world, will prove a cockney.
I prithee now, ungird thy strangeness, and tell me what
I shall vent to my lady. Shall I vent to her that thou   15
art coming?

Sebastian
I prithee, foolish Greek, depart from me;
There's money for thee; if you tarry longer
I shall give worse payment.

Clown
By my troth, thou hast an open hand. These wise men   20
that give fools money get themselves a good

175

22. *after fourteen years' purchase.* The value of land was calculated at twelve annual rentals. One was paying dearly at fourteen rentals. Feste is probably despising Sebastian for giving him such a large 'bribe' – he takes it as a sign of weakness in Sebastian, almost as an admission of defeat. (Feste's observation will be spoken as an 'aside'.)

24. *There's for you:* 'Take that!'

27. *Hold:* stop.

28–9. *in some of your coats.* Today we say, 'in your shoes'.

31–2. *I'll go another way to work with him.* Sir Andrew realizes that he must try something else, having come off the worse in this latest encounter.
32. *battery.* The legal term for 'physical assault on the person'.
33–4. *it's no matter for that:* 'it doesn't matter.'

37. *iron:* sword. *well flesh'd:* experienced in fighting.

42. *malapert:* impudent.

report – after fourteen years' purchase.

[Enter SIR ANDREW, SIR TOBY, and FABIAN]

Sir Andrew
Now, sir, have I met you again?
[Striking SEBASTIAN] There's for you.

Sebastian
Why, there's for thee, and there, and there.   25
Are all the people mad?

Sir Toby
Hold, sir, or I'll throw your dagger o'er the house.
[Holding SEBASTIAN]

Clown
This will I tell my lady straight. I would not be in some
of your coats for two-pence.

[Exit]

Sir Toby
Come on, sir; hold.   30

Sir Andrew
Nay, let him alone. I'll go another way to work with
him; I'll have an action of battery against him, if there
be any law in Illyria; though I struck him first, yet it's
no matter for that.

Sebastian
Let go thy hand.   35

Sir Toby
Come, sir, I will not let you go. Come, my young
soldier, put up your iron; you are well flesh'd. Come
on.

Sebastian
I will be free from thee. What wouldst thou now?
If thou dar'st tempt me further, draw thy sword.   40
[Draws]

Sir Toby
What, what? Nay, then I must have an ounce or two
of this malapert blood from you.   *[Draws]*

45. *Will it ever be thus?* Olivia says this with almost weary resignation – 'Will you never change your ways?' The rhetorical outburst that follows must make Sir Toby feel even more rejected than if Olivia had remonstrated with him in everyday terms. It is as if she has been offering hospitality to her uncle only out of charity, perhaps keeping up some sort of pretence to herself that his grossness might be cured. But this pretence is now shattered, and Olivia casts him off almost as if she could never have seriously regarded him as a kinsman. (This incident may suggest, in a small way, the rejection of Falstaff by Prince Hal, in the second part of *Henry IV*.)

48. How effective that, in the middle of her fiery dismissal of the others, Olivia should show such tender concern for 'Cesario'!

49. *Rudesby:* lout.

49–57. Perhaps Olivia is secretly glad of an opportunity – which she has not had to initiate – for fresh and close contact with 'Viola'. There is little reason for her suggestion – to make amends for Sebastian's rough treatment – that they should return to the house, and even less that they should pass the time hearing of Sir Toby's other misdemeanours.

50. *sway:* influence (you).

51. *uncivil:* discourteous; ***extent:*** assault (a legal term).

53. *fruitless:* 'pointless' probably, rather than 'unsuccessful'.

54. *botch'd up:* 'put together anyhow' (in a rough way).

56. *deny:* refuse. ***Beshrew:*** Curse. The shrew was commonly held to possess malevolent qualities.)

57. A difficult line – the meaning probably is that Sir Toby, by his rough treatment of Sebastian ('Cesario', of course, in Olivia's mind), **started** or startled Olivia. Being so in love, Olivia would feel the outrage as if levelled against herself.

58. *What relish is in this?* 'What does this taste like?' 'What am I to make of this?' ***How runs the stream?*** has much the same significance.

59. *Or . . . or.* We would say 'Either . . . or.'

60. *Lethe:* a river of the Underworld in ancient Greek mythology. To drink its water induced forgetfulness of one's past life on earth, ***steep:*** immerse. ***still*** is used adverbially here; the modern order of words would be: 'Let fancy steep my senses in Lethe still' – 'Let my imagination continue to lull my senses, so that I forget reality.'

61. *If it be thus to dream:* 'If this is what dreaming is like.'

62. *Would thou'dst be rul'd by me:* 'I wish you would accept my advice.' 'Would' (or more usually 'Would that') was a common way of introducing a wish, and meant 'I wish that . . .'

[Enter OLIVIA]

Olivia
   Hold, Toby; on thy life, I charge thee hold.
Sir Toby
   Madam!
Olivia
   Will it be ever thus? Ungracious wretch,   45
   Fit for the mountains and the barbarous caves,
   Where manners ne'er were preach'd! Out of my sight!
   Be not offended, dear Cesario—
   Rudesby, be gone!

   [Exeunt SIR TOBY, SIR ANDREW, and FABIAN]

                   I prithee, gentle friend,
   Let thy fair wisdom, not thy passion, sway   50
   In this uncivil and unjust extent
   Against thy peace. Go with me to my house,
   And hear thou there how many fruitless pranks
   This ruffian hath botch'd up, that thou thereby
   Mayst smile at this. Thou shalt not choose but go;   55
   Do not deny. Beshrew his soul for me!
   He started one poor heart of mine in thee.
Sebastian
   What relish is in this? How runs the stream?
   Or I am mad, or else this is a dream.
   Let fancy still my sense in Lethe steep;   60
   If it be thus to dream, still let me sleep!
Olivia
   Nay, come, I prithee. Would thou'dst be rul'd by
     me!
Sebastian
   Madam, I will.
Olivia
                   O, say so, and so be!

             [Exeunt]

SCENE II

The sequel to this promising encounter between Olivia and Sebastian is delayed, in order to make way for a scene of a very different kind. Perhaps it is only the pleasurable anticipation that has just been aroused that tides us over this next shabby piece of Malvolio-baiting. By this time, with Olivia's (and Sebastian's) fortunes so obviously drawing to a climax, we may have begun to lose interest in Malvolio's fate. With his humiliation already effected, he has little further to do dramatically. The inclusion, therefore, of this scene may strike us as a forcing of the humour of the Malvolio plot – little more than a concession to the cruder elements in the audience. This is perhaps a good illustration of the intrinsic contrast between the two kinds of comedy brought together in *Twelfth Night* – the Comedy of Humours seems to have exhausted itself, while Shakespeare's 'character-development' approach has not yet reached its prime.

2. *Sir Topas the curate*. The title 'Sir' was commonly applied to a priest. (Viola says she would rather 'go with sir priest than sir knight', in Act III, Scene iv.) The name 'Thopas' was chosen by Chaucer for the knight in the tale he ascribes to himself, in *The Canterbury Tales*. Also, the precious stone, the topaz, was used in treating lunacy. Malvolio is to be treated, as before, as one possessed by a devil; and, dressed as a priest, Feste will drive the point home more convincingly. Whereas earlier, the thought that Malvolio might really be devil-possessed, threw Maria into a certain panic, she has no qualms now about initiating this latest torment.

3. *the whilst:* in the meantime.

5. Feste plays on the two meanings of *dissemble*. He uses it first simply as 'disguise', but then in an unfavourable sense – 'behave deceptively'. He is having a 'dig' at the clergy, who, by very reason of their high calling, must always run the risk of being termed hypocritical.

6. *tall:* good; *become:* suit.

7. *function:* i.e. of the priest. *lean enough.* A hard-working student would have little time or money to live comfortably or grow fat.

8. *to be said:* to be called.

9. *housekeeper:* Either 'one who stays at home (leading a quiet, law-abiding life)', or 'a hospitable person'. *goes as fairly as to say:* 'is as good as being called.' Feste seems to mean that, for all his ordinariness, he is just as good as the scholarly parson he is impersonating.

10. *competitors:* partners.

11. *Jove bless thee*. For this use of 'Jove' instead of 'God', see note on Act III, Scene iv, line 71.

12. *Bonos dies:* good day. *old hermit of Prague:* a typical Feste invention, which sounds almost authentic.

14. *King Gorboduc*. A legendary British King. (The first English tragedy in blank verse was about him.) Feste clearly enjoys playing this part, in which he can positively revel in pseudo-scholarship, interlaced, however, with enough genuine learning to convince Malvolio that he is a bona-fide priest.

SCENE II

Olivia's house

[Enter MARIA *and* CLOWN*]*

Maria

Nay, I prithee, put on this gown and this beard; make
him believe thou art Sir Topas the curate; do it quickly.
I'll call Sir Toby the whilst.

[Exit]

Clown

Well, I'll put it on, and I will dissemble myself in't;
and I would I were the first that ever dissembled in   5
such a gown. I am not tall enough to become the
function well nor lean enough to be thought a good
student; but to be said an honest man and a good
housekeeper goes as fairly as to say a careful man and
a great scholar. The competitors enter.   10

[Enter SIR TOBY *and* MARIA*]*

Sir Toby

Jove bless thee, Master Parson.

Clown

Bonos dies, Sir Toby; for as the old hermit of Prague,
that never saw pen and ink, very wittily said to a niece
of King Gorboduc 'That that is is'; so I, being Master
Parson, am Master Parson; for what is 'that' but that,   15
and 'is' but is?

Sir Toby

To him, Sir Topas.

Clown

What ho, I say! Peace in this prison!

Sir Toby

The knave counterfeits well; a good knave.

21–2. *Malvolio the lunatic.* Malvolio's chief fault was in thinking too highly of himself, and in this way welcoming untruth. It was a sort of 'sin against the light', as all self-conceit must be in some measure. The mental torture to which he is now subjected – being made to feel that he can no longer rely on the plain evidence of his senses, and that his very reasoning powers are false – is therefore highly appropriate, if excessively severe. The effect it actually has upon Malvolio is, however, to throw him entirely upon the resources of his own reason. There is nothing else for him to grasp except the plain functioning of reason. And this, we may like to believe, is the beginning of his cure – whether Maria and the others intended that it should turn out like this, or were simply out for one final laugh at his expense. (We have to admire Malvolio for his heroic defiance of what to most of us would have seemed unanswerable opposition.)

24. *hyperbolical:* excessively bad. The expected word would be 'diabolical' – devilish. But Feste's use of *hyperbolical* is not entirely out of place. (Literally, Feste's phrase means 'excessive fiend').

25. *Talkest thou nothing but of ladies?* This kind of wilful misunderstanding is a familiar humorous device, and particularly effective if it substitutes something that is as inappropriate as in this instance. (Malvolio is the last person we would describe as a lady's man!)

30. *dishonest.* Satan is referred to in the Bible as the 'Father of Lies'. Feste's humour here consists in claiming to speak with restraint, but in fact, addressing 'the Devil' quite bluntly.

32–3. *Say'st thou that house is dark?* Feste's simple plan is to contradict Malvolio flatly at every point, in such a way as to persuade him that he must be quite out of his mind ('seeing things' as we say). The darkness of Malvolio's 'prison' was to him the one central fact of his life just then. So this is the reality that Feste proceeds to deny. But he goes further – he mixes sense with nonsense in such a way as to shatter, if possible, Malvolio's very hold upon sanity. A less tough victim would have surrendered to such nightmarish treatment.

35. *barricadoes:* barricades. This is intentional nonsense; a barricade is designed solely to block up an opening, and seal it off – not to let in the light!

36. *clerestories:* windows set high up in the walls of a church or hall, their chief purpose being to let in plenty of light. *south north.* An impossible compass direction, of course, but, again, delivered with apparent authority.

37. *lustrous as ebony.* The third of Feste's paradoxes – ebony is black, so what sort of light shines through them?

38. *obstruction:* i.e. of the light.

41–2. *no darkness but ignorance.* Part of the effect of this valid observation is to imply to Malvolio that the darkness he experiences is simply the projection of his own inner darkness or ignorance.

43. *Egyptians in their fog.* Probably a reference to the 'plague' of darkness that afflicted the Egyptians at the time of the Israelites' exodus (see *Exodus*, Chapter 10).

Malvolio [Within]
    Who calls there?   20
Clown
    Sir Topas the curate, who comes to visit Malvolio the
    lunatic.
Malvolio
    Sir Topas, Sir Topas, good Sir Topas, go to my lady.
Clown
    Out, hyperbolical fiend! How vexest thou this man!
    Talkest thou nothing but of ladies?   25
Sir Toby
    Well said, Master Parson.
Malvolio
    Sir Topas, never was man thus wronged. Good Sir
    Topas, do not think I am mad; they have laid me here
    in hideous darkness.
Clown
    Fie, thou dishonest Satan! I call thee by the most   30
    modest terms, for I am one of those gentle ones that
    will use the devil himself with courtesy. Say'st thou
    that house is dark?
Malvolio
    As hell, Sir Topas.
Clown
    Why, it hath bay windows transparent as barricadoes,   35
    and the clerestories toward the south north are as
    lustrous as ebony; and yet complainest thou of
    obstruction?
Malvolio
    I am not mad, Sir Topas, I say to you this house is
    dark.   40
Clown
    Madman, thou errest. I say there is no darkness but
    ignorance; in which thou art more puzzled than the
    Egyptians in their fog.

44. Malvolio's mental powers show no weakening – the old intractable spirit is still active.

47. He will welcome any opportunity to prove, in honest argument, that he is as sane as they are. *constant question* is a question of hard fact, not just opinion, which Feste could twist to suit himself.

48. *Pythagoras:* a philosopher of Ancient Greece, who taught the doctrine of Transmigration of Souls – that, at death, the soul entered the body of some other living creature, human or otherwise. (He is chiefly remembered today for his mathematical propositions.)

50. *Grandam:* grandmother. *haply:* by chance.

53. A reasonable and tactful reply!

56–7. But Feste is adamant – Malvolio must accept Pythagoras' theory before Feste will admit that he is in his right mind (*allow of thy wits*).

60. Sir Toby says this teasingly, but with admiration for Feste's success in 'bringing off' the deception.

61. *for all waters:* 'ready for anything'.

62–3. Maria's comment is perfectly true; but the disguise was really for the audience's entertainment.

65–9. We can well understand Sir Toby's misgivings. This treatment of Olivia's steward would have been a risky thing to attempt in any circumstances, but quite foolhardy in view of Sir Toby's present low standing with his niece.

66. *deliver'd:* set free.

67. *I am now so far in offence with my niece:* 'I'm now so much in my niece's bad books,' 'I've done so much which has offended her.'

68–9. *to the upshot:* to its conclusion, *by and by:* shortly.

Malvolio

I say this house is as dark as ignorance, though ignorance were as dark as hell; and I say there was never   45
man thus abus'd. I am no more mad than you are;
make the trial of it in any constant question.

Clown

What is the opinion of Pythagoras concerning wild
fowl?

Malvolio

That the soul of our grandam might haply inhabit a   50
bird.

Clown

What think'st thou of his opinion?

Malvolio

I think nobly of the soul, and no way approve his
opinion.

Clown

Fare thee well. Remain thou still in darkness: thou   55
shalt hold th' opinion of Pythagoras ere I will allow
of thy wits; and fear to kill a woodcock, lest thou
dispossess the soul of thy grandam. Fare thee well.

Malvolio

Sir Topas, Sir Topas!

Sir Toby

My most exquisite Sir Topas!   60

Clown

Nay, I am for all waters.

Maria

Thou mightst have done this without thy beard and
gown: he sees thee not.

Sir Toby

To him in thine own voice, and bring me word how
thou find'st him. I would we were well rid of this   65
knavery. If he may be conveniently deliver'd, I would
he were; for I am now so far in offence with my niece
that I cannot pursue with any safety this sport to the
upshot. Come by and by to my chamber.

70–7. Feste's song has the same mocking effect on Malvolio as the one sung earlier by Sir Toby and himself, in Act II, Scene iii. In each case the intention is to treat Malvolio as if he isn't there, or at least doesn't matter. In this present instance, it is particularly hurtful, for Malvolio is in great desperation, and yet he can get no response or reaction of any kind from Feste till the end of his song. The words of the song itself are not going to help either – Malvolio's pursuit of Olivia has been ill-fated enough already, and he doesn't need a song to remind him that women can be unfaithful.

73. *perdy:* 'par Dieu.' (A softer version, since it's in a foreign language, of the literal 'By God,' which was too profane for common usage.)

79. *help me to:* 'please fetch me.'

80. *thankful:* deserving of thanks. If Feste will do him this kindness, then Malvolio (*as I am a gentleman*) will, by rewarding him, deserve his thanks (for the reward).

81. Feste pretends that he has only just recognized the voice.

83. 'Alas, sir, how is it that you are out of your mind?' *besides:* out of. *five wits:* normal faculties. The Elizabethans listed them as follows: commonsense, imagination, fancy, estimation and memory.

86. *But:* Only. Feste is getting his own back now, for Malvolio's earlier scorn of him and of all professional fools (Act I, Scene v). So there is more in his reply here than just a play on the two meanings of 'fool'.

88. *propertied:* used as their property, for their own ends.

90. *face me out of my wits.* A most apt description of the way Feste has, by barefaced lies, tried to convince Malvolio that he must be mad.

[Exeunt SIR TOBY *and* MARIA]

Clown [Sings]
  Hey, Robin, jolly Robin,   70
  Tell me how thy lady does.
Malvolio
  Fool!
Clown [Sings]
  My lady is unkind, perdy.
Malvolio
  Fool!
Clown [Sings]
  Alas, why is she so?   75
Malvolio
  Fool I say!
Clown [Sings]
  She loves another – Who calls, ha?
Malvolio
  Good fool, as ever thou wilt deserve well at my hand,
  help me to a candle, and pen, ink, and paper; as I am
  a gentleman, I will live to be thankful to thee for't.   80
Clown
  Master Malvolio?
Malvolio
  Ay, good fool.
Clown
  Alas, sir, how fell you besides your five wits?
Malvolio
  Fool, there was never man so notoriously abus'd; I am
  as well in my wits, fool, as thou art.   85
Clown
  But as well? Then you are mad indeed, if you be no
  better in your wits than a fool.
Malvolio
  They have here propertied me; keep me in darkness,
  send ministers to me, asses, and do all they can to face
  me out of my wits.   90

91. *Advise you:* Take care. ('Advisedly' means 'after due consideration.')

92–4. The sudden change of voice and manner is a well-used comic device, and parsonical tones have always been 'good for a laugh'. The artificial order (object-subject-verb) of ***thy wits the heavens restore***, and the stilted ***Endeavour thyself to sleep*** stress further the contrast Feste wants to make between himself as Clown and himself as Sir Topas.

94. *bibble-babble:* senseless talk.

96–8. Feste pretends to be now himself, now Sir Topas, changing his voice (and possibly – for our benefit, since Malvolio can see none of this – his position on the stage, and even part of his disguise) in rapid alternation. This bit of lightning conversation with himself can be very amusing.
Maintain . . . fellow is by Sir Topas.
Who, I . . . Sir Topas by Feste.
Marry, amen – Sir Topas.
I will, sir, I will – Feste.

100. *shent:* blamed. Feste means that he shouldn't really be talking to someone like Malvolio.

105. *Well-a-day:* Alas. ***that:*** if. 'It would be a bad look-out if you were' (that is to say if other people were as mad as Malvolio!).

107. *convey what I will set down:* 'take what I am going to write.'

110–11. Perhaps Feste's most ingenious question – 'Are you mad, or just pretending to be?'

113. *till I see his brains.* This could mean several things: 'Till I see some evidence of his intelligence,' or 'Till he is dead' (in other words, 'never'), or most likely, 'Till I have the unmistakable medical proof in front of me.'

115. *requite:* repay.

Clown

Advise you what you say: the minister is here. *[Speaking as* SIR TOPAS*]* Malvolio, Malvolio, thy wits the heavens restore! Endeavour thyself to sleep, and leave thy vain bibble-babble.

Malvolio

Sir Topas! 95

Clown

Maintain no words with him, good fellow. – Who, I, sir? Not I, sir. God buy you, good Sir Topas. – Marry, amen. – I will, sir, I will.

Malvolio

Fool, fool, fool, I say!

Clown

Alas, sir, be patient. What say you, sir? I am shent for 100 speaking to you.

Malvolio

Good fool, help me to some light and some paper. I tell thee I am as well in my wits as any man in Illyria.

Clown

Well-a-day that you were, sir! 105

Malvolio

By this hand, I am. Good fool, some ink, paper, and light; and convey what I will set down to my lady. It shall advantage thee more than ever the bearing of letter did.

Clown

I will help you to't. But tell me true, are you not mad 110 indeed, or do you but counterfeit?

Malvolio

Believe me, I am not; I tell thee true.

Clown

Nay, I'll ne'er believe a madman till I see his brains. I will fetch you light and paper and ink.

Malvolio

Fool, I'll requite it in the highest degree; I prithee 115

117. Feste's song refers to the old morality plays, in which 'Vice' – probably the prototype of the professional jester, and similarly portrayed – would, as part of his routine, leap upon the Devil and beat him with a wooden (*of lath*) dagger till he cried out. He would also make a show of cutting the Devil's nails with the dagger (*Pare thy nails*).

128. *goodman*. This word, followed by the name of a person's occupation, served as a term of address.

SCENE III

The fresh air and sunshine, which tally so exactly with Sebastian's hopefulness, are in strong contrast with Malvolio's darkness and frustration. What dramatic purpose is served by this? Is it solely for our benefit, to cheer us up after the questionable goings-on in the last scene?

1–2. By using his senses, Sebastian seeks to convince himself that he is not just imagining his present good fortune. (Is this intended as a further contrast? – Malvolio was almost brow-beaten into giving up all trust in *his* senses.)

6. *there he was:* 'he had been there.' *credit:* general opinion.

8. *counsel:* advice. *golden service:* 'service so valuable as to deserve generous (golden) reward.' As he goes on to say, Sebastian needs Antonio's clear-headedness to help him out of his confusion.

9–21. The argument here is involved – which is not inappropriate, since Sebastian is extremely confused by what is happening to him, and not likely to express himself over-simply.

9–10. *soul . . . sense.* The higher and the lower human faculties. *disputes well.* They are both in agreement, that Sebastian's present situation may be the result of a misunderstanding (*error*) but it does not mean that he has gone mad (*no madness*).

11. *accident:* that which has actually happened. *flood:* fulness, 'the wonderful way things have turned out.'

12. *instance:* example, precedent. *discourse:* reasoning, 'normal experience, both outward and inward.' This seems to take us back to *soul* and *sense* in line 9, and is repeated by *eyes* and *reason* in lines 13 and 14.

be gone.
Clown [Singing]

> I am gone, sir,
> And anon, sir,
> I'll be with you again,
> In a trice,
> Like to the old Vice,   120
> Your need to sustain;
> Who with dagger of lath,
> In his rage and his wrath,
> Cries, Ah, ha! to the devil,
> Like a mad lad,   125
> Pare thy nails, dad.
> Adieu, goodman devil.

[Exit]

SCENE III

Olivia's garden

[Enter SEBASTIAN]

Sebastian
> This is the air; that is the glorious sun;
> This pearl she gave me, I do feel't and see't;
> And though 'tis wonder that enwraps me thus,
> Yet 'tis not madness. Where's Antonio, then?
> I could not find him at the Elephant;
> Yet there he was; and there I found this credit,   5
> That he did range the town to seek me out.
> His counsel now might do me golden service;
> For though my soul disputes well with my sense
> That this may be some error, but no madness,
> Yet doth this accident and flood of fortune   10
> So far exceed all instance, all discourse,

14–16. *persuades me . . . the lady's mad:* 'persuades me that neither I nor the lady is mad.' (Literally, 'persuades me to believe anything else except that I and the lady are mad.') In other words, what is happening is so 'out of this world' that Sebastian is inclined to distrust his common-sense when it tells him that this is probably just a case of misunderstanding.

16–19. But the alternative is not satisfactory either, for Sebastian cannot wholly believe that Olivia *is* mad, because of the obviously sane way she manages her household.

17. *sway her house:* 'run her house' is how we would put it today.

18. 'Handle business matters, making sure things are properly carried out.'

21. *deceivable:* 'not what it seems.'

22. *Blame not this haste of mine.* It seems to be Olivia's fate to be landed in situations where, for all her would-be dignity and poise, she finds herself doing all the wrong things. It is not surprising that she feels she must apologize for acting with such indecent haste, and producing a priest so precipitately to officiate at their betrothal.

24. *chantry:* a small private chapel, with a priest permanently resident. (People of means often endowed a chantry and priest, so that Mass could be said regularly on their behalf.) *by:* nearby.

26. *Plight:* pledge, solemnly promise. *of your faith:* 'that you will be faithful.'

27–8. *That my most jealous and too doubtful soul May live at peace.* Olivia's jealousy and uncertainty would make her suspicious and anxious, but once he is 'secured' by betrothal she can relax. Though not complete wedlock, betrothal was solemnly binding, much more so than our modern 'engagement'.

28. *He:* the priest.

29. *Whiles:* until ('While'='until' in North of England conversation still.) *come to note:* be made public.

30. *What time:* At which time.

31. *According to my birth:* 'As befits my social status.'

34. *father:* a traditional term of address for a priest.

35. *fairly note:* 'look favourably upon.'

That I am ready to distrust mine eyes
And wrangle with my reason, that persuades me
To any other trust but that I am mad,   15
Or else the lady's mad; yet if 'twere so,
She could not sway her house, command her
    followers,
Take and give back affairs and their dispatch
With such a smooth, discreet, and stable bearing,
As I perceive she does. There's something in't   20
That is deceivable. But here the lady comes.

[Enter OLIVIA and PRIEST]

Olivia
Blame not this haste of mine. If you mean well,
Now go with me and with this holy man
Into the chantry by; there, before him
And underneath that consecrated roof,   25
Plight me the full assurance of your faith,
That my most jealous and too doubtful soul
May live at peace. He shall conceal it
Whiles you are willing it shall come to note,
What time we will our celebration keep   30
According to my birth. What do you say?
Sebastian
I'll follow this good man, and go with you;
And, having sworn truth, ever will be true.
Olivia
Then lead the way, good father; and heavens so
    shine
That they may fairly note this act of mine!   35

[Exeunt]

ACT FIVE SCENE I

The resolving of all the confusions that have been building up since the play began – *Twelfth Night* has more than most – is the inevitable business of this final act. Traditionally, this must take place in the presence of someone of highest rank (in this case the Duke Orsino). He alone will be in a position to administer whatever is required of justice and reconciliation, and to guarantee permanence and stability. Orsino has this further reason to be present at the dénouement, since he is as closely implicated in the confusion as anyone else. Apart from some initial clowning, the whole of the action serves this end – to gather together the whole company, introducing, explaining and reconciling. Malvolio alone stands outside the final happy reunion (from choice, however) though Sir Toby's and Sir Andrew's leave-taking is under almost as heavy a cloud.

1. *as:* if. *his letter.* i.e. the one Malvolio has written, from 'prison'.

3. *anything:* 'Whatever you ask.'

5–6. *desire my dog again:* i.e. want to have it back.

8. *trappings:* literally, 'trivial ornaments.' (Why does Feste so describe himself and Fabian?)

9. *I know thee well.* When did Orsino and Feste first meet?

10. *for:* because of.

ACT FIVE
SCENE I

Before olivia's house

[Enter CLOWN and FABIAN]

Fabian
Now, as thou lov'st me, let me see his letter.

Clown
Good Master Fabian, grant me another request.

Fabian
Anything.

Clown
Do not desire to see this letter.

Fabian
This is to give a dog, and in recompense desire my   5
dog again.

[Enter DUKE, VIOLA, CURIO and LORDS]

Duke
Belong you to the Lady Olivia, friends?

Clown
Ay, sir, we are some of her trappings.

Duke
I know thee well. How dost thou, my good fellow?

Clown
Truly, sir, the better for my foes and the worse for my   10
friends.

Duke
Just the contrary: the better for thy friends.

Clown
No, sir, the worse.

Duke
How can that be?

18. *abused:* deceived.
19. *your . . . your:* 'the ones we are talking about.'

26–7. A neat pun – *double-dealing* normally means 'acting dishonestly', but here Feste also uses it to mean 'making the gift twice as large.'

29. *grace* (God's special help) is a theological antithesis to *flesh and blood* (man's natural, unrefined instincts). Since Orsino has described Feste's argument (about what he should give him) as *ill counsel*, and therefore not to be listened to, Feste, in order to win his point, has to urge him to ignore conscience (*Put your grace in your pocket*) and obey his natural instincts – and Feste's request at the same time! This is all purely in fun; neither of them is taking any of it seriously.

33–6. Quick as ever, Feste calls to mind four separate examples of 'threes', to cajole Orsino into adding yet another coin to the two already given. (When he first met Viola, Feste followed the same tactics. How much did he scrounge from her?)

33. *Primo, secundo, tertio:* First, second, third. Probably refers to a contemporary schoolboys' game. *play:* 'throw', probably, rather than 'game'.

35. *Saint Bennet:* a well-known church (probably one that used to stand near the Globe Theatre, and was destroyed in the Great Fire of London), and with an obviously familiar triple chime.

37. *throw:* (literally 'throw of the dice'), attempt.

39–40. *awake my bounty.* Orsino's metaphor here is almost unconscious – it simply adds a certain graciousness to his half-promise.

Clown

Marry, sir, they praise me and make an ass of me. Now 15
my foes tell me plainly I am an ass; so that by my
foes, sir, I profit in the knowledge of myself, and by
my friends I am abused; so that, conclusions to be as
kisses, if your four negatives make your two affirma-
tives, why then, the worse for my friends, and the 20
better for my foes.

Duke

Why, this is excellent.

Clown

By my troth, sir, no; though it please you to be one
of my friends.

Duke

Thou shalt not be the worse for me. There's gold. 25

Clown

But that it would be double-dealing, sir, I would you
could make it another.

Duke

O, you give me ill counsel.

Clown

Put your grace in your pocket, sir, for this once, and
let your flesh and blood obey it. 30

Duke

Well, I will be so much a sinner to be a double-dealer.
There's another.

Clown

Primo, secundo, tertio, is a good play; and the old
saying is 'The third pays for all'. The triplex, sir, is a
good tripping measure; or the bells of Saint Bennet, 35
sir, may put you in mind – one, two, three.

Duke

You can fool no more money out of me at this throw;
if you will let your lady know I am here to speak with
her, and bring her along with you, it may awake my
bounty further. 40

41-5. But Feste's reply is perhaps his best demonstration of quick-thinking in the whole play. He won't let it be just a conventional turn of speech, but at once develops the idea of sleep and waking, to serve as a slight but ingenious reminder that he hopes for Orsino's undivided generosity. For if the Duke's bounty will need to be awakened, this implies that it will have gone to sleep – which will suit Feste admirably, since he doesn't want it to be exercised in any other direction but his own! So *lullaby to your bounty* he says, 'keep a tight hold on your money – till I come back!' (*I will awake it anon*).

46. Serious things now take over, with the arrival, under escort, of Antonio, to answer his charge before the Duke. The dialogue, then, is continued in verse, which is sustained until, as a timely relaxation, Sir Andrew appears with news of less dignified happenings. Antonio's affairs, interesting enough in themselves, have always subserved dramatically the fortunes of first, Sebastian, and now, Viola. To extract the full flavour from Viola's plight – a necessary prelude to the happy ending – there must be an intensifying of her ordeal, a 'piling-up', as never before, of undeserved suffering. (Many heroines are seen on the very brink of disaster and disgrace before their final rescue!) So she must once again bear the brunt of Antonio's scorn, and then (a worse ordeal, we may imagine) the hatred of her dearly loved Orsino, the cause in each case being the unfaithfulness they so wrongly suspect. To this we can add the bewilderment she suffers when Olivia insists that she had already become her husband, and when Sir Toby and Sir Andrew insist that it is she who has just assaulted them. But if Viola is to be reinstated with the full acclaim of the whole company – and this is the chief point now – she must submit to this public scrutiny.

Notice how Viola's greeting of Antonio's appearance brings out her innate warm-heartedness. She recalls his kindness only – nothing of his fierce incriminations.

47-72. But now, for a while, all thought is for Antonio for his own sake. Courtly matters recede, and the man's world of battle and violence takes over.

49. *Vulcan:* the Roman god of fire.

50. *baubling:* trifling, insignificant.

51. *unprizable:* of no value.

52. *scathful:* harmful. *grapple:* joining in battle.

53. *bottom:* ship. (The figure of speech used here – a part of something when the whole of it is meant – is called synecdoche. Ships are also referred to as 'sails', in the same way.) The fact that Antonio took on a much more powerful opponent emphasized his courage.

54. 'Even those who resented his victory and bewailed their losses.'

55. *What's the matter?* 'Come to the point.'

57. *Phoenix:* the ship's name. *fraught:* cargo. *Candy:* Candia, the old name for Crete.

Clown

Marry, sir, lullaby to your bounty till I come again. I go, sir; but I would not have you to think that my desire of having is the sin of covetousness. But, as you say, sir, let your bounty take a nap; I will awake it anon.   45

[Exit. Enter ANTONIO *and* OFFICERS*]*

Viola

Here comes the man, sir, that did rescue me.

Duke

That face of his I do remember well;
Yet when I saw it last it was besmear'd
As black as Vulcan in the smoke of war.
A baubling vessel was he captain of,   50
For shallow draught and bulk unprizable,
With which such scathful grapple did he make
With the most noble bottom of our fleet
That very envy and the tongue of loss
Cried fame and honour on him. What's the matter?   55

First Officer

Orsino, this is that Antonio
That took the Phoenix and her fraught from Candy;
And this is he that did the Tiger board
When your young nephew Titus lost his leg.

60. *desperate of shame and state.* An involved phrase, which loses much in prosaic rendering. The impression gained is of someone who has 'come down in the world' and has stopped caring what other people think – just the sort of person to fall foul of the authorities!

61. *brabble:* brawl. *apprehend:* arrest.

62. Ever generous, Viola intervenes on Antonio's behalf, pointing out he took her part in the 'duel' (*drew on my side*) and attributing even his highly offensive charges against her to some temporary mental aberration (*distraction*).

65. *Notable:* Well-known, notorious.

66–8. Which concerns Orsino most, Antonio's piracy and his disorderly conduct, or his foolhardiness in putting himself right into his enemies' hands?

67. *dear:* dire.

69. *Be pleas'd that I . . .:* 'Please let me . . .'

71. *on base and ground enough:* 'with good enough reason.' Having cleared up this point of honour, Antonio goes on to voice his indignation against Viola. (It is clear that his sense of betrayal still dominates all other feelings.)

72. *A witchcraft.* In Antonio's mind, the whole episode, from his rescue of Sebastian, to this present bitter experience, must have been brought about by some evil power working against him – otherwise how could his own single-minded generosity have provoked such an inhuman reaction in the one he has befriended?

75. *redeem.* The word implies rescue of someone from a situation from which he could not have saved himself – in this case, certain death from drowning.

77. *retention:* holding back. (Almost the same as *restraint*).

78. *All his in dedication:* 'Entirely out of devotion to him.'

79. *pure:* purely. *of:* because of. *his love:* my love for him.

80. *adverse:* hostile.

81. *drew:* drew my sword.

84. *face me out of his acquaintance.* Malvolio accused Feste and the others of trying to 'face him out of his wits'. The meaning is the same here – when Viola protested (the audience, but not Antonio, know how sincerely) that she had no idea who he was, Antonio took it to be a particularly barefaced piece of deception.

85–6. A most effective expression. In a moment (*While one would wink*) Antonio felt he had become a complete stranger. This feeling of separation we tend to describe in spatial terms (e.g., 'miles apart') but Antonio's *twenty years removed* is perhaps more effective. *denied me:* 'refused to give me.'

87. *to:* for.

Here in the streets, desperate of shame and state,   60
In private brabble did we apprehend him.

Viola

He did me kindness, sir; drew on my side;
But in conclusion put strange speech upon me.
I know not what 'twas but distraction.

Duke

Notable pirate, thou salt-water thief!   65
What foolish boldness brought thee to their mercies
Whom thou, in terms so bloody and so dear,
Hast made thine enemies?

Antonio

                  Orsino, noble sir,
Be pleas'd that I shake off these names you give me:
Antonio never yet was thief or pirate,   70
Though I confess, on base and ground enough,
Orsino's enemy. A witchcraft drew me hither:
That most ingrateful boy there by your side
From the rude sea's enrag'd and foamy mouth
Did I redeem; a wreck past hope he was.   75
His life I gave him, and did thereto add
My love without retention or restraint,
All his in dedication; for his sake,
Did I expose myself, pure for his love,
Into the danger of this adverse town;   80
Drew to defend him when he was beset;
Where being apprehended, his false cunning,
Not meaning to partake with me in danger,
Taught him to face me out of his acquaintance,
And grew a twenty years removed thing   85
While one would wink; denied me mine own purse,
Which I had recommended to his use
Not half an hour before.

Viola

                 How can this be?

Duke

When came he to this town?

91. *No int'rim* (interim): 'without any break.' *not a minute's vacancy:* 'without the space of a minute (spent otherwise).'

93–6. These lines bring out very well Orsino's continuing passion for Olivia. She has only to make her appearance, and he turns away momentarily from everything else, as if it had never existed. It is only on second thoughts that he even recollects what Antonio has just been saying. He needs that split-second (between *fellow* and *fellow*) before he can re-apply his attention and see how impossible Antonio's story is.

97–8. *What would my lord . . . seem serviceable?* is no more than a polite way of saying: 'What can I do for you?' *but that he may not have:* 'except that which he cannot have' – meaning, of course, her love. Her earlier refusal to respond to his suit is now, she believes, strengthened beyond all question, by her newly contracted betrothal to somebody else.
99. What was the arrangement, in fact, with Sebastian – about which Viola can, of course, know nothing?

103. Viola's courtesy towards the Duke is impeccable. She won't answer Olivia simply because Orsino is waiting to say something. *My duty* (of deference towards my master) *hushes me:* keeps me quiet.
104. *aught to the old tune:* 'anything like your usual remarks.'
105. *fat and fulsome.* A fine alliterative phrase, both physical and figurative. This is exactly how Olivia feels now about the Duke's over-eloquent addresses.
106. *howling after music.* (Does she have in mind the way music sets some dogs howling?) Courtship from anyone – not just Orsino – will grate on her ears after Sebastian's promises of life-long fidelity.
107–8. *constant . . . to perverseness:* implies that Olivia has been consistent (*constant*) only in her stubbornness (*perverseness*). *uncivil:* discourteous. Olivia is being unnecessarily brutal just now.

109. *ingrate:* ungrateful. *unauspicious:* not responding favourably.

Antonio

To-day, my lord; and for three months before, 90
No int'rim, not a minute's vacancy,
Both day and night did we keep company.

[Enter OLIVIA and ATTENDANTS]

Duke

Here comes the Countess; now heaven walks on
  earth.
But for thee, fellow – fellow, thy words are
  madness.
Three months this youth hath tended upon me— 95
But more of that anon. Take him aside.

Olivia

What would my lord, but that he may not have,
Wherein Olivia may seem serviceable?
Cesario, you do not keep promise with me.

Viola

Madam? 100

Duke

Gracious Olivia—

Olivia

What do you say, Cesario? Good my lord—

Viola

My lord would speak; my duty hushes me.

Olivia

If it be aught to the old tune, my lord,
It is as fat and fulsome to mine ear 105
As howling after music.

Duke

                        Still so cruel?

Olivia

Still so constant, lord.

Duke

What, to perverseness? You uncivil lady,
To whose ingrate and unauspicious altars
My soul the faithfull'st off'rings hath breath'd out 110
That e'er devotion tender'd! What shall I do?

203

112. How should Olivia say this line? *become:* suit.

113–27. Orsino is so beside himself that he even speaks of murder. Rejecting this (he has not the *heart to do it*), he directs his anger instead against Viola. He has no doubt now where Olivia's affections lie, and hints at ruthless counter-measures.

114. *Egyptian thief:* a robber chief, Thyamis, who, when threatened with capture and probable death himself, attempted to kill one of his captives with whom he had fallen in love, so that they might be re-united in the next life. This was a popular story in Shakespeare's time.

116. *savours nobly:* 'has something noble about it.' *hear me this:* hear this from me.

117. *non-regardance:* literally 'the act of not regarding'. To 'regard' someone meant to have a certain opinion about him; and so 'non-regardance' (no opinion at all) implies that someone or something is insignificant. *faith:* good faith, sincerity (rather than faithfulness). Orsino will naturally resent Olivia's failure to appreciate his sincere offers of love.

118. *instrument.* Whom does he mean?

119. *screws.* What does his description of his 'rival's' success with Olivia gain by his use of this word? *my true place.* What does this tell us about Orsino?

120. *Live you* is an imperative. He tells her to go on (*still*) being hard-hearted (*the marble-breasted tyrant*) if she is so indifferent to his own affection.

121. *minion:* a scornful term applying to any servile dependant; and most apt if in fact 'Cesario', a mere page, had become Olivia's lover.

122. *tender:* regard.

123–4. A loved-one was often spoken of as being 'in the eye of' the lover, as if the lover's eyes gaze so fondly that the other's image becomes permanently fixed there. *in his master's spite:* in spite of his master.

125. *ripe in:* ready for.

127. Olivia's heart is black (like the *raven*) in contrast with her appearance of innocence (*dove*).

128–9. In spite of his threat to use her cruelly, simply to get his own back on Olivia, Viola has nothing but love and loyalty for her master. *jocund:* joyful. *apt:* ready. (Notice the use of the adverb *willingly* after the two adjectives.) *To do:* to cause, give. Orsino's *rest* is contrasted with the *thousand deaths* Viola is willing to die to bring it about.

130. This is Viola's first public affirmation of love for Orsino. But notice how it has come about. Unlike his own carefully thought-out words and occasions, this has come out suddenly, under the pressure of circumstances, with all the more spontaneity, probably, for that reason. (In the same way, Olivia suddenly found herself speaking openly about *her* love for Viola.) And even now, she is ostensibly expressing a young man's affectionate loyalty to his master. This is a most subtle moment – she may not yet be allowing even herself to think of her love for Orsino in any other way. For she is still committed (permanently, she must believe) to this 'sex-less' rôle, and so her attachment to the Duke may still (even in her own consciousness) be limited and 'de-fused'.

Olivia
    Even what it please my lord, that shall become him.
Duke
    Why should I not, had I the heart to do it,
    Like to the Egyptian thief at point of death,
    Kill what I love? – a savage jealousy   115
    That sometime savours nobly. But hear me this:
    Since you to non-regardance cast my faith,
    And that I partly know the instrument
    That screws me from my true place in your favour,
    Live you the marble-breasted tyrant still;   120
    But this your minion, whom I know you love,
    And whom, by heaven I swear, I tender dearly,
    Him will I tear out of that cruel eye
    Where he sits crowned in his master's spite.
    Come, boy, with me; my thoughts are ripe in
        mischief: 125
    I'll sacrifice the lamb that I do love
    To spite a raven's heart within a dove.
Viola
    And I, most jocund, apt, and willingly,
    To do you rest, a thousand deaths would die.
Olivia
    Where goes Cesario?
Viola
                After him I love   130

133. *witnesses above:* Either 'the stars,' or, more Christianly, 'God and His angels'. The sense is the same – such a gross act of duplicity would simply cry out for divine retribution.
134. *Punish . . .:* 'May you punish . . .' *tainting.* True love can be shared with one other person only; otherwise it gets spoiled.
135. *beguil'd:* deceived.

137. *Hast thou forgot thyself?* To 'forget oneself' normally means to behave without proper restraint. But here it implies an almost literal forgetfulness of one's very identity. *Is it so long?* Olivia knows exactly when the betrothal took place. The point she is making is that it must be a lot longer ago, if Viola has already forgotten all about it.

138. *Come, away!* This is said to Viola.

139. But Olivia cannot just stand by, silent, and acquiesce in her 'husband's' dismissal. Her actual use of the word brings things at once to a head.

142. *the baseness of thy fear.* Olivia implies that 'his' present fear is not worthy of him. But it is a momentary failing she speaks of and not the fatal weakness of character such a phrase would normally signify.
143. *propriety:* identity. to *strangle* this, through fear, means to be too diffident to assert oneself.
144. *fortunes.* The enhanced status of being married to a Countess seems to be Olivia's meaning in this and the next line.
146. 'Your present greatness will match your previous fear.'

149. *what:* that which.
150. *ripe:* ready. (Olivia refers to their previous plan to keep the betrothal secret till there was a suitable opportunity for the full marriage rite.)

More than I love these eyes, more than my life,
More, by all mores, than e'er I shall love wife.
If I do feign, you witnesses above
Punish my life for tainting of my love!

Olivia
Ay me, detested! How am I beguil'd!   135

Viola
Who does beguile you? Who does do you wrong?

Olivia
Hast thou forgot thyself? Is it so long?
Call forth the holy father.

[Exit an ATTENDANT*]*

Duke
                Come, away!

Olivia
Whither, my lord? Cesario, husband, stay.

Duke
Husband?

Olivia
          Ay, husband; can he that deny?   140

Duke
Her husband, sirrah?

Viola
             No, my lord, not I.

Olivia
Alas, it is the baseness of thy fear
That makes thee strangle thy propriety.
Fear not, Cesario, take thy fortunes up;
Be that thou know'st thou art, and then thou art   145
As great as that thou fear'st.

[Enter PRIEST*]*

                O, welcome, father!
Father, I charge thee, by thy reverence,
Here to unfold – though lately we intended
To keep in darkness what occasion now
Reveals before 'tis ripe – what thou dost know   150
Hath newly pass'd between this youth and me.

152–7. The priest 'spells out' in order the various parts of the betrothal rite.

153. *joinder:* joining.

154. *Attested:* Certified. *close:* union.

157. *Seal'd in my function:* 'duly completed by me in my capacity as priest.' *by my testimony.* Simply to be witness of the betrothal was no small part of the priest's rôle.

158–9. Very characteristically, the priest thinks in this way of the passage of time.

160–5. Orsino's scathing attack upon Viola would be amply justified if what Olivia and the priest have just said, were true – and there is no reason for him to think otherwise.

161. *grizzle:* sprinkling of grey. *case:* body (that which encloses or 'encases' the soul), or skin (which encloses the body).

163. *trip:* false step. Orsino means that Viola's double-dealing will be her own undoing, so that she won't live long enough to have any grey hairs.

164–5. His final scornful dismissal is probably Viola's most painful experience.

166–7. Olivia seems to mean that Viola should not rely upon oaths but upon what *little faith* she has in the midst of all her *fear*.

168. Sir Andrew's entrance, dramatically most opportune, postpones the solving of the puzzle, until full and final capital can be made out of Viola's mistaken identity, with Sir Toby and his cronies, and with Antonio and Sebastian. So Orsino's tirade, and Viola's and Olivia's protests, are 'frozen' – they must live with their torturing uncertainties for a little longer.

169. *presently:* at once.

172. *coxcomb.* Normally, this means the jester's cap, designed to resemble a cock's 'comb'. Here it is used facetiously for 'head'.

176. *incardinate.* Sir Andrew thinks he is saying 'incarnate' (='in human form').

Priest
>A contract of eternal bond of love,
>Confirm'd by mutual joinder of your hands,
>Attested by the holy close of lips,
>Strengthen'd by interchangement of your rings   155
>And all the ceremony of this compact
>Seal'd in my function, by my testimony;
>Since when, my watch hath told me, toward my
>   grave,
>I have travell'd but two hours.

Duke
>O thou dissembling cub! What wilt thou be,   160
>When time hath sow'd a grizzle on thy case?
>Or will not else thy craft so quickly grow
>That thine own trip shall be thine overthrow?
>Farewell, and take her; but direct thy feet
>Where thou and I henceforth may never meet.   165

Viola
>My lord, I do protest—

Olivia
>   O, do not swear!
>Hold little faith, though thou hast too much fear.

[Enter SIR ANDREW]

Sir Andrew
>For the love of God, a surgeon!
>Send one presently to Sir Toby.

Olivia
>What's the matter?   170

Sir Andrew
>Has broke my head across, and has given Sir Toby a
>bloody coxcomb too. For the love of God, your help!
>I had rather than forty pound I were at home.

Olivia
>Who has done this, Sir Andrew?

Sir Andrew
>The Count's gentleman, one Cesario. We took him for 175
>a coward, but he's the very devil incardinate.

209

178. *Od's lifelings.* This is one of the many oaths we have noted, where the name of God is 'disguised' in reverence. The suffix '-ling' has a diminutive force.

178–9. *for nothing:* 'for no good reason, without provocation.'

179–80. *that that I did, I was set on to do't by Sir Toby.* Even if there has been something provocative in his behaviour, it was Sir Toby's idea, not his own.

181–3. Viola is naturally baffled by this – she knows about the first part of their encounter but nothing of its violent conclusion. *bespake you fair:* 'answered you quite reasonably.'

184–8. Sir Andrew's reaction to this is very amusing. We must imagine his aggrieved tone, and, no doubt, some rueful handling of his sore head. *set nothing by:* 'don't take seriously.' *tickl'd:* beaten. *othergates:* otherwise.

190. Sir Toby is never over-deferential. He seems to have gained for himself that degree of licence so often accorded to people of his kind. He is so put out now that he brushes aside Orsino's enquiry almost rudely. *That's all one:* 'What does it matter?' *there's th'end on't:* 'That's all there is to it.' How well the contrast between him and Sir Andrew is brought out in their respective comments about their injuries! Sir Andrew almost whines in protest, whereas Sir Toby shows his annoyance by 'biting everyone's head off'. It is rather sad that this is the point at which he takes his leave. There has been a likeable side to him, and he has done as much as anyone in the play to stimulate humour. But it is not easy to remember this now, as he blusters out, insulting his friends and spurning the help that is offered. (Is it perhaps that Shakespeare wishes us never to make the fatal error – he would regard it as such – of giving our final approval to such a rogue?)

191. *Sot:* fool. *Dick Surgeon.* This seems a deliberately unceremonious way of addressing him.

192. *agone:* ago.

193. *set:* fixed (in a drunken stare).

194. *passy measures pavin:* A corruption of the Italian 'passamezzo pavana'. The pavan was a stately dance; Sir Toby prefers the livelier measures.

195. Does he realize that this description of the Surgeon applies better to himself?

198–9. The moment of 'disenchantment' does not yet seem to have arrived for Sir Andrew. His offer is in all sincerity, *be dress'd:* 'have our wounds dressed.'

200–1. This is ingratitude and callousness at their worst. All these things are true about Sir Andrew; but why should Sir Toby face him

Duke

My gentleman, Cesario?

Sir Andrew

Od's lifelings, here he is! You broke my head for
nothing; and that that I did, I was set on to do't by
Sir Toby.   180

Viola

Why do you speak to me? I never hurt you.
You drew your sword upon me without cause;
But I bespake you fair and hurt you not.

[Enter SIR TOBY and CLOWN]

Sir Andrew

If a bloody coxcomb be a hurt, you have hurt me; I
think you set nothing by a bloody coxcomb. Here 185
comes Sir Toby halting; you shall hear more; but if he
had not been in drink, he would have tickl'd you
othergates than he did.

Duke

How now, gentleman? How isn't with you?

Sir Toby

That's all one; has hurt me, and there's th' end on't. 190
Sot, didst see Dick Surgeon, sot?

Clown

O, he's drunk, Sir Toby, an hour agone; his eyes were
set at eight i' th' morning.

Sir Toby

Then he's a rogue and a passy measures pavin. I hate
a drunken rogue.   195

Olivia

Away with him. Who hath made this havoc with
them?

Sir Andrew

I'll help you, Sir Toby, because we'll be dress'd
together.

Sir Toby

Will you help – an ass-head and a coxcomb and a 200

211

with them now? After all, they have provided Sir Toby with his entertainment, and he has, all through the play, carefully nurtured them for this very purpose. Is 'gull' left to the end because Sir Toby despises it most?

203. Sebastian's appearance now, like Sir Andrew's a little earlier, has the effect of switching our attention forward once again. The central reconciliation, which, apart from Malvolio and his fortunes, will bring everything else into line and harmony, can be delayed no longer. Now at last, Viola and her brother come face to face – the first time since their separation in the wreck. Note the continuity: the last thing in everyone's mind has been the unexplained assault upon Sir Toby and Sir Andrew. So Sebastian's first comment is about this; this minor point is to be cleared up first. It is followed by his reconciliation with Antonio; then, keeping, as it were, the best till last, the joyful recognition between brother and sister with a happy ending for both.

205. *with wit and safety:* 'if I were to take sensible steps for my own safety.' (He was after all acting in self-defence.)

206. Why in fact did Olivia look 'strangely' (distantly) at him?

208. *for:* for the sake of.

209. *so late ago:* 'such a little while ago.'

210. *habit:* dress. (Why did these have to be the same?)

211. *perspective:* an optical instrument which produced a stereoscopic effect. When two pictures were looked at through it, they appeared as one. Orsino describes the sudden appearance together of the twins as a *natural perspective* because its effect is equally fantastic but without artificial aid. *is and is not.* What they see is actually there, and yet it seems an impossibility.

215. *Fear'st thou that . . . ?* From this question, we can deduce that Antonio's first reaction is (quite understandably) to recoil, as one does when confronted by what seems a supernatural event.

216–18. A most effective description of identical twinship.

220. *Do I stand there?* Sebastian only now catches sight of his sister.

221–2. *deity . . . here and everywhere.* One of the divine attributes is generally held to be 'omnipresence' – being in all places at the same time.

224. *Of charity:* 'Out of the goodness of your heart, tell me . . .' Still unsure of what all this means, Sebastian expresses his unconscious need of kindly treatment.

225. *What countryman:* 'What country are you from?'

knave, a thin fac'd knave, a gull?

Olivia

Get him to bed, and let his hurt be look'd to.

[Exeunt CLOWN, FABIAN, SIR TOBY, and SIR ANDREW,
Enter SEBASTIAN]

Sebastian

I am sorry, madam, I have hurt your kinsman;
But, had it been the brother of my blood,
I must have done no less with wit and safety.   205
You throw a strange regard upon me, and by that
I do perceive it hath offended you.
Pardon me, sweet one, even for the vows
We made each other but so late ago.

Duke

One face, one voice, one habit, and two persons!   210
A natural perspective, that is and is not.

Sebastian

Antonio, O my dear Antonio!
How have the hours rack'd and tortur'd me
Since I have lost thee!

Antonio

Sebastian are you?

Sebastian

              Fear'st thou that, Antonio?   215

Antonio

How have you made division of yourself?
An apple cleft in two is not more twin
Than these two creatures. Which is Sebastian?

Olivia

Most wonderful!

Sebastian

Do I stand there? I never had a brother;   220
Nor can there be that deity in my nature
Of here and everywhere. I had a sister
Whom the blind waves and surges have devour'd.
Of charity, what kin are you to me?
What countryman, what name, what parentage?   225

227. *Such a Sebastian* Like the one standing in front of her.

228. *So . . . suited:* 'dressed like you.'

229–30. Viola still finds it hard to believe that spirits *can* appear in this way – actually wearing the clothes of a once-living person. Her chief reaction to it is to fear the worst. *A spirit I am indeed.* He reassures her, that he *is* a spirit, but a body also – like every other human being.

231. *in that dimension grossly clad. Grossly* because the body was thought of as 'gross' or heavy, dull and base, by comparison with the spirit.

233. *Were you . . .*; 'If you were . . .'; *as the rest goes even:* 'as the rest of the evidence seems to agree.'

236–42. The next bit of dialogue, with its incomplete lines, catches their mood of excitement and near-certainty.

240. *lively:* fresh. (The day of his father's death is still very vivid in Sebastian's memory.)

241. *finished . . . his mortal act:* died.

243. *lets:* hinders, prevents. 'If nothing stands in the way of our happiness.'

244. *But:* except. *usurp'd.* Male attire is not properly hers.

246. *jump:* agree. (What further confirmation can Viola have in mind, apart from allowing her brother to see her in familiar female dress?)

249. *weeds:* clothing.

251. 'All that has happened to me.'

253. *So comes it . . .:* 'So it comes about (that) . . .

Viola

    Of Messaline; Sebastian was my father.
    Such a Sebastian was my brother too;
    So went he suited to his watery tomb;
    If spirits can assume both form and suit,
    You come to fright us.

Sebastian

                 A spirit I am indeed,   230
    But am in that dimension grossly clad
    Which from the womb I did participate.
    Were you a woman, as the rest goes even,
    I should my tears let fall upon your cheek,
    And say 'Thrice welcome, drowned Viola!'   235

Viola

    My father had a mole upon his brow.

Sebastian

    And so had mine.

Viola

    And died that day when Viola from her birth
    Had number'd thirteen years.

Sebastian

    O, that record is lively in my soul!   240
    He finished indeed his mortal act
    That day that made my sister thirteen years.

Viola

    If nothing lets to make us happy both
    But this my masculine usurp'd attire,
    Do not embrace me till each circumstance   245
    Of place, time, fortune, do cohere and jump
    That I am Viola; which to confirm,
    I'll bring you to a captain in this town,
    Where lie my maiden weeds; by whose gentle help
    I was preserv'd to serve this noble Count.   250
    All the occurrence of my fortune since
    Hath been between this lady and this lord.

Sebastian [To OLIVIA]

    So comes it, lady, you have been mistook;
    But nature to her bias drew in that.

254–7. Nature, by providing identical twins, male and female, has 'come to the rescue,' and what would have been a disaster has turned out perfectly. Her wooing of the wrong person will have served as a perfectly adequate prelude to her mature love for the right person!

259–60. After his reassurance to the still bewildered Olivia, the Duke says these lines more to himself than anyone else. *glass:* a reference back to *perspective* (line 211).

260. *share in this most happy wreck.* The *wreck* is indeed producing happiness at last – for Sebastian and Olivia. It may surprise us that Orsino can already see a happy outcome for himself, too. (His rapid detachment from Olivia, and attachment to Viola, is one of the less credible parts of the play. We are, however, somewhat prepared for this: Orsino has always been presented to us as one whose emotions are less deeply involved than he himself claims or believes.)

262. From this, we might infer that Viola's impact upon him has been considerably greater than even he at the time recognized. He has no difficulty in calling her words to mind.

263. Now, for the first time, Viola can voice her feelings for him in full womanly affection, *overswear:* swear with even greater solemnity and insistence.

264. *as true in soul:* 'as wholeheartedly.'

265. *orbed continent:* the sun.

269. *upon some action:* because of some legal action. (This is the first time we hear of it. What purpose is served in the play by this? Is it simply a link-up with Malvolio, to bring him again into the picture?)

270. *in durance:* in custody. *at Malvolio's suit:* at Malvolio's instigation (in the sense probably that Malvolio took legal action against him).

272. *enlarge:* set free. (Compare 'at large'.)

273. *now I remember me:* 'now I come to think of it.' (Malvolio's fortunes have been crowded right out of her mind, till this moment.)

274. *distract:* distracted. (As we have noticed before, she still has a good deal of feeling left for her steward, even if it is now only pity.)

275. *extracting:* drawing away (my thoughts) from everything else. (It seems to take up the idea of *distract*.)

276. *his:* his frenzy. (Lines 275–6 could well be an 'aside'.) The arrival of Feste, and Fabian, and the letter, focuses attention still further upon Malvolio.

278. *Belzebub:* the Devil's chief assistant, or, perhaps, the Devil himself. *holds . . . at the stave's end:* 'barely keeps at bay.' (A staff or stave was useful in keeping one's enemies at a distance.) They still think of Malvolio – or pretend to – as being devil-possessed.

There remains now only the clearing up of Malvolio's troubles; everything else is potentially set to rights. The letter he has composed from his 'cell' therefore, re-opens his whole case. Otherwise, like Olivia, we too might have forgotten about him. The play virtually ends with Malvolio's final protest – himself against the whole assembled company – and their verdict upon him. The last words, however, are for the Duke to deliver, as the conventional ending. But these, by themselves, are not enough; the main plot needs to be rounded off a little more smoothly; and this in fact is what is seen to while Malvolio is being fetched.

You would have been contracted to a maid;   255
Nor are you therein, by my life, deceiv'd;
You are betroth'd both to a maid and man.

Duke

Be not amaz'd; right noble is his blood.
If this be so, as yet the glass seems true,
I shall have share in this most happy wreck.   260
[To VIOLA*]* Boy, thou hast said to me a thousand
        times
Thou never shouldst love woman like to me.

Viola

And all those sayings will I overswear;
And all those swearings keep as true in soul
As doth that orbed continent the fire   265
That severs day from night.

Duke

                                Give me thy hand;
And let me see thee in thy woman's weeds.

Viola

The captain that did bring me first on shore
Hath my maid's garments. He, upon some action,
Is now in durance, at Malvolio's suit,   270
A gentleman and follower of my lady's.

Olivia

He shall enlarge him. Fetch Malvolio hither;
And yet, alas, now I remember me,
They say, poor gentleman, he's much distract.

[Re-enter CLOWN, *with a letter, and* FABIAN*]*

A most extracting frenzy of mine own   275
From my remembrance clearly banish'd his.
How does he, sirrah?

Clown

Truly, madam, he holds Belzebub at the stave's end

280–1. *to-day morning:* this morning, *epistles* and *gospels* are the Church names for those parts of Holy Scripture read, one of each, in the Holy Communion Service or Mass, which customarily took place in the early morning. Feste is playing on the two usages of *epistle* (Malvolio's letter is an epistle) to provide his facetious excuse for delay. *it skills not:* 'it makes no difference.'

284. *delivers:* 'reads the words of.'

287. *I do but read madness.* Is there a hint here at something deeper – a wistful defence of jesting, which exists solely to imitate human foibles, so that the jester's madness is always in that sense our own?

288. *as it ought to be.* Madmen's words ought to be delivered madly. It is clear that Feste has begun to read in a really crazy way, perhaps shrieking.

289. *allow vox:* allow me to speak. (*vox* is the Latin for 'voice'.)

291–3. A further quibble on the same point – he must be mentally alert to be able to convey Malvolio's madness through his actual tone of voice and his gestures; *to read his right wits:* 'to reproduce his true state.'

292. *perpend:* consider.

294. *Read it you:* 'You read it.'

298. *benefit:* natural gift.

299–300. *semblance:* show. (Malvolio refers to the uncharacteristic dress and mannerisms he was tricked into adopting.)

301. *myself much right . . . you much shame.* He hopes that when the contents of the letter are divulged, that will clear him, and cause her some shame. (We might have expected 'and' rather than *or*.)

302. *I leave my duty a little unthought of:* 'I am somewhat neglecting my duty to you.' (He means his duty of due deference to his mistress – he should not speak so frankly to her.)

303. *out of:* out of a sense of.

as well as a man in his case may do. Has here writ a
letter to you; I should have given't you to-day morning, 280
but as a madman's epistles are no gospels, so it skills
not much when they are deliver'd.

Olivia

Open't, and read it.

Clown

Look then to be well edified when the fool delivers
the madman. *[Reads madly]* 'By the Lord, madam—' 285

Olivia

How now! Art thou mad?

Clown

No, madam, I do but read madness.
An your ladyship will have it as it ought to be, you
must allow vox.

Olivia

Prithee read i' thy right wits. 290

Clown

So I do, Madonna; but to read his right wits is to
read thus; therefore perpend, my Princess, and give
ear.

Olivia [To FABIAN]

Read it you, sirrah.

Fabian [Reads]

'By the Lord, madam, you wrong me, and the world 295
shall know it. Though you have put me into darkness
and given your drunken cousin rule over me, yet
have I the benefit of my sense as well as your ladyship. I have your own letter that induced me to the
semblance I put on, with the which I doubt not but 300
to do myself much right or you much shame. Think
of me as you please. I leave my duty a little unthought
of, and speak out of my injury.

THE MADLY-US'D MALVOLIO.'

Olivia

Did he write this?

306. *savours not much of:* 'doesn't sound like.' (Literally 'has no taste of.')

308–18. While Fabian is off-stage, Olivia and Orsino confirm their relationship. This is done briefly, almost perfunctorily. The excitement of the play is all in its tensions and 'impossible' situations – once these are resolved, the drama is virtually exhausted, and there is little to be gained by dwelling on the sequel.
308. *these things further thought on:* 'when you have thought more about these things.'
308–9. Olivia will be a sister in view of the union obviously impending between him and the sister of her own Sebastian.
310. *th' alliance:* i.e. of herself and Orsino, as 'brother and sister', which will come about when he and Viola are duly joined together. ***on't:*** of it.
311. *proper:* own. She makes this offer perhaps in Sebastian's name. As Viola's next of kin, he will have some obligation to make this provision for his sister's wedding.
312. *apt:* ready.
313. *quits:* sets free (from service as his page).
314. *mettle:* essential character.
318. Olivia and Viola can freely and happily embrace.

321–37. If anything, Malvolio's stature now is greater than before. There is a dignity, even if a stiff and cold one, and a certain integrity. He is, for better or worse, still himself – disillusioned in the matter of his hoped-for alliance with Olivia, but not broken by his humiliation. He feels his injuries keenly – he makes no secret about that – but he seeks no favours of anyone; his only request is that Olivia shall explain her conduct.
325. *Write from it:* 'Write differently.' ***in hand or phrase:*** in actual handwriting or style.

Clown
    Ay, Madam.   305
Duke
    This savours not much of distraction.
Olivia
    See him deliver'd, Fabian; bring him hither.

                [Exit FABIAN]

    My lord, so please you, these things further thought
        on,
    To think me as well a sister as a wife,
    One day shall crown th' alliance on't, so please you, 310
    Here at my house, and at my proper cost.
Duke
    Madam, I am most apt t'embrace your offer.
    [To VIOLA] Your master quits you; and, for your
        service done him,
    So much against the mettle of your sex,
    So far beneath your soft and tender breeding,   315
    And since you call'd me master for so long,
    Here is my hand; you shall from this time be
    Your master's mistress.
Olivia
                   A sister! You are she.

      [Re-enter FABIAN, with MALVOLIO]

Duke
    Is this the madman?
Olivia
               Ay, my lord, this same.
    How now, Malvolio!   320
Malvolio
    Madam, you have done me wrong,
    Notorious wrong.
Olivia
             Have I, Malvolio? No.
Malvolio
    Lady, you have. Pray you peruse that letter.
    You must not now deny it is your hand;
    Write from it if you can, in hand or phrase;   325

327. *Well, grant it then.* Olivia has not recovered herself sufficiently to contradict him, so he assumes that she admits authorship.

328. *modesty:* moderation, simple expression.

332. *the lighter people.* How would Sir Toby have reacted to this?

336. *geck:* fool.

339. *character:* handwriting.

342. *cam'st.* Malvolio is the subject of this verb, not Maria.

343–4. *pre-suppose'd Upon thee:* 'suggested before-hand, for you to adopt.' *Prithee, be content.* Olivia checks in advance a protest Malvolio is obviously about to make at this point.

345. *shrewdly:* cruelly. 'What they have done has turned out most cruelly for you.'

346. *grounds:* reason.

347. *plaintiff:* the injured party who pleads his cause in a court of law.

349. Fabian in a sense speaks for us all. They must not allow the happy atmosphere to be spoiled. To ensure this, he is quite prepared to accept his own share of the blame.

352. *wonder'd at:* 'found so wonderful.'

355. *upon:* because of. *parts:* characteristics.

356. *conceiv'd against him:* 'thought him guilty of.'

357. *importance:* importunity. (To 'importune' is persistently to urge or pester.)

359. *sportful:* playful, good-humoured. (This is intended to take the 'sting' out of *malice*.)

360. *pluck on:* induce.

Or say 'tis not your seal, not your invention;
You can say none of this. Well, grant it then,
And tell me, in the modesty of honour,
Why you have given me such clear lights of favour,
Bade me come smiling and cross-garter'd to you,   330
To put on yellow stockings, and to frown
Upon Sir Toby and the lighter people;
And, acting this in an obedient hope,
Why have you suffer'd me to be imprison'd,
Kept in a dark house, visited by the priest,   335
And made the most notorious geck and gull
That e'er invention play'd on? Tell me why.

Olivia

Alas, Malvolio, this is not my writing,
Though, I confess, much like the character;
But out of question 'tis Maria's hand.   340
And now I do bethink me, it was she
First told me thou wast mad; then cam'st in smiling,
And in such forms which here were pre-suppos'd
Upon thee in the letter. Prithee, be content;
This practice hath most shrewdly pass'd upon thee,   345
But, when we know the grounds and authors of it,
Thou shalt be both the plaintiff and the judge
Of thine own cause.

Fabian

    Good madam, hear me speak,
And let no quarrel nor no brawl to come   350
Taint the condition of this present hour,
Which I have wonder'd at. In hope it shall not,
Most freely I confess myself and Toby
Set this device against Malvolio here,
Upon some stubborn and uncourteous parts   355
We had conceiv'd against him. Maria writ
The letter, at Sir Toby's great importance,
In recompense whereof he hath married her.
How with a sportful malice it was follow'd
May rather pluck on laughter than revenge,   360

361–2. There have been faults on both sides, and Fabian asks that they be fairly weighed. Fabian has been given some very significant lines to deliver. He has to strike a sober note, and hint at a larger justice than has frequently been evident. What he says is some justification in effect of the whole play. He does it with dignity and a certain finality. He brings in a sanity which helps to offset Feste's unbridled sneers and Malvolio's savage reply.

363. *baffl'd:* brought to public ridicule.

364–70. Fabian has spoken fairly, Olivia pityingly, but Feste positively taunts his victim. In this he serves two purposes. There are, in every audience, those for whom a subtle revenge is not enough, and who insist that every possible advantage shall be taken of the 'villain' once he is down. Such are delighted when Feste throws Malvolio's earlier strictures (almost perfectly remembered) back in his face. They have been waiting for just such a moment, and would feel cheated without it. Feste's words also have their necessary part in the working out of the 'Humours' element, which presents us with stereotyped characters, and an equally fixed scale of punishment and reward. Created as such, Malvolio must, for his unmitigated self-love, receive and carry away with him the full weight of scorn and ridicule. But because *Twelfth Night* is only partly a 'Comedy of Humours', we are spared the spectacle, at the end, of wholesale condemnation of him. Instead, Feste's unholy glee, while catering for certain elements in the audience – perhaps in each one of us – is relieved by a more enlightened humaneness from other quarters. To hold these two distinctive concepts in balance is one of the play's greatest achievements.

365. *thrown*. The original letter said *thrust*.

366. *interlude:* a short play within the main one.

367. *that's all one*. Compare line 190.

370. *whirligig:* a spinning top. The idea is that just as any one point on a rotating object is bound to come round again to where it started, so, if one waits long enough, all wrong-doing will meet with its proper punishment. (It is the same as 'the wheel coming full circle', a fairly familiar image.) The clown's function, as we have noticed, was to stand back from events, from time to time, and comment shrewdly, even cynically, but always to good effect. This line of his makes some amends for the personal invective preceding it.

371. So Malvolio finally leaves us, indifferent to affection and offering none, neither giving nor seeking forgiveness.

372–3. But, in welcome contrast, both Olivia and Orsino are prepared to receive him back into the 'family circle'. ***notoriously abus'd:*** disgracefully ill-treated.

373. *entreat him to a peace:* 'try to persuade him to make friends.'

374. We hope this is not Orsino's only reason for wanting Malvolio calmed down!

375. *golden time*. An interesting and very Shakespearian phrase. 'The occasion that will crown all that has gone before with happy fulfilment.' ***convents:*** either, 'summons': or 'is convenient'.

    If that the injuries be justly weigh'd
    That have on both sides pass'd.

Olivia
    Alas, poor fool, how have they baffl'd thee!

Clown
    Why, 'Some are born great, some achieve greatness,
    and some have greatness thrown upon them'. I was 365
    one, sir, in this interlude – one Sir Topas, sir; but that's
    all one. 'By the Lord, fool, I am not mad!' But do you
    remember – 'Madam, why laugh you at such a barren
    rascal? An you smile not, he's gagg'd'? And thus the
    whirligig of time brings in his revenges.   370

Malvolio
    I'll be reveng'd on the whole pack of you.

[Exit]

Olivia
    He hath been most notoriously abus'd.

Duke
    Pursue him, and entreat him to a peace;
    He hath not told us of the captain yet.
    When that is known, and golden time convents,   375

376. solemn combination. This is probably kept deliberately vague to include both the actual marriages and the closer relationship between all four that will result.

377. souls: selves.

380. habits: clothes.

381. fancy's queen: because she receives the full homage of his love *fancy* = love.)

382–401. This kind of ending was quite familiar on the Elizabethan stage, and is not without its counterpart in modern entertainment. Music has played a significant part in *Twelfth Night*, and the songs have contributed in their own right to the mood and action. This concluding piece, addressed to the audience, and most likely accompanied by a little dance, is an odd mixture of doggerel and shrewd insight. It captures the wistfulness that haunts so much of the clown's more obvious banter and crudeness. In it, Feste traces step by step the frustrations of his own mean existence, from boyhood to old age, its futility brought out in each second and fourth line, where wind and rain keep up their burden of sublime indifference. But the song does no more than hint gently at this. The ending of the piece, however, brings us back to the business of the moment. The world will go on as it always has, but the play is over; and the clown, on behalf of the whole company, hopes we have enjoyed it.

382. and. This is superfluous; it may have been inserted by a playhouse musician.

384. The child's only experience then of the folly of life was through his playthings.

388. knaves and thieves. Feste seems to put himself before us as a rogue, on the 'wrong side of the law'. (In spite of the plurals here, and further on, Feste is speaking of himself throughout, at least ostensibly.)

390. to wive: to be married.

394–7. This clumsy stanza seems to suggest that the singer and his wife always went to bed drunk. (**toss-pots:** drunkards.)

A solemn combination shall be made
Of our dear souls. Meantime, sweet sister,
We will not part from hence. Cesario, come;
For so you shall be while you are a man;
But when in other habits you are seen,   380
Orsino's mistress, and his fancy's queen.

[Exeunt all but the CLOWN*]*

*[*CLOWN *sings]*

When that I was and a little tiny boy,
   With hey, ho, the wind and the rain,
A foolish thing was but a toy,
   For the rain it raineth every day.   385

But when I came to man's estate,
   With hey, ho, the wind and the rain,
'Gainst knaves and thieves men shut their gate,
   For the rain it raineth every day.

But when I came, alas! to wive,   390
   With hey, ho, the wind and the rain,
By swaggering could I never thrive,
   For the rain it raineth every day.

But when I came unto my beds,
   With hey, ho, the wind and the rain,   395
With toss-pots still had drunken heads,
   For the rain it raineth every day.

A great while ago the world begun,
   With hey, ho, the wind and the rain,
But that's all one, our play is done,   400
   And we'll strive to please you every day.

[Exit]

SUMMING UP

We'll strive to please you every day, the Clown sings before his final bow at the end of the play. This is more than a polite convention. It sets out the essential purpose of all playwrights. All the other things they may wish to do through their plays depend on how effectively they can win over, and hold on to, the interest and goodwill of the people who have come to watch. (The value of a play can never be entirely divorced from its commercial success.)

In the Introduction, it was suggested that *Twelfth Night* has had a long history of stage success largely because it includes so many different kinds of entertainment, so that there is always something happening to amuse or excite. We are now in a position to look more closely at these sources of entertainment, and see how effectively they have been integrated, to provide something for all tastes and yet give to each scene an obvious part in the overall movement.

The Duke's wooing of Olivia, and its outcome, with which the play opens and closes, provides (along with Malvolio's temperament, and the shipwreck of the twins) the starting-point of the whole action. In itself, it has great humorous potential. It is presented as a basically superficial relationship, with an excess of romanticized passion that invites ridicule. To prick the bubble of self-importance has always been a function (the greatest, perhaps) of comedy; and *Twelfth Night* does it relentlessly. It motivates not only the baiting of Malvolio, and the gentler teasing of Sir Andrew, but may be detected also in the humiliations, or at least embarrassments, of Olivia and Orsino. The Duke not only has his very fulsome love-messages scoffed at, but finds that his supplanter is his own trusted 'page'. All his patronizing of Cesario – 'You're too young to understand what it means to be deeply in love' – recoils on himself when he discovers that Olivia in fact prefers Cesario, for all 'his' youthfulness.

His subsequent rapid detachment from Olivia, though unnoticed by those around him (his rank would preclude comments from them, anyway) is for us a rare moment. It gives us the satisfaction – hard to justify, perhaps – of seeing him topple from his pedestal. 'What about your claims of life-long fidelity now?' we want to say to him. 'What kind of passionate devotion is this, if you can transfer it in a moment to someone else?' But these are subtler delights for us as we watch. No one up to now, except Olivia herself, and Feste, perhaps, can bring himself to point out, let alone laugh at, Orsino's pretentiousness. But its debunking is, for all that, an integral part of the play's larger comment on life.

Olivia comes in for the same treatment. She, too, is seen as resolute and inflexible; nothing is going to break *her* purpose of mourning and unworldliness. Indeed, this is how she is first introduced to us – a grief-stricken sister to whom male company is repugnant. But, once again, the poetic justice of life asserts itself, by knocking aside her defences with nothing more substantial than a beard-less youth 'not yet old enough for a man'. And even then, it could have been any other youth – but instead it turns out to be the page of the very man she has so confidently refused. This is Cupid's traditional revenge, to humble most ruthlessly those who most stoutly resist; and, in fiction at any rate, those who profess indifference to love are often the first to succumb.

But perhaps the chief source of pleasure for us, both gay and poignant, is in Viola's special situation, and her relationships with Olivia and Orsino. The device that brings these three together is in essence simple enough, and is the foundation of scores of successful plays. As long as there is a happy final sorting-out, then there is no limit to the amount of torture, suspense and mockery that can be extracted, when A woos B, who instead of reciprocating, falls for C, who, equally unaccommodating, pursues A. The refinements added in the Olivia-Viola-Orsino triangle contribute almost as much again to this basic theme. The most obvious of these is Viola's male disguise, which, once adopted, she feels she must retain. (This would, in Shakespeare's time, have an additional, if extrinsic, appeal – there would, in those days when boy-actors took all the female parts, have been a sort of double disguise. Thus, a boy would be playing Viola, who, in turn, is disguised back again as a boy!)

Within the play itself, Viola's disguise – originally adopted, it will be remembered, as a protective measure – is in fact the cause of all her distresses. It throws her into an intimate relationship with the Duke, who, all unsuspecting, extends to her a warm affection. To this she can only respond falsely as a male, when all the time she as a woman is growing fonder of him. From this are derived some of her most heartrending moments, and some of her most brilliant displays of quick thinking, when she copes with Orsino's unintentionally embarrassing questions, or evades Olivia's mistaken amorousness. This she does, to her huge credit, not simply by verbal skill – this might not be so difficult – but by maintaining a deep sincerity, so that not only does she ward off awkward remarks, but manages at the same time and through the same words, to express her deepest emotions.

This contrasts significantly with Olivia's and Orsino's excessive displays of largely simulated emotion, and emphasizes the essentially heroic qualities in Viola. For although she is put before us as hardly mature enough for grand purposes – her youthful naïvety is perhaps her greatest charm – yet there is a nobility about her, and an integrity which cannot be hidden.

There must be few heroines of fiction who so completely capture our affection. It is not simply that we admire her sterling worth – that might, as so often, evoke a cold, even grudging response. But there is something about her very defencelessness, and even her embarrassments – both of them consequences of her youth – that induces in us a fond, almost patronizing, attitude. Her humiliations bring her down to our level; there are no vices in her to do this, and most of us are a little daunted by heroes or heroines too far above us. From the moment Viola begins her precarious progress, we are staunchly on her side, and the more appreciative, as from the inside, of her suspense.

Quite apart from any personal identification with those involved, there is a humorous satisfaction of a quite special kind, in this mistaken wooing of woman by woman. It is handled innocently enough, in its courtly setting. (It is worth noting, in view of contemporary preoccupation with homosexual relationships, often the source of crude humour, that these encounters in *Twelfth Night* depend for their humour on a completely 'normal' view of sexual love – something that can happen only between man and woman. Viola's alarm when Olivia falls for her, and her sense of hopelessness when she herself falls for Orsino, would make little impact except in a clearly defined, 'black and white' context of normality.)

Within these limits, if such they are, the most is made of the situation. The humour is delicate, as much by implication as by overt comment. There is suspense, when discovery of Viola's secret appears imminent. There is a light-hearted playing-off of one sex against the other, as when Orsino pompously asserts male superiority in the matter of capacity for deep emotion. There is a clever reversing of the normal rôles of the sexes in courtship (starting with Olivia's defiant pursuit of 'Cesario' and ending with Sebastian's cheerful submission). There is the more down-to-earth contrast between the sexes in the face of physical danger, when Viola succumbs to female panic at the thought of fighting a duel.

All this is straightforward 'family entertainment' – the rivalry and disparity between the sexes have always been a favourite source of humour. We are made to laugh at ourselves, as one or other of the two halves of the human race. No individual need feel singled out – it is all men and all women who are being subjected to this mocking.

The pricking of the bubble of self-importance is only part of the humour in the main plot. It is the whole purpose in the case of Malvolio. It is, moreover, handled almost scientifically, in accordance with the principles of treatment found in the Comedy of Humours. The subtleties that were so effectively used in the love-triangle have no part to play when it comes to Malvolio and his one-track personality. This is not to say that the actual scheming for his downfall is not brilliantly conceived, but nothing about Malvolio himself is left in doubt and the counter-measures are presented as natural and inevitable. The principle involved is again simple enough. Just as Viola was so presented as to win our affection, so that we insist, as it were, upon her final vindication and happiness, so Malvolio is presented, just as persuasively, in such a way as to incur our vehement dislike, and our demand for his downfall. He is as double-dyed as any villain of melodrama; he may not constitute a physical threat to anyone, but his entire personality precludes our affection. Pride, however it shows itself, is bound to alienate our sympathies; the utterly proud person cannot hope to retain our affection, since his sole desire is to set himself beyond our reach.

The pleasure, then, that we get from Malvolio's rough handling is that of seeing justice done, and, as such, it might be thought to strengthen our moral sense. (In simple traditional stories, it is the 'baddies' who have to get punished in the end.) It is the same instinct as used to be satisfied in the old Miracle Plays when the audience vowed vengeance on Judas the Traitor, or in any public execution or witch-hunt. As long as the villain in question is exaggerated to the point where we need not identify ourselves with him, then we feel free to wish upon him the full rigours of justice. Whether we ought to react in this way is another matter: modern audiences, certainly, are less disposed to view this sort of thing uncritically.

We become, then, so confirmed in our desire for vengeance that we look for the perfect settling of accounts – and this is what we get. The fact that Malvolio gets his deserts is only half our pleasure The other and greater part of our enjoyment is in the way it is achieved. It is the ingeniousness that so perfectly matches punishment with crime that appeals most. It is present in most types of humour, this gift for selecting the right circumstances to bring out a victim's weaknesses most pointedly. We cannot conceive a bait more tempting, for such a one as Malvolio, than the faked letter; nor a more illuminating arrangement than his spied-on soliloquy in the garden. The comparative failure (for us today) of the dark-room scene is largely because it is attempting the impossible. The ingeniousness of Malvolio's deception, culminating in his grotesquely coy addresses to Olivia, is at a high level. The point has been made brilliantly, and anything further on the same lines is likely to seem an anticlimax.

In analysing the humorous impact of the Malvolio episode, we must not overlook the use made of another elementary comic device, that of contrast. When they successfully deceive Malvolio, it is not only supposed to be 'good for his soul'. It also involves him in a way of behaviour and dress that is ludicrously out of character. We laugh at him for believing that Olivia is madly in love with him; but we laugh far more when, to secure her love, he struggles to fit his staid, morose self into the debonair mould suggested by Maria's letter. We laugh at Malvolio because he is so cleverly deceived, and deserves to be. What happens to Sir Andrew has only partly the same appeal. Though we could never pretend that he has admirable qualities, yet there is nothing vicious about him We pity rather than blame him. There is, then, no question of getting their own back on him when the others subject him to their pranks. They do it simply because he is such a 'sitting target'. This may strike us as far less excusable, but the effect is at least to take much of the sting out of their treatment of him. He is spared the knowledge that they, his friends, are plotting behind his back; he never even realizes that he is being ridiculed. And this, of course, for those who perpetrate such tricks, is the crowning delight – to have brought off such outrageous deceptions, and flattered the victim so successfully, that he accepts it all in perfect faith.

The delight that Shakespeare's contemporaries apparently found in the reactions of the simpleton when dazzled by what he regards as sophisticated behaviour, is something we do not so widely share: perhaps we are growing more charitable towards the unpolished, or less enchanted by 'civilized' values. In Sir Andrew's case, however, this motif is handled with restraint. It is not so much his lack of social grace that is ridiculed, as his own reaction to his lack of it. His pathetic craving for acceptability is what seems to interest Shakespeare more than his silly mistakes. This is not a major fault in Sir Andrew, but it shows a petty-mindedness, and we despise it more for that reason. He is, however ineffectually, a social climber in his own way, and most of us are quite content to leave him to Sir Toby's unscrupulous manipulations. There is a certain subtlety in the depiction of Sir Andrew that is lacking in the case of Malvolio. He is allowed to grow before our eyes, and we can begin to appreciate his nature from our own scene-by-scene observation, without having to depend on the opinion of others in the play: Malvolio comes to us readymade, by comparison. Sir Andrew's fluctuation between foolish confidence and spineless timidity needs to be dramatized if its finer points are not to be missed. By contrast, Malvolio's reactions are always well-pronounced and reasonably predictable. Sir Andrew's first appearance makes it obvious what sort of a person he is, in broad outline. Yet a lot of the time he is on the edge of things; and only if we watch him, and bother to listen to his remarks (feeble and repetitive though they often are) do we appreciate what has gone into the making of him. By the time he is required to perform his major rôle as Viola's opponent in the duel, he has grown upon us as a credible individual, who can give to the occasion all that it needs.

He may be regarded as the sort of 'fool's zany', or 'stooge', Malvolio refers to so disparagingly – with Sir Toby as the fool. He certainly has little independent existence apart from Sir Toby whom he regards so highly and uncritically. Everything his 'master' says or does is material for imitation; and knowing this, Sir Toby keeps him well supplied. The physical contrast between them follows this same pattern. Sir Toby is portly, and vigorously hearty, for all his dissolute ways; while Sir Andrew is correspondingly thin and unaggressive. It needs little wit to appreciate such an oddly assorted pair. But unlike the real-life clown, Sir Toby exercises his zany as much for his own as for other people's entertainment. It often seems as if he has Sir Andrew there as a kind of comic stand-by, to be turned to when other humour is temporarily unavailable. (We notice this especially when they hatch the duel-plot as a kind of stop-gap after the successful conclusion of the letter-reading in the garden.) Fabian's comment on this use Sir Toby makes of Sir Andrew – *This is a dear manakin to you* – is very much to the point. We may well feel that Sir Andrew is handled as cruelly in this respect as Malvolio. He is treated as a nonentity, which is perhaps the worst thing any human being can suffer at the hands of another. It is his heartlessness towards his friend, not his attack upon Malvolio (a worthy opponent, anyway), that loses for Sir Toby any lasting place in our affection.

Sir Andrew, then, is as necessary in the play as Malvolio. Neither must become the sole butt for ridicule or enmity. They have a common bond in their gullibility, which provides one kind of stock humour, straightforward and innocent enough in itself, but the similarity of function ends there. Malvolio's fortunes alone would not be sufficient to make a Shakespearian comedy. So Sir Andrew comes, as it were, to the rescue, and extends the scope of this kind of deception. But again, if Sir Andrew were the only victim, then the sheer callousness of his treatment would strike too gloomy a note. We need to be able to alternate between the two: neither by himself could sustain us contentedly for long. (It is not surprising that an attempt in 1703 to combine Malvolio and Sir Andrew into one character, in a version of *Twelfth Night* intended as script for an opera or masque, had so little success.)

Our analysis of the humour of the play cannot omit the uncomplicated scenes devoted to Sir Toby, Maria, Fabian and Feste, and Sir Andrew. In sheer time alone, these make a major contribution to our entertainment. The squabbling and banter, wisecracking and horseplay that we can usually depend on when they hold the stage, appeals to most audiences. Merely reading their words, we could be forgiven for wondering whether Shakespearian audiences brought a good deal more intelligence to their theatre-going than we sometimes do: 'What about the groundlings?' we might ask, 'How could they possibly work out such subtleties of wit?' No more successfully, probably, than we can today, by simply reading the play, but once the words are spoken by real people on the stage, and the humour enacted, then enough of its drive and point gets through. We can always afford to miss the occasional puns or quips, which often exist only as extras, anyway, in this kind of comedy. When Sir Toby coaxes Sir Andrew to forget his cautiousness and dance so spiritedly, we have only to watch, to be amused. And when Sir Andrew and Viola try so desperately to avoid having to fight each other, the words they use matter little – what we see is enough. This is a play, then, with an ample supply of comic situations, all of them satisfactorily placed so as at least to appear integral parts of the action, and not just funny incidents with the play built round them! They are not without appropriate and often brilliant dialogue, but they depend for their success only minimally upon words, and never upon verbal subtlety alone.

It is, however, when we turn to what Feste brings to the play, that we are most conscious of the distance in time between ourselves and the Elizabethans. Feste is a real person in his own right, but he is still a professional jester. Whatever he contributes is in this capacity, which, though giving him entrée into every situation yet necessarily limits his appeal for us today, since we know no modern equivalent. Further, his very stock-in-trade is Elizabethan wit, which may impress us by its cleverness, but is hardly what we consider side-splitting. Many of Feste's purely professional antics we can appreciate, however. We can see for ourselves when he exercises his privilege of poking irreverent fun at his social superiors. It is obvious what is going on, even if the full scope of his wit evades us. A lot of his chatter is bound to seem idle, in the sense that we needn't be listening to it all the time – a little of it goes a long way! He is obliged, professionally, to keep up a constant flow of banter, and we can treat it at times with no more attentiveness than if it were mere background effect. Even to Elizabethans, such forced humour must surely have become monotonous if that were all that a clown could offer. (We know today that humour is very much more than comic script, and that the personality of the comedian contributes as much, if not more, to the entertainment.) We can be sure that those clowns who stayed in office must have combined in themselves a ready wit and a buoyant temperament. Their job must have been far more testing than that of the comedian in the scripted stage-show, or the circus clown with his painted smile. They had to improvise constantly, and interpret their patrons' moods from moment to moment – and this in an age when there was little redress against high-handed employers. Shakespeare's Feste shows this quality of resourcefulness. There is no one of note, except Antonio, on whom he doesn't sharpen his wits; and his encounters with people are often used as a pleasant introduction to a scene. They are useful, further, in establishing (on our behalf, as it were) a link between the several parts and people of the play. They give to the performance a certain unity, quite apart from its dramatic wholeness. For the clown in Shakespeare acts rather in the way that the Chorus did in Greek Drama – he enhances the sense of participation, as a kind of middleman between actors and audience. His mere presence in a scene – familiar and predictable – ensures for us a sense of belonging, and serves as a reminder that it is, after all, 'our' play, with 'our' amusement as its prime purpose. His profession sets him outside the normal conventions. He can appear truly himself, in any situation, and not be faulted for impertinence. This very detachment from the rest of the players tends to make him one of us.

At a deeper level, this detachment is reflected in the wisdom of the comments he makes. There are times when the man emerges from behind the motley, and his facetious remarks give place to a shrewdness that has nothing artificial about it. For, as we have noted, the clown shares some of the playwright's own function of observing humanity; and he has to contend with the same occasional obloquy. This is probably why much of *Twelfth Night* is occupied with the clown's profession. Malvolio's first words question the whole *raison d'être* of professional jesting. Feste more than once has to defend himself and his kind. Olivia obviously finds him a great solace, and Orsino is glad of his wistful songs. It is left for Viola to sum up the true measure of his art.

It is virtually impossible not to be aware of the clown as a key figure in the play. He may not be the sole purveyor of humour, nor even of the most brilliant parts of it. Even his specific clowning rôle is at times filled equally well by others in his absence. But, however contrived his methods often are, and however poorly they may compare with those rarer scenes of heroism and pathos, yet he epitomizes a major function in Shakespeare's comedies – to look squarely at life and ourselves, and to enjoy what we find to be laughable.

THEME INDEX

Mistaken Identity. The fact of the twinship between Viola and Sebastian: II i 16, 17 and 23–4; III iv 367–71. Neither Viola nor Sebastian knows of the other's survival: I ii 4–5; III iv 361–4; II i 19–21.

Humorous situations resulting from the confusion. Sebastian taken for Viola: by Feste, IV i 1–10; by Sir Toby, IV i 23–6; by Olivia, IV i 48–57; Sebastian's reaction, IV i 58–61; IV iii. Viola taken for Sebastian: by Antonio, III iv 300–2.

Distressing situations resulting from the confusion. Viola taken for Sebastian: by Antonio, III iv 319–25, 334–9 and 352–3; V i 72–8; Viola's reactions, generous and forgiving: III iv 329–34; V i 62–4.

Viola's disguise as Cesario (a blessing and a curse). The purpose and plan: I ii 41–4, 55–61; its initial success: I iv 1–4, 24–8 and 29–36. The effect on Olivia. Begins to fall in love: I v 266, 268–71 and 282–7. Viola suspects: II ii 15, 16; despairs: II ii 31–9. Olivia grows bolder, but still only hints: III i 106–8; declares outright: III i 147–50; helplessly in love: III iv 209.

Viola and Orsino. Viola hints at love: I iv 5–7; states plainly: I iv 41–2.

Orsino unsuspectingly confides in her: I iv 12–14; II iv 14–19, 22–40. Viola professes love, but indirectly: II iv 88–91, 105–9; Openly declares it: V i 128–9, 130–4.

Viola's involvement in the duel: Her 'unmanliness' noted: III ii 58–9; Sir Toby frightens her with the challenge: III iv 212–7, 226–31. Viola's reaction: III iv 232–6, 261–3.

The confusion is cleared up. Initial bewilderment: V i 206, 226–230; Antonio and Sebastian reunited: V i 212–8; 226–230; Antonio and Sebastian reunited: V i 212–8; gradual dawning of recognition: V i 230–47; the humour of Olivia's betrothal: V i 253–7.

Various attitudes to love. Romanticized and exaggerated. Orsino 'enjoys' his lovesickness, overestimating the intensity of his own feelings: I i 1–23; II iv 72–7.

Olivia's 'dramatized' grief for her brother: I i 25–33; I ii 39–41.

Olivia's embarrassing love for Viola: I v 278–87, 297–300; which she cannot or will not restrain: III i 147–54; her greedy insistence: IV i 54–5; iii 22–8.

Orsino's rapid switch from Olivia to Viola: V i 259–62. Sincere, selfless love. Viola genuinely grieves for lost brother: I ii 1–7; III iv 361–4, 371–2; pities Olivia: II ii 23–4, 36–7; 'Heroic', self-effacing love for Orsino; prepared to restrain her feelings (unlike Olivia): II iv 89–91, 107–9. Ready to suffer for it: V i 128–34; generous and forgiving towards Antonio: III iv 329–34; V i 62–4.

Loyal, 'heroic' friendship between Sebastian and Antonio: II i 3–7, 44–5; III iii 11–13, 13–18.

Sebastian's uninhibited acceptance of Olivia: IV i 60–1; IV iii 32–3.

Sir Andrew's diffident way of wooing Olivia, under pressure from Sir Toby: I iii 13–15, 96–9.

Malvolio's loveless wooing of Olivia, just to enhance his social status. (He is excited not because of her womanly charms but because he believes she had singled him out.) II v 32, 44–6 and throughout letter-reading.

Sir Toby's love for Maria, ostensibly out of admiration for her cleverness: II v 11, 12, 170 and 172–3. His casual marriage: V i 356–8.

Various types of humour. 'Knock-about' humour. Sir Andrew introduced to Maria and persuaded to dance: I iii; the late night carousal, interrupted by Malvolio: II iii; the duel: III iv.

Hoax. Against Malvolio. The planning of the letter: II iii. The visit by 'Sir Thopas': IV ii.

Against Sir Andrew: The 'selling' to him of the idea of challenging Viola: III ii; keeping him to it: III iv.

Exaggeration, 'tall story', bare-faced flattery and

deception. Against Malvolio: the content of the letter: II v.

'Sir Thopas's' cross-questioning: IV ii.

Against Sir Andrew: I iii 115–24; III ii 9, 15–26, and 29–34; iv 138–75, 264–9.

Against Viola: III iv 21–4, 255–60.

Verbal wit, puns, riddles, repartee: Sir Toby and Maria score points off Sir Andrew: I iii.

Feste and Maria: I v 4–12; Feste and Olivia: I v 34–48, 61–6. Sir Toby and Sir Andrew: II iii 1–12. Feste and Viola: III i 1–10, 31–6. Feste and Orsino: V i 10–41. Feste and Olivia: V i 278–93.

Subtle humour, verbal sparring (less obvious and superficial than in (4) above, but much more dramatically significant). Frequent dramatic irony, chiefly between Viola and Olivia: I v 160–300; III i 93–162. And between Viola and Orsino: I iv 29–34; II iv 21–34, 103–5 and 119–212.

Characters

Orsino
Typical courtly lover, takes himself too seriously, exaggerates his feelings even to himself, somewhat 'cushioned' from the realities of life. Yet courteous, gentle and considerate, and just: I v 247–51; V i 1–40, 306 and 373.

Olivia
Like Orsino, 'plays the game of love' according to the courtly conventions. Unlike Orsino, she is shrewd, sophisticated and self-possessed, with a sense of humour, until Viola's arrival puts an end to all this. Genuinely concerned for Malvolio and Sir Toby in their need, though equally able to 'give them a piece of her mind' when they deserve it: I v 232–7; III iv 56–60; V i 202; IV i 44–8; I v 84–90.

Viola

Entirely sincere but with a seasoning of youthful irreverence and mischievousness. Generous, forgiving and loyal. Her reactions are always entirely feminine, notably with Olivia: I v; Orsino: II iv; and in the duel: III iv. She has more to put up with than anyone else, but has not time nor inclination for self-pity. Anyone less youthful or 'outgoing' would have made heavy going of her ordeal, and made too heavy demands on our sympathies.

Sebastian

A credible twin brother to Viola. Equally sincere, loyal and generous, but being a man, less calculating and more naïve than his sister, and without her sense of fun. (Compare their respective encounters with Feste: IV i 1–12 and III i 1–53.)

Malvolio

His lack of 'shading' has been noticed, and his chief characteristics are obvious. Note Olivia's assessment: I v 84–90 and Maria's: II iii 138–44. Within the action of the play, he is motivated chiefly by ambition and self-interest; but shows great courage and stubbornness in the face of wholesale opposition: III iv 119–21; V i 321–2, 371.

Sir Toby

Initially likeable for his expansive good humour and resourcefulness, which tend to put him at the centre of so many of the most amusing scenes. But quite unscrupulous in his treatment of others: III ii 49–50. He despises weak-mindedness in others (obviously Sir Andrew) even though turning it to his own advantage and entertainment. He can take command of a situation when he bothers to exert himself: II iii 107–9; III iv 92–5. He is hardly ever ruffled, but deeply resents it when he is – he is not a good loser: V i 190–5.

Sir Andrew
The perfect victim for Sir Toby's heartless jests and dishonesty. A feeble person in all ways, with no large faults, but no virtues either, except self-disparagement. Characteristically he trails hopefully behind Sir Toby and the others in their exuberance, never quite managing to contribute anything valid of his own: II v 170–95; II iii 18–24.

Maria
A vigorous little woman, with little outwardly to suggest the toughness within. She is not cowed by Malvolio's over-bearing ways, and has him weighed up: II iii 138–44. Her drive and inventiveness are responsible for the plot against him, and she is idolized by Sir Toby and the others for it: II v 11, 12, and 170–95. Yet she is woman enough to have scruples when Malvolio falls too heavily into the trap: III iv 89, 90 and 100–2.

Feste
The professional faithfully discharging his clowning function, and loyally defending his profession: I v 29–33. His humour is innocent enough and impersonal to everyone except Malvolio, to whom he shows personal malice, especially when he gets his own back at the end: V i 364–70.

Fabian
In a sense included simply to augment the group around Sir Toby. Three are usually better than two as an audience (as in the garden scene); and Sir Toby must have someone with whom to share his enjoyment of Sir Andrew, when Maria or Feste is occupied elsewhere. We could regard him as a less frivolous version of Feste: II v.

Antonio

A refreshing contrast to the atmosphere of artificiality pervading much of the play. Obviously a man of action with a high regard for loyalty. His devoted attachment to the young Sebastian is one of many examples of male friendship in Shakespeare and literature generally. In *Twelfth Night*, it adds a sturdy, independent dimension to the complexities of the main plot: II i; III iii; III iv 300–360.

Shakespeare: Words and Phrases

adapted from the Collins English Dictionary

abate 1 VERB to abate here means to lessen or diminish ❏ *There lives within the very flame of love/A kind of wick or snuff that will abate it* (*Hamlet 4.7*) 2 VERB to abate here means to shorten ❏ *Abate thy hours* (*A Midsummer Night's Dream 3.2*) 3 VERB to abate here means to deprive ❏ *She hath abated me of half my train* (*King Lear 2.4*)

abjure VERB to abjure means to renounce or give up ❏ *this rough magic I here abjure* (*Tempest 5.1*)

abroad ADV abroad means elsewhere or everywhere ❏ *You have heard of the news abroad* (*King Lear 2.1*)

abrogate VERB to abrogate means to put an end to ❏ *so it shall praise you to abrogate scurrility* (*Love's Labours Lost 4.2*)

abuse 1 NOUN abuse in this context means deception or fraud ❏ *What should this mean? Are all the rest come back?/Or is it some abuse, and no such thing?* (*Hamlet 4.7*) 2 NOUN an abuse in this context means insult or offence ❏ *I will be deaf to pleading and excuses/Nor tears nor prayers shall purchase out our abuses* (*Romeo and Juliet 3.1*) 3 NOUN an abuse in this context means using something improperly ❏ *we'll digest/Th'abuse*

of distance (*Henry II Chorus*) 4 NOUN an abuse in this context means doing something which is corrupt or dishonest ❏ *Come, bring them away: if these be good people in a commonweal that do nothing but their abuses in common houses, I know no law: bring them away.* (*Measure for Measure 2.1*)

abuser NOUN the abuser here is someone who betrays, a betrayer ❏ *I ... do attach thee/For an abuser of the world* (*Othello 1.2*)

accent NOUN accent here means language ❏ *In states unborn, and accents yet unknown* (*Julius Caesar 3.1*)

accident NOUN an accident in this context is an event or something that happened ❏ *think no more of this night's accidents* (*A Midsummer Night's Dream 4.1*)

accommodate VERB to accommodate in this context means to equip or to give someone the equipment to do something ❏ *The safer sense will ne'er accommodate/His master thus.* (*King Lear 4.6*)

according ADJ according means sympathetic or ready to agree ❏ *within the scope of choice/Lies* *my consent and fair according voice* (*Romeo and Juliet 1.2*)

account NOUN account often means judgement (by God) or reckoning ❏ *No reckoning made, but sent to my account/ With all my imperfections on my head* (*Hamlet 1.5*)

accountant ADJ accountant here means answerable or accountable ❏ *his offence is… /Accountant to the law* (*Measure for Measure 2.4*)

ace NOUN ace here means one or first referring to the lowest score on a dice ❏ *No die, but an ace, for him; for he is but one./ Less than an ace, man; for he is dead; he is nothing.* (*A Midsummer Night's Dream 5.1*)

acquit VERB here acquit means to be rid of or free of. It is related to the verb quit ❏ *I am glad I am so acquit of this tinderbox* (*The Merry Wives of Windsor 1.3*)

afeard ADJ afeard means afraid or frightened ❏ *Nothing afeard of what thyself didst make* (*Macbeth 1.3*)

affiance NOUN affiance means confidence or trust ❏ *O how hast thou with jealousy infected/ The sweetness of affiance* (*Henry V 2.2*)

affinity NOUN in this context, affinity means important connections, or relationships with important people ❏ *The Moor replies/ That he you hurt is of great fame in Cyprus,/ And great affinity* (*Othello 3.1*)

agnize VERB to agnize is an old word that means that you recognize or acknowledge something ❏ *I do agnize/ A natural and prompt alacrity I find in hardness* (*Othello 1.3*)

ague NOUN an ague is a fever in which the patient has hot and cold

shivers one after the other ❏ *This is some monster of the isle with four legs, who hath got … an ague* (*The Tempest 2.2*)

alarm, alarum NOUN an alarm or alarum is a call to arms or a signal for soldiers to prepare to fight ❏ *Whence cometh this alarum and the noise?* (*Henry VI part I 1.4*)

Albion NOUN Albion is another word for England ❏ *but I will sell my dukedom,/ To buy a slobbery and a dirty farm In that nook-shotten isle of Albion* (*Henry V 3.5*)

all of all PHRASE all of all means everything, or the sum of all things ❏ *The very all of all* (*Love's Labours Lost 5.1*)

amend VERB amend in this context means to get better or to heal ❏ *at his touch… They presently amend* (*Macbeth 4.3*)

anchor VERB if you anchor on something you concentrate on it or fix on it ❏ *My invention … Anchors on Isabel* (*Measure for Measure 2.4*)

anon ADV anon was a common word for soon ❏ *You shall see anon how the murderer gets the love of Gonzago's wife* (*Hamlet 3.2*)

antic 1 ADJ antic here means weird or strange ❏ *I'll charm the air to give a sound/ While you perform your antic round* (*Macbeth 4.1*) 2 NOUN in this context antic means a clown or a strange, unattractive creature ❏ *If black, why nature, drawing an antic,/ Made a foul blot* (*Much Ado About Nothing 3.1*)

apace ADV apace was a common word for quickly ❏ *Come apace* (*As You Like It 3.3*)

apparel NOUN apparel means clothes or clothing ❑ *one suit of apparel* (*Hamlet 3.2*)

appliance NOUN appliance here means cure ❑ *Diseases desperate grown/ By desperate appliance are relieved* (*Hamlet 4.3*)

argument NOUN argument here means a topic of conversation or the subject ❑ *Why 'tis the rarest argument of wonder that hath shot out in our latter times* (*All's Well That Ends Well 2.3*)

arrant ADJ arrant means absolute, complete. It strengthens the meaning of a noun ❑ *Fortune, that arrant whore* (*King Lear 2.4*)

arras NOUN an arras is a tapestry, a large cloth with a picture sewn on it using coloured thread ❑ *Behind the arras I'll convey myself/ To hear the process* (*Hamlet 3.3*)

art 1 NOUN art in this context means knowledge ❑ *Their malady convinces/ The great essay of art* (*Macbeth 4.3*) 2 NOUN art can also mean skill as it does here ❑ *He ... gave you such a masterly report/ For art and exercise in your defence* (*Hamlet 4.7*) 3 NOUN art here means magic ❑ *Now I want/ Spirits to enforce, art to enchant* (*The Tempest 5 Epilogue*)

assay 1 NOUN an assay was an attempt, a try ❑ *Make assay./ Bow, stubborn knees* (*Hamlet 3.3*) 2 NOUN assay can also mean a test or a trial ❑ *he hath made assay of her virtue* (*Measure for Measure 3.1*)

attend (on/upon) VERB attend on means to wait for or to expect ❑ *Tarry I here, I but attend on death* (*Two Gentlemen of Verona 3.1*)

auditor NOUN an auditor was a member of an audience or someone who listens ❑ *I'll be an auditor* (*A Midsummer Night's Dream 3.1*)

aught NOUN aught was a common word which meant anything ❑ *if my love thou holdest at aught* (*Hamlet 4.3*)

aunt 1 NOUN an aunt was another word for an old woman and also means someone who talks a lot or a gossip ❑ *The wisest aunt telling the saddest tale* (*A Midsummer Night's Dream 2.1*) 2 NOUN aunt could also mean a mistress or a prostitute ❑ *the thrush and the jay/ Are summer songs for me and my aunts/ While we lie tumbling in the hay* (*The Winter's Tale 4.3*)

avaunt EXCLAM avaunt was a common word which meant go away ❑ *Avaunt, you curs!* (*King Lear 3.6*)

aye ADV here aye means always or ever ❑ *Whose state and honour I for aye allow* (*Richard II 5.2*)

baffle VERB baffle meant to be disgraced in public or humiliated ❑ *I am disgraced, impeached, and baffled here* (*Richard II 1.1*)

bald ADJ bald means trivial or silly ❑ *I knew 'twould be a bald conclusion* (*The Comedy of Errors 2.2*)

ban NOUN a ban was a curse or an evil spell ❑ *Sometimes with lunatic bans... Enforce their charity* (*King Lear 2.3*)

barren ADJ barren meant empty or hollow ❑ *now I let go your hand, I am barren.* (*Twelfth Night 1.3*)

base ADJ base is an adjective that means unworthy or dishonourable ❑ *civet is of a baser birth than tar* (*As You Like It 3.2*)

base 1 ADJ base can also mean of low social standing or someone who was not part of the ruling class ❑ *Why brand they us with 'base'?* (*King Lear 1.2*) 2 ADJ here base means poor quality ❑ *Base cousin,/ Darest thou break first?* (*Two Noble Kinsmen 3.3*)

bawdy NOUN bawdy means obscene or rude ❑ *Bloody, bawdy villain!* (*Hamlet 2.2*)

bear in hand PHRASE bear in hand means taken advantage of or fooled ❑ *This I made good to you In our last conference, passed in probation with you/ How you were borne in hand* (*Macbeth 3.1*)

beard VERB to beard someone was to oppose or confront them ❑ *Com'st thou to beard me in Denmark?* (*Hamlet 2.2*)

beard, in one's PHRASE if you say something in someone's beard you say it to their face ❑ *I will verify as much in his beard* (*Henry V 3.2*)

beaver NOUN a beaver was a visor on a battle helmet ❑ *O yes, my lord, he wore his beaver up* (*Hamlet 1.2*)

become VERB if something becomes you it suits you or is appropriate to you ❑ *Nothing in his life became him like the leaving it* (*Macbeth 1.4*)

bed, brought to PHRASE to be brought to bed means to give birth ❑ *His wife but yesternight was brought to bed* (*Titus Andronicus 4.2*)

bedabbled ADJ if something is bedabbled it is sprinkled ❑ *Bedabbled with the dew, and torn with briers* (*A Midsummer Night's Dream 3.2*)

Bedlam NOUN Bedlam was a word used for Bethlehem Hospital which was a place the insane were sent to ❑ *The country give me proof and precedent/ Of Bedlam beggars* (*King Lear 2.3*)

bed-swerver NOUN a bed-swerver was someone who was unfaithful in marriage, an adulterer ❑ *she's/ A bed-swerver* (*Winter's Tale 2.1*)

befall 1 VERB to befall is to happen, occur or take place ❑ *In this same interlude it doth befall/ That I present a wall* (*A Midsummer Night's Dream 5.1*) 2 VERB to befall can also mean to happen to someone or something ❑ *fair befall thee and thy noble house* (*Richard III 1.3*)

behoof NOUN behoof was an advantage or benefit ❑ *All our surgeons/ Convent in their behoof* (*Two Noble Kinsmen 1.4*)

beldam NOUN a beldam was a witch or old woman ❑ *Have I not reason, beldams as you are?* (*Macbeth 3.5*)

belike ADV belike meant probably, perhaps or presumably ❑ *belike he likes it not* (*Hamlet 3.2*)

bent 1 NOUN bent means a preference or a direction ❑ *Let me work,/ For I can give his humour true bent,/ And I will bring him to the Capitol* (*Julius Caesar 2.1*) 2 ADJ if you are bent on something you are determined to do it ❑ *for now I am bent to know/ By the worst means the worst.* (*Macbeth 3.4*)

beshrew VERB beshrew meant to curse or wish evil on someone ❑ *much beshrew my manners and my pride/ If Hermia meant to say Lysander lied* (*A Midsummer Night's Dream 2.2*)

betime (s) ADV betime means early ❑ *To business that we love we rise betime* (Antony and Cleopatra 4.4)

bevy NOUN bevy meant type or sort, it was also used to mean company ❑ *many more of the same bevy* (Hamlet 5.2)

blazon VERB to blazon something meant to display or show it ❑ *that thy skill be more to blazon it* (Romeo and Juliet 2.6)

blind ADJ if you are blind when you do something you are reckless or do not care about the consequences ❑ *are you yet to your own souls so blind/ That two you will war with God by murdering me* (Richard III 1.4)

bombast NOUN bombast was wool stuffing (used in a cushion for example) and so it came to mean padded out or long-winded. Here it means someone who talks a lot about nothing in particular ❑ *How now my sweet creature of bombast* (Henry IV part I 2.4)

bond 1 NOUN a bond is a contract or legal deed ❑ *Well, then, your bond, and let me see* (Merchant of Venice 1.3) 2 NOUN bond could also mean duty or commitment ❑ *I love your majesty/ According to my bond* (King Lear 1.1)

bottom NOUN here bottom means essence, main point or intent ❑ *Now I see/ The bottom of your purpose* (All's Well That Ends Well 3.7)

bounteously ADV bounteously means plentifully, abundantly ❑ *I prithee, and I'll pay thee bounteously* (Twelfth Night 1.2)

brace 1 NOUN a brace is a couple or two ❑ *Have lost a brace of kinsmen* (Romeo and Juliet 5.3) 2 NOUN if you are in a brace position it means you are ready ❑ *For that it stands not in such warlike brace* (Othello 1.3)

brand VERB to mark permanantly like the markings on cattle ❑ *the wheeled seat/ Of fortunate Caesar ... branded his baseness that ensued* (Anthony and Cleopatra 4.14)

brave ADJ brave meant fine, excellent or splendid ❑ *O brave new world/ That has such people in't* (The Tempest 5.1)

brine NOUN brine is sea-water ❑ *He shall drink nought brine, for I'll not show him/ Where the quick freshes are* (The Tempest 3.2)

brow NOUN brow in this context means appearance ❑ *doth hourly grow/ Out of his brows* (Hamlet 3.3)

burden 1 NOUN the burden here is a chorus ❑ *I would sing my song without a burden* (As You Like It 3.2) 2 NOUN burden means load or weight (this is the current meaning) ❑ *the scarfs and the bannerets about thee did manifoldly dissuade me from believing thee a vessel of too great a burden* (All's Well that Ends Well 2.3)

buttons, in one's PHRASE this is a phrase that means clear, easy to see ❑ *Tis in his buttons he will carry't* (The Merry Wives of Windsor 3.2)

cable NOUN cable here means scope or reach ❑ *The law ... Will give her cable* (Othello 1.2)

cadent ADJ if something is cadent it is falling or dropping ❑ *With cadent tears fret channels in her cheeks* (King Lear 1.4)

canker VERB to canker is to decay, become corrupt ❏ *And, as with age his body uglier grows,/So his mind cankers* (*The Tempest 4.1*)

canon, from the PHRASE from the canon is an expression meaning out of order, improper ❏ *Twas from the canon* (*Coriolanus 3.1*)

cap-a-pie ADV cap-a-pie means from head to foot, completely ❏ *I am courtier cap-a-pie* (*The Winter's Tale 4.4*)

carbonadoed ADJ if something is carbonadoed it is cut or scored (scratched) with a knife ❏ *it is your carbonadoed* (*All's Well That Ends Well 4.5*)

carouse VERB to carouse is to drink at length, party ❏ *They cast their caps up and carouse together* (*Anthony and Cleopatra 4.12*)

carrack NOUN a carrack was a large old ship, a galleon ❏ *Faith, he tonight hath boarded a land-carrack* (*Othello 1.2*)

cassock NOUN a cassock here means a military cloak, long coat ❏ *half of the which dare not shake the snow from off their cassocks lest they shake themselves to pieces* (*All's Well That Ends Well 4.3*)

catastrophe NOUN catastrophe here means conclusion or end ❏ *pat he comes, like the catastrophe of the old comedy* (*King Lear 1.2*)

cautel NOUN a cautel was a trick or a deceptive act ❏ *Perhaps he loves you now/And now no soil not cautel doth besmirch* (*Hamlet 1.2*)

celerity NOUN celerity was a common word for speed, swiftness ❏ *Hence hath offence his quick celerity/When it is borne in high authority* (*Measure for Measure 4.2*)

chafe NOUN chafe meant anger or temper ❏ *this Herculean Roman does become/The carriage of his chafe* (*Anthony and Cleopatra 1.3*)

chanson NOUN chanson was an old word for a song ❏ *The first row of the pious chanson will show you more* (*Hamlet 2.2*)

chapman NOUN a chapman was a trader or merchant ❏ *Not uttered by base sale of chapman's tongues* (*Love's Labours Lost 2.1*)

chaps, chops NOUN chaps (and chops) was a word for jaws ❏ *Which ne'er shook hands nor bade farewell to him/Till he unseamed him from the nave to th' chops* (*Macbeth 1.2*)

chattels NOUN chattels were your moveable possessions. The word is used in the traditional marriage ceremony ❏ *She is my goods, my chattels* (*The Taming of the Shrew 3.3*)

chide VERB if you are chided by someone you are told off or reprimanded ❏ *Now I but chide, but I should use thee worse* (*A Midsummer Night's Dream 3.2*)

chinks NOUN chinks was a word for cash or money ❏ *he that can lay hold of her/Shall have the chinks* (*Romeo and Juliet 1.5*)

choleric ADJ if something was called choleric it meant that they were quick to get angry ❏ *therewithal unruly waywardness that infirm and choleric years bring with them* (*King Lear 1.1*)

chuff NOUN a chuff was a miser,

someone who clings to his or her money ❏ *ye fat chuffs* (*Henry IV part I 2.2*)

cipher NOUN cipher here means nothing ❏ *Mine were the very cipher of a function* (*Measure for Measure 2.2*)

circummured ADJ circummured means that something is surrounded with a wall ❏ *He hath a garden circummured with brick* (*Measure for Measure 4.1*)

civet NOUN a civet is a type of scent or perfume ❏ *Give me an ounce of civet* (*King Lear 4.6*)

clamorous ADJ clamorous means noisy or boisterous ❏ *Be clamorous and leap all civil bounds* (*Twelfth Night 1.4*)

clangour, clangor NOUN clangour is a word that means ringing (the sound that bells make) ❏ *Like to a dismal clangour heard from far* (*Henry VI part III 2.3*)

cleave VERB if you cleave to something you stick to it or are faithful to it ❏ *Thy thoughts I cleave to* (*The Tempest 4.1*)

clock and clock, 'twixt PHRASE from hour to hour, without stopping or continuously ❏ *To weep 'twixt clock and clock* (*Cymbeline 3.4*)

close ADJ here close means hidden ❏ *Stand close; this is the same Athenian* (*A Midsummer Night's Dream 3.2*)

cloud NOUN a cloud on your face means that you have a troubled, unhappy expression ❏ *He has cloud in's face* (*Anthony and Cleopatra 3.2*)

cloy VERB if you cloy an appetite you satisfy it ❏ *Other women cloy/The appetites they feed* (*Anthony and Cleopatra 2.2*)

cock-a-hoop, set PHRASE if you set cock-a-hoop you become free of everything ❏ *You will set cock-a-hoop* (*Romeo and Juliet 1.5*)

colours NOUN colours is a word used to describe battle-flags or banners. Sometimes we still say that we nail our colours to the mast if we are stating which team or side of an argument we support ❏ *the approbation of those that weep this lamentable divorce under her colours* (*Cymbeline 1.5*)

combustion NOUN combustion was a word meaning disorder or chaos ❏ *prophesying ... Of dire combustion and confused events* (*Macbeth 2.3*)

comely ADJ if you are or something is comely you or it is lovely, beautiful, graceful ❏ *O, what a world is this, when what is comely/Envenoms him that bears it!* (*As You Like It 2.3*)

commend VERB if you commend yourself to someone you send greetings to them ❏ *Commend me to my brother* (*Measure for Measure 1.4*)

compact NOUN a compact is an agreement or a contract ❏ *what compact mean you to have with us?* (*Julius Caesar 3.1*)

compass 1 NOUN here compass means range or scope ❏ *you would sound me from my lowest note to the top of my compass* (*Hamlet 3.2*) 2 VERB to compass here means to achieve, bring about or make happen ❏ *How now shall this be compassed?/Canst thou bring me to the party?* (*Tempest 3.2*)

comptible ADJ comptible is an old word meaning sensitive ❑ *I am very comptible, even to the least sinister usage.* (Twelfth Night 1.5)

confederacy NOUN a confederacy is a group of people usually joined together to commit a crime. It is another word for a conspiracy ❑ *Lo, she is one of this confederacy!* (A Midsummer Night's Dream 3.2)

confound VERB if you confound something you confuse it or mix it up; it also means to stop or prevent ❑ *A million fail, confounding oath on oath.* (A Midsummer Night's Dream 3.2)

contagion NOUN contagion is an old word for disease or poison ❑ *hell itself breathes out/ Contagion to this world* (Hamlet 3.2)

contumely NOUN contumely is an old word for an insult ❑ *the proud man's contumely* (Hamlet 3.1)

counterfeit 1 VERB if you counterfeit something you copy or imitate it ❑ *Meantime your cheeks do counterfeit our roses* (Henry VI part I 2.4) 2 VERB in this context counterfeit means to pretend or make believe ❑ *I will counterfeit the bewitchment of some popular man* (Coriolanus)

coz NOUN coz was a shortened form of the word cousin ❑ *sweet my coz, be merry* (As You Like It 1.2)

cozenage NOUN cozenage is an old word meaning cheating or a deception ❑ *Thrown out his angle for my proper life,/ And with such coz'nage* (Hamlet 5.2)

crave VERB crave used to mean to beg or request ❑ *I crave your pardon* (The Comedy of Errors 1.2)

crotchet NOUN crotchets are strange ideas or whims ❑ *thou hast some strange crotchets in thy head now* (The Merry Wives of Windsor 2.1)

cuckold NOUN a cuckold is a man whose wife has been unfaithful to him ❑ *As there is no true cuckold but calamity* (Twelfth Night 1.5)

cuffs, go to PHRASE this phrase meant to fight ❑ *the player went to cuffs in the question* (Hamlet 2.2)

cup VERB in this context cup is a verb which means to pour drink or fill glasses with alcohol ❑ *cup us til the world go round* (Anthony and Cleopatra 2.7)

cur NOUN cur is an insult meaning dog and is also used to mean coward ❑ *Out, dog! out, cur! Thou drivest me past the bounds/ Of maiden's patience* (A Midsummer Night's Dream 3.2)

curiously ADV in this context curiously means carefully or skilfully ❑ *The sleeves curiously cut* (The Taming of the Shrew 4.3)

curry VERB curry means to flatter or to praise someone more than they are worth ❑ *I would curry with Master Shallow that no man could better command his servants* (Henry IV part II 5.1)

custom NOUN custom is a habit or a usual practice ❑ *Hath not old custom made this life more sweet/ Than that of painted pomp?* (As You Like It 2.1)

cutpurse NOUN a cutpurse is an old word for a thief. Men used to carry their money in small bags (purse) that hung from their belts; thieves would cut the purse from the belt and steal their money ❑ *A cutpurse of the empire and the rule* (Hamlet 3.4)

dainty ADJ dainty used to mean splendid, fine ❑ *Why, that's my dainty Ariel!* (*Tempest 5.1*)

dally VERB if you dally with something you play with it or tease it ❑ *They that dally nicely with words may quickly make them wanton* (*Twelfth Night 3.1*)

damask COLOUR damask is a light-red or pink colour ❑ *Twas just the difference/Betwixt the constant red and mingled damask* (*As You Like It 3.5*)

dare 1 VERB dare means to challeng or, confront ❑ *He goes before me, and still dares me on* (*A Midsummer Night's Dream 3.3*) 2 VERB dare in this context means to present, deliver or inflict ❑ *all that fortune, death, and danger dare* (*Hamlet 4.4*)

darkly ADV darkly was used in this context to mean secretly or cunningly ❑ *I will go darkly to work with her* (*Measure for Measure 5.1*)

daw NOUN a daw was a slang term for idiot or fool (after the bird jackdaw which was famous for its stupidity) ❑ *Yea, just so much as you may take upon a knife's point and choke a daw withal* (*Much Ado About Nothing 3.1*)

debile ADJ debile meant weak or feeble ❑ *And debile minister great power* (*All's Well That Ends Well 2.3*)

deboshed ADJ deboshed was another way of saying corrupted or debauched ❑ *Men so disordered, deboshed and bold* (*King Lear 1.4*)

decoct VERB to decoct was to heat up, warm something ❑ *Can sodden water,/A drench for sur-rained jades*

... Decoct their cold blood to such valiant heat? (*Henry V 3.5*)

deep-revolving ADJ deep-revolving here uses the idea that you turn something over in your mind when you are thinking hard about it and so means deep-thinking, meditating ❑ *The deep-revolving Buckingham/No more shall be the neighbour to my counsels* (*Richard III 4.2*)

defect NOUN defect here means shortcoming or something that is not right ❑ *Being unprepared/Our will became the servant to defect* (*Macbeth 2.1*)

degree 1 NOUN degree here means rank, standing or station ❑ *Should a like language use to all degrees,/ And mannerly distinguishment leave out/Betwixt the prince and beggar* (*The Winter's Tale 2.1*) 2 NOUN in this context, degree means extent or measure ❑ *her offence/Must be of such unnatural degree* (*King Lear 1.1*)

deify VERB if you deify something or someone you worship it or them as a God ❑ *all.. deifying the name of Rosalind* (*As You Like It 3.2*)

delated ADJ delated here means detailed ❑ *the scope/Of these delated articles* (*Hamlet 1.2*)

delicate ADJ if something was described as delicate it meant it was of fine quality or valuable ❑ *thou wast a spirit too delicate* (*The Tempest 1.2*)

demise VERB in this context demise means to transmit, give or convey ❑ *what state ... Canst thou demise to any child of mine?* (*Richard III 4.4*)

deplore VERB to deplore means to express with grief or sorrow ❑ *Never more/ Will I my master's tears to you deplore* (*Twelfth Night 3.1*)

depose VERB if you depose someone you make them take an oath, or swear something to be true ❑ *Depose him in the justice of his cause* (*Richard II 1.3*)

depositary NOUN a depositary is a trustee ❑ *Made you ... my depositary* (*King Lear 2.4*)

derive 1 VERB to derive means to comes from or to descend (it usually applies to people) ❑ *No part of it is mine,/ This shame derives itself from unknown loins.* (*Much Ado About Nothing 4.1*) 2 VERB if you derive something from someone you inherit it ❑ *Treason is not inherited ...Or, if we derive it from our friends/ What's that to me?* (*As You Like It 1.3*)

descry VERB to see or catch sight of ❑ *The news is true, my lord. He is descried* (*Anthony and Cleopatra 3.7*)

desert 1 NOUN desert means worth or merit ❑ *That dost in vile misproson shackle up/ My love and her desert* (*All's Well That Ends Well 2.3*) 2 ADJ desert is used here to mean lonely or isolated ❑ *if that love or gold/ Can in this desert place buy entertainment* (*As You LIke It 2.4*)

design 1 VERB to design means to indicate or point out ❑ *we shall see/ Justice design the victor's chivalry* (*Richard II 1.1*) 2 NOUN a design is a plan, an intention or an undertaking ❑ *hinder not the honour of his design* (*All's Well That Ends Well 3.6*)

designment NOUN a designment was a plan or undertaking ❑ *The desperate tempest hath so bang'd the Turks,/ That their designment halts* (*Othello 2.1*)

despite VERB despite here means to spite or attempt to thwart a plan ❑ *Only to despite them I will endeavour anything* (*Much Ado About Nothing 2.2*)

device NOUN a device is a plan, plot or trick ❑ *Excellent, I smell a device* (*Twelfth Night 2.3*)

disable VERB to disable here means to devalue or make little of ❑ *he disabled my judgement* (*As You Like It 5.4*)

discandy VERB here discandy means to melt away or dissolve ❑ *The hearts ... do discandy , melt their sweets* (*Anthony and Cleopatra 4.12*)

disciple VERB to disciple is to teach or train ❑ *He ...was/ Discipled of the bravest* (*All's Well That Ends Well 1.2*)

discommend VERB if you discommend something you criticize it ❑ *my dialect which you discommend so much* (*King Lear 2.2*)

discourse NOUN discourse means conversation, talk or chat ❑ *which part of it I'll waste/ With such discourse as I not doubt shall make it/ Go quick away* (*The Tempest 5.1*)

discover VERB discover used to mean to reveal or show ❑ *the Prince discovered to Claudio that he loved my niece* (*Much Ado About Nothing 1.2*)

disliken VERB disguise, make unlike ❑ *disliken/ The truth of your own seeming* (*The Winter's Tale 4.4*)

dismantle VERB to dismantle is to remove or take away ❑ *Commit a thing so monstrous to dismantle/*

So many folds of favour (*King Lear 1.1*)

disponge VERB disponge means to pour out or rain down ❑ *The poisonous damp of night disponge upon me* (*Anthony and Cleopatra 4.9*)

distrain VERB to distrain something is to confiscate it ❑ *My father's goods are all distrained and sold* (*Richard II 2.3*)

divers ADJ divers is an old word for various ❑ *I will give out divers schedules of my beauty* (*Twelfth Night 1.5*)

doff VERB to doff is to get rid of or dispose ❑ *make our women fight/ To doff their dire distresses* (*Macbeth 4.3*)

dog VERB if you dog someone or something you follow them or it closely ❑ *I will rather leave to see Hector than not to dog him* (*Troilus and Cressida 5.1*)

dotage NOUN dotage here means infatuation ❑ *Her dotage now I do begin to pity* (*A Midsummer NIght's Dream 4.1*)

dotard NOUN a dotard was an old fool ❑ *I speak not like a dotard nor a fool* (*Much Ado About Nothing 5.1*)

dote VERB to dote is to love, cherish, care without seeing any fault ❑ *And won her soul; and she, sweet lady, dotes,/ Devoutly dotes, dotes in idolatry* (*A Midsummer Night's Dream 1.1*)

doublet NOUN a doublet was a man's close-fitting jacket with short skirt ❑ *Lord Hamlet, with his doublet all unbraced* (*Hamlet 2.1*)

dowager NOUN a dowager is a widow ❑ *Like to a step-dame or a dowage* (*A Midsummer Night's Dream 1.1*)

dowdy NOUN a dowdy was an ugly woman ❑ *Dido was a dowdy* (*Romeo and Juliet 2.4*)

dower NOUN a dower (or dowery) is the riches or property given by the father of a bride to her husband-to-be ❑ *Thy truth then by they dower* (*King Lear 1.1*)

dram NOUN a dram is a tiny amount ❑ *Why, everything adheres together that no dram of a scruple* (*Twelfth Night 3.4*)

drift NOUN drift is a plan, scheme or intention ❑ *Shall Romeo by my letters know our drift* (*Romeo and Juliet 4.1*)

dropsied ADJ dropsied means pretentious ❑ *Where great additions swell's and virtues none/ It is a dropsied honour* (*All's Well That Ends Well 2.3*)

drudge NOUN a drudge was a slave, servant ❑ *If I be his cuckold, he's my drudge* (*All's Well That Ends Well 1.3*)

dwell VERB to dwell sometimes meant to exist, to be ❑ *I'd rather dwell in my necessity* (*Merchant of Venice 1.3*)

earnest ADJ an earnest was a pledge to pay or a payment in advance ❑ *for an earnest of a greater honour/ He bade me from him call thee Thane of Cawdor* (*Macbeth 1.3*)

ecstasy NOUN madness ❑ *This is the very ecstasy of love* (*Hamlet 2.1*)

edict NOUN law or declaration ❑ *It stands as an edict in destiny.* (*A Midsummer Night's Dream 1.1*)

egall ADJ egall is an old word meaning equal ❏ *companions/ Whose souls do bear an egall yoke of love* (Merchant of Venice 2.4)

eisel NOUN eisel meant vinegar ❏ *Woo't drink up eisel?* (Hamlet 5.1)

eke, eke out VERB eke meant to add to, to increase. Eke out nowadays means to make something last as long as possible – particularly in the sense of making money last a long time ❏ *Still be kind/ And eke out our performance with your mind* (Henry V Chorus)

elbow, out at PHRASE out at elbow is an old phrase meaning in poor condition – as when your jacket sleeves are worn at the elbow which shows that it is an old jacket ❏ *He cannot, sir. He's out at elbow* (Measure for Measure 2.1)

element NOUN elements were thought to be the things from which all things were made. They were: air, earth, water and fire ❏ *Does not our lives consist of the four elements?* (Twelfth Night 2.3)

elf VERB to elf was to tangle ❏ *I'll ... elf all my hairs in knots* (King Lear 2.3)

embassy NOUN an embassy was a message ❏ *We'll once more hear Orsino's embassy.* (Twelfth Night 1.5)

emphasis NOUN emphasis here means a forceful expression or strong statement ❏ *What is he whose grief/ Bears such an emphasis* (Hamlet 5.1)

empiric NOUN an empiric was an untrained doctor sometimes called a quack ❏ *we must not ... prostitute our past-cure malady/ To empirics* (All's Well That Ends Well 2.1)

emulate ADJ emulate here means envious ❏ *pricked on by a most emulate pride* (Hamlet 1.1)

enchant VERB to enchant meant to put a magic spell on ❏ *Damn'd as thou art, thou hast enchanted her,/ For I'll refer me to all things of sense* (Othello 1.2)

enclog VERB to enclog was to hinder something or to provide an obstacle to it ❏ *Traitors enscarped to enclog the guitless keel* (Othello 1.2)

endure VERB to endure was to allow or to permit ❏ *and will endure/ Our setting down before't.* (Macbeth 5.4)

enfranchise VERB if you enfranchised something you set it free ❏ *Do this or this;/ Take in that kingdom and enfranchise that;/ Perform't, or else we damn thee.'* (Anthony and Cleopatra 1.1)

engage VERB to engage here means to pledge or to promise ❏ *This to be true I do engage my life* (As You Like It 5.4)

engaol VERB to lock up or put in prison ❏ *Within my mouth you have engaoled my tongue* (Richard II 1.3)

engine NOUN an engine was a plot, device or a machine ❏ *their promises, enticements, oaths, tokens, and all these engines, of lust, are not the things they go under* (All's Well That Ends Well 3.5)

englut VERB if you were engulfed you were swallowed up or eaten whole ❏ *For certainly thou art so near the gulf,/ Thou needs must be englutted.* (Henry V 4.3)

enjoined ADJ enjoined describes people joined together for the same reason ❏ *Of enjoined penitents/*

There's four or five (All's Well That Ends Well 3.5)

entertain 1 VERB to entertain here means to welcome or receive ❑ *Approach, rich Ceres, her to entertain.* (The Tempest 4.1) 2 VERB to entertain in this context means to cherish, hold in high regard or to respect ❑ *and I quake,/ Lest thou a feverous life shouldst entertain/ And six or seven winters more respect/ Than a perpetual honour.* (Measure for Measure 3.1) 3 VERB to entertain means here to give something consideration ❑ *But entertain it,/ And though you think me poor, I am the man/ Will give thee all the world.* (Anthony and Cleopatra 2.7) 4 VERB to entertain here means to treat or handle ❑ *your highness is not entertained with that ceremonious affection as you were wont* (King Lear 1.4)

envious ADJ envious meant spiteful or vindictive ❑ *he shall appear to the envious a scholar* (Measure for Measure 3.2)

ere PREP ere was a common word for before ❑ *ere this I should ha' fatted all the region kites* (Hamlet 2.2)

err VERB to err means to go astray, to make a mistake ❑ *And as he errs, doting on Hermia's eyes* (A Midsummer Night's Dream 1.1)

erst ADV erst was a common word for once or before ❑ *that erst brought sweetly forth/ The freckled cowslip* (Henry V 5.2)

eschew VERB if you eschew something you deliberately avoid doing it ❑ *What cannot be eschewed must be embraced* (The Merry Wives of Windsor 5.5)

escote VERB to escote meant to pay for, support ❑ *How are they escoted?* (Hamlet 2.2)

estimable ADJ estimable meant appreciative ❑ *I could not with such estimable wonder over-far believe that* (Twelfth Night 2.1)

extenuate VERB extenuate means to lessen ❑ *Which by no means we may extenuate* (A Midsummer Night's Dream 1.1)

fain ADV fain was a common word meaning gladly or willingly ❑ *I would fain prove so* (Hamlet 2.2)

fall NOUN in a voice or music fall meant going higher and lower ❑ *and so die/ That strain again! it had a dying fall* (Twelfth Night 1.1)

false ADJ false was a common word for treacherous ❑ *this is counter, you false Danish dogs!* (Hamlet 4.5)

fare VERB fare means to get on or manage ❑ *I fare well* (The Taming of the Shrew Introduction 2)

feign VERB to feign was to make up, pretend or fake ❑ *It is the more like to be feigned* (Twelfth Night 1.5)

fie EXCLAM fie was an exclamation of disgust ❑ *Fie, that you'll say so!* (Twelfth Night 1.3)

figure VERB to figure was to symbolize or look like ❑ *Wings and no eyes, figure unheedy haste* (A Midsummer Night's Dream 1.1)

filch VERB if you filch something you steal it ❑ *With cunning hast thou filch'd my daughter's heart* (A Midsummer Night's Dream 1.1)

flout VERB to flout something meant to scorn it ❑ *Why will you suffer her to flout me thus?* (A Midsummer Night's Dream 3.2)

fond ADJ fond was a common word meaning foolish ❑ *Shall we their fond pageant see?* (*A Midsummer Night's Dream 3.2*)

footing 1 NOUN footing meant landing on shore, arrival, disembarkation ❑ *Whose footing here anticipates our thoughts/A se'nnight's speed.* (*Othello 2.1*) 2 NOUN footing also means support ❑ *there your charity would have lacked footing* (*Winter's Tale 3.3*)

forsooth ADV in truth, certainly, truly
❑ *I had rather, forsooth, go before you like a man* (*The Merry Wives of Windsor 3.2*)

forswear VERB if you forswear you lie, swear falsely or break your word ❑ *he swore a thing to me on Monday night, which he forswore on Tuesday morning* (*Much Ado About Nothing 5.1*)

freshes NOUN a fresh is a fresh water stream ❑ *He shall drink nought brine, for I'll not show him/Where the quick freshes are.* (*Tempest 3.2*)

furlong NOUN a furlong is a measure of distance. It is the equivalent on one eight of a mile ❑ *Now would I give a thousand furlongs of sea for an acre of barren ground* (*Tempest 1.1*)

gaberdine NOUN a gaberdine is a cloak ❑ *My best way is to creep under his gaberdine* (*Tempest 2.2*)

gage NOUN a gage was a challenge to duel or fight ❑ *There is my gage, Aumerle, in gage to thine* (*Richard II 4.1*)

gait NOUN your gait is your way of walking or step ❑ *I know her by her gait* (*Tempest 4.1*)

gall VERB to gall is to annoy or irritate ❑ *Let it not gall your patience, good Iago,/That I extend my manners* (*Othello 2.1*)

gambol NOUN frolic or play ❑ *Hop in his walks, and gambol in his eyes* (*A Midsummer Night's Dream 3.1*)

gaskins NOUN gaskins is an old word for trousers ❑ *or, if both break, your gaskins fall.* (*Twelfth Night 1.5*)

gentle ADJ gentle means noble or well-born ❑ *thrice-gentle Cassio!* (*Othello 3.4*)

glass NOUN a glass was another word for a mirror ❑ *no woman's face remember/Save from my glass, mine own* (*Tempest 3.1*)

gleek VERB to gleek means to make a joke or jibe ❑ *Nay, I can gleek upon occasion* (*A Midsummer Night's Dream 3.1*)

gust NOUN gust meant taste, desire or enjoyment. We still say that if you do something with gusto you do it with enjoyment or enthusiasm ❑ *the gust he hath in quarrelling* (*Twelfth Night 1.3*)

habit NOUN habit means clothes ❑ *You know me by my habit* (*Henry V 3.6*)

heaviness NOUN heaviness means sadness or grief ❑ *So sorrow's heaviness doth heavier grow/For debt that bankrupt sleep doth sorrow owe* (*A Midsummer Night's Dream 3.2*)

heavy ADJ if you are heavy you are said to be sad or sorrowful ❑ *Away from light steals home my heavy son* (*Romeo and Juliet 1.1*)

hie VERB to hie meant to hurry ❑ *My husband hies him home* (*All Well That Ends Well 4.4*)

hollowly ADV if you did something hollowly you did it insincerely ❑ *If hollowly invert/What best is boded me to mischief!* (Tempest 3.1)

holy-water, court PHRASE if you court holy water you make empty promises, or make statements which sound good but have no real meaning ❑ *court holy-water in a dry house is better than this rain-water out o'door* (King Lear 3.2)

howsoever ADV howsoever was often used instead of however ❑ *But howsoever strange and admirable* (A Midsummer Night's Dream 5.1)

humour NOUN your humour was your mood, frame of mind or temperament ❑ *it fits my humour well* (As You Like It 3.2)

ill ADJ ill means bad ❑ *I must thank him only,/Let my remembrance suffer ill report* (Antony and Cleopatra 2.2)

indistinct ADJ inseparable or unable to see a difference ❑ *Even till we make the main and the aerial blue/An indistinct regard.* (Othello 2.1)

indulgence NOUN indulgence meant approval ❑ *As you from crimes would pardoned be,/Let your indulgence set me free* (The Tempest Epilogue)

infirmity NOUN infirmity was weakness or fraility ❑ *Be not disturbed with my infirmity* (The Tempest 4.1)

intelligence NOUN here intelligence means information ❑ *Pursue her; and for this intelligence/If I have thanks* (A Midsummer Night's Dream 1.1)

inwards NOUN inwards meant someone's internal organs ❑ *the thought whereof/Doth like a poisonous mineral gnaw my inwards* (Othello 2.1)

issue 1 NOUN the issue of a marriage are the children ❑ *To thine and Albany's issues,/Be this perpetual* (King Lear 1.1) 2 NOUN in this context issue means outcome or result ❑ *I am to pray you, not to strain my speech,/To grosser issues* (Othello)

kind NOUN kind here means situation or case ❑ *But in this kind, wanting your father's voice,/The other must be held the worthier.* (A Midsummer Night's Dream 1.1)

knave NOUN a knave was a common word for scoundrel ❑ *How absolute the knave is!* (Hamlet 5.1)

league NOUN A distance. A league was the distance a person could walk in one hour ❑ *From Athens is her house remote seven leagues* (A Midsummer Night's Dream 1.1)

lief, had as ADJ I had as lief means I should like just as much ❑ *I had as lief the town crier spoke my lines* (Hamlet 1.2)

livery NOUN livery was a costume, outfit, uniform usually worn by a servant ❑ *You can endure the livery of a nun* (A Midsummer Night's Dream 1.1)

loam NOUN loam is soil containing decayed vegetable matter and therefore good for growing crops and plants ❑ *and let him have some plaster, or some loam, or some rough-cast about him, to signify wall* (A Midsummer Night's Dream 3.1)

lusty ADJ lusty meant strong ❑ *and oared/Himself with his good arms in lusty stroke/To th' shore* (The Tempest 2.1)

maidenhead NOUN maidenhead means chastity or virginity ❏ *What I am, and what I would, are as secret as maidenhead* (*Twelfth Night 1.5*)

mark VERB mark means to note or pay attention to ❏ *Where sighs and groans,/ Are made not marked* (*Macbeth 4.3*)

marvellous ADJ very or extremely ❏ *here's a marvellous convenient place for our rehearsal* (*A Midsummer Night's Dream 3.1*)

meet ADJ right or proper ❏ *tis most meet you should* (*Macbeth 5.1*)

merely ADV completely or entirely ❏ *Love is merely a madness* (*As You Like It 3.2*)

misgraffed ADJ misgraffed is an old word for mismatched or unequal ❏ *Or else misgraffed in respect of years* (*A Midsummer Night's Dream 1.1*)

misprision NOUN a misprision meant an error or mistake ❏ *Misprision in the highest degree!* (*Twelfth Night 1.5*)

mollification NOUN mollification is appeasement or a way of preventing someone getting angry ❏ *I am to hull here a little longer. Some mollification for your giant* (*Twelfth Night 1.5*)

mouth, cold in the PHRASE a well-known saying of the time which meant to be dead ❏ *What, must our mouths be cold?* (*The Tempest 1.1*)

murmur NOUN murmur was another word for rumour or hearsay ❏ *and then 'twas fresh in murmur* (*Twelfth Night 1.2*)

murrain NOUN murrain was another word for plague, pestilence ❏ *A murrain on your monster, and the devil take your fingers!* (*The Tempest 3.2*)

neaf NOUN neaf meant fist ❏ *Give me your neaf, Monsieur Mustardseed* (*A Midsummer Night's Dream 4.1*)

nice 1 ADJ nice had a number of meanings here it means fussy or particular ❏ *An therefore, goaded with most sharp occasions,/ Which lay nice manners by, I put you to/ The use of your own virtues* (*All's Well That Ends Well 5.1*) 2 ADJ nice here means critical or delicate ❏ *We're good… To set so rich a man/ On the nice hazard of one doubtful hour?* (*Henry IV part 1*) 3 ADJ nice in this context means carefully accurate, fastidious ❏ *O relation/ Too nice and yet too true!* (*Macbeth 4.3*) 4 ADJ trivial, unimportant ❏ *Romeo .. Bid him bethink/ How nice the quarrel was* (*Romeo and Juliet 3.1*)

nonpareil NOUN if you are nonpareil you are without equal, peerless ❏ *though you were crown'd/ The nonpareil of beauty!* (*Twelfth Night 1.5*)

office NOUN office here means business or work ❏ *Speak your office* (*Twelfth Night 1.5*)

outsport VERB outsport meant to overdo ❏ *Let's teach ourselves that honorable stop,/ Not to outsport discretion.* (*Othello 2.2*)

owe VERB owe meant own, possess ❏ *Lend less than thou owest* (*King Lear 1.4*)

paragon 1 VERB to paragon was to surpass or excede ❏ *he hath achieved a maid/ That paragons description and wild fame* (*Othello 2.1*) 2 VERB to paragon could also mean to compare with ❏ *I will give thee* *bloody teeth If thou with Caesar paragon again/ My man of men (Anthony and Cleopatra 1.5)*

pate NOUN pate is another word for head ❑ *Back, slave, or I will break thy pate across (The Comedy of Errors 2.1)*

paunch VERB to paunch someone is to stab (usually in the stomach). Paunch is still a common word for a stomach ❑ *Batter his skull, or paunch him with a stake (The Tempest 3.2)*

peevish ADJ if you are peevish you are irritable or easily angered ❑ *Run after that same peevish messenger (Twelfth Night 1.5)*

peradventure ADV perhaps or maybe ❑ *Peradventure this is not Fortune's work (As You Like It 1.2)*

perforce 1 ADV by force or violently ❑ *my rights and royalties,/ Plucked from my arms perforce (Richard II 2.3)* 2 ADV necessarily ❑ *The hearts of men, they must perforce have melted (Richard II 5.2)*

personage NOUN personage meant your appearance ❑ *Of what personage and years is he? (Twelfth Night 1.5)*

pestilence NOUN pestilence was a common word for plague or disease ❑ *Methought she purg'd the air of pestilence! (Twelfth Night 1.1)*

physic NOUN physic was medicine or a treatment ❑ *'tis a physic/ That's bitter to sweet end (Measure for Measure 4.6)*

place NOUN place means a person's position or rank ❑ *Sons, kinsmen, thanes,/ And you whose places are the nearest (Macbeth 1.4)*

post NOUN here a post means a messenger ❑ *there are twenty weak and wearied posts/ Come from the north (Henry IV part II 2.4)*

pox NOUN pox was a word for any disease during which the victim had blisters on the skin. It was also a curse, a swear word ❑ *The pox of such antic, lisping, affecting phantasims (Romeo and Juliet 2.4)*

prate VERB to prate means to chatter ❑ *if thou prate of mountains (Hamlet 5.1)*

prattle VERB to prattle is to chatter or talk without purpose ❑ *I prattle out of fashion, and I dote In mine own comforts (Othello 2.1)*

precept NOUN a precept was an order or command ❑ *and my father's precepts I therein do forget. (The Tempest 3.1)*

present ADJ present here means immediate ❑ *We'll put the matter to the present push (Hamlet 5.1)*

prithee EXCLAM prithee is the equivalent of please or may I ask – a polite request ❑ *I prithee, and I'll pay thee bounteously (Twelfth Night 1.2)*

prodigal NOUN a prodigal is someone who wastes or squanders money ❑ *he's a very fool, and a prodigal (Twelfth Night 1.3)*

purpose NOUN purpose is used here to mean intention ❑ *understand my purposes aright (King Lear 1.4)*

quaff VERB quaff was a common word which meant to drink heavily or take a big drink ❑ *That quaffing and drinking will undo you (Twelfth Night 1.3)*

quaint 1 ADJ clever, ingenious ❏ *with a quaint device* (*The Tempest* 3.3) 2 ADJ cunning ❏ *I'll… tell quaint lies* (*Merchant of Venice* 3.4) 3 ADJ pretty, attractive ❏ *The clamorous owl, that nightly hoots and wonders/At our quaint spirit* (*A Midsummer Night's Dream* 2.2)

quoth VERB an old word which means say ❏ *'Tis dinner time.' quoth I* (*The Comedy of Errors* 2.1)

rack NOUN a rack described clouds or a cloud formation ❏ *And, like this insubstantial pageant faded,/ Leave not a rack behind* (*The Tempest* 4.1)

rail VERB to rant or swear at. It is still used occasionally today ❏ *Why do I rail on thee* (*Richard II* 5.5)

rate NOUN rate meant estimate, opinion ❏ *My son is lost, and, in my rate, she too* (*The Tempest* 2.1)

recreant NOUN recreant is an old word which means coward ❏ *Come, recreant, come, thou child* (*A Midsummer Night's Dream* 3.2)

remembrance NOUN remembrance is used here to mean memory or recollection ❏ *our remembrances of days foregone* (*All's Well That Ends Well* 1.3)

resolute ADJ firm or not going to change your mind ❏ *You are resolute, then?* (*Twelfth Night* 1.5)

revels NOUN revels means celebrations or a party ❏ *Our revels now are ended* (*The Tempest* 4.1)

rough-cast NOUN a mixture of lime and gravel (sometimes shells too) for use on an outer wall ❏ *and let him have some plaster, or some loam, or some rough-cast about him, to signify wall* (*A Midsummer Night's Dream* 3.1)

sack NOUN sack was another word for wine ❏ *My man-monster hath drowned his tongue in sack.* (*The Tempest* 3.2)

sad ADJ in this context sad means serious, grave ❏ *comes me the Prince and Claudio… in sad conference* (*Much Ado About Nothing* 1.3)

sampler NOUN a piece of embroidery, which often showed the family tree ❏ *Both on one sampler, sitting on one cushion* (*A Midsummer Night's Dream* 3.2)

saucy ADJ saucy means rude ❏ *I heard you were saucy at my gates* (*Twelfth Night* 1.5)

schooling NOUN schooling means advice ❏ *I have some private schooling for you both.* (*A Midsummer Night's Dream* 1.1)

seething ADJ seething in this case means boiling – we now use seething when we are very angry ❏ *Lovers and madmen have such seething brains* (*A Midsummer Night's Dream* 5.1)

semblative ADJ semblative means resembling or looking like ❏ *And all is semblative a woman's part.* (*Twelfth Night* 1.4)

several ADJ several here means separate or different ❏ *twenty several messengers* (*Anthony and Cleopatra* 1.5)

shrew NOUN An annoying person or someone who makes you cross ❏ *Bless you, fair shrew.* (*Twelfth Night* 1.3)

shroud VERB to shroud is to hide or shelter ❏ *I will here, shroud till the dregs of the storm be past* (*The Tempest 2.2*)

sickleman NOUN a sickleman was someone who used a sickle to harvest crops ❏ *You sunburnt sicklemen, of August weary* (*The Tempest 4.1*)

soft ADV soft here means wait a moment or stop ❏ *But, soft, what nymphs are these* (*A Midsummer Night's Dream 4.1*)

something ADV something here means somewhat or rather ❏ *Be something scanter of your maiden presence* (*Hamlet 1.3*)

sooth NOUN truly ❏ *Yes, sooth; and so do you* (*A Midsummer Night's Dream 3.2*)

spleen NOUN spleen means fury or anger ❏ *That, in a spleen, unfolds both heaven and earth* (*A Midsummer Night's Dream 1.1*)

sport NOUN sport means recreation or entertainment ❏ *I see our wars/ Will turn unto a peaceful comic sport* (*Henry VI part I 2.2*)

strain NOUN a strain is a tune or a musical phrase ❏ *and so die/That strain again! it had a dying fall* (*Twelfth Night 1.1*)

suffer VERB in this context suffer means perish or die ❏ *but an islander that hath lately suffered by a thunderbolt.* (*The Tempest 2.2*)

suit NOUN a suit is a petition, request or proposal (marriage) ❏ *Because she will admit no kind of suit* (*Twelfth Night 1.2*)

sup VERB to sup is to have supper ❏ *Go know of Cassio where he supped tonight* (*Othello 5.1*)

surfeit NOUN a surfeit is an amount which is too large ❏ *If music be the food of love, play on;/Give me excess of it, that, surfeiting,/ The appetite may sicken* (*Twelfth Night 1.1*)

swain NOUN a swain is a suitor or person who wants to marry ❏ *take this transformed scalp/From off the head of this Athenian swain* (*A Midsummer Night's Dream 4.1*)

thereto ADV thereto meant also ❏ *If she be black, and thereto have a wit* (*Othello 2.1*)

throstle NOUN a throstle was a name for a song-bird ❏ *The throstle with his note so true* (*A Midsummer Night's Dream 3.1*)

tidings NOUN tidings meant news ❏ *that upon certain tidings now arrived, importing the mere perdition of the Turkish fleet* (*Othello 2.2*)

transgress VERB if you transgress you break a moral law or rule of behaviour ❏ *Virtue that transgresses is but patched with sin* (*Twelfth Night 1.5*)

troth, by my PHRASE this phrase means I swear or in truth or on my word ❏ *By my troth, Sir Toby, you must come in earlier o' nights* (*Twelfth Night 1.3*)

trumpery NOUN trumpery means things that look expensive but are worth nothing (often clothing) ❏ *The trumpery in my house, go bring it hither/For stale catch these thieves* (*The Tempest 4.1*)

twink NOUN In the wink of an eye or no time at all ❏ *Ay, with a twink* (*The Tempest 4.1*)

undone ADJ if something or someone is undone they are ruined, destroyed, brought down ❑ *You have undone a man of fourscore three* (*The Winter's Tale 4.4*)

varlets NOUN varlets were villains or ruffians ❑ *Say again: where didst thou leave these varlets?* (*The Tempest 4.1*)

vaward NOUN the vaward is an old word for the vanguard, front part or earliest ❑ *And since we have the vaward of the day* (*A Midsummer Night's Dream 4.1*)

visage NOUN face ❑ *when Phoebe doth behold/ Her silver visage in the watery glass* (*A Midsummer Night's Dream 1.1*)

voice NOUN voice means vote ❑ *He has our voices* (*Coriolanus 2.3*)

waggish ADJ waggish means playful ❑ *As waggish boys in game themselves forswear* (*A Midsummer Night's Dream 1.1*)

wane VERB to wane is to vanish, go down or get slighter. It is most often used to describe a phase of the moon ❑ *but, O, methinks, how slow/ This old moon wanes* (*A Midsummer Night's Dream 1.1*)

want VERB to want means to lack or to be without ❑ *a beast that wants discourse of reason/ Would have mourned longer* (*Hamlet 1.2*)

warrant VERB to assure, promise, guarantee ❑ *I warrant your grace* (*As You Like It 1.2*)

welkin NOUN welkin is an old word for the sky or the heavens ❑ *The starry welkin cover thou anon/ With drooping fog as black as Acheron* (*A Midsummer Night's Dream 3.2*)

wench NOUN wench is an old word for a girl ❑ *Well demanded, wench* (*The Tempest 1.2*)

whence ADV from where ❑ *Whence came you, sir?* (*Twelfth Night 1.5*)

wherefore ADV why ❑ *Wherefore, sweetheart? what's your metaphor?* (*Twelfth Night 1.3*)

wide-chopped ADJ if you were wide-chopped you were big-mouthed ❑ *This wide-chopped rascal* (*The Tempest 1.1*)

wight NOUN wight is an old word for person or human being ❑ *She was a wight, if ever such wight were* (*Othello 2.1*)

wit NOUN wit means intelligence or wisdom ❑ *thou didst conclude hairy men plain dealers, without wit* (*The Comedy of Errors 2.2*)

wits NOUN wits mean mental sharpness ❑ *we that have good wits have much to answer for* (*As You Like It 4.1*)

wont ADJ to wont is to be in the habit of doing something regularly ❑ *When were you wont to use my sister thus?* (*The Comedy of Errors 2.2*)

wooer NOUN a wooer is a suitor, someone who is hoping to marry ❑ *and of a foolish knight that you brought in one night here to be her wooer* (*Twelfth Night 1.3*)

wot VERB wot is an old word which means know or learn ❑ *for well I wot/ Thou runnest before me* (*A Midsummer Night's Dream 3.2*)